# Artificial Intelligence

# Introductions to Modern Psychology

# Artificial Intelligence
## An introduction

**Alan Garnham**

**Routledge & Kegan Paul**
London and New York

First published in 1988 by
Routledge & Kegan Paul Ltd
11 New Fetter Lane, London EC4P 4EE

Published in the USA by
Routledge & Kegan Paul Inc.
in association with Methuen Inc.
29 West 35th Street, New York, NY 10001

Set in Baskerville
by Hope Services Ltd.
and printed in Great Britain
by T. J. Press Ltd,
Padstow, Cornwall

Library of Congress Cataloging in Publication Data
Garnham, Alan, 1954–
Artificial intelligence: an introduction / Alan Garnham.
p. cm. — (Introductions to modern psychology)
Bibliography: p.
Includes index.
1. Artificial intelligence.   I. Title.   II. Series.
Q335.G36 1987
006.3 – dc19

British Library CIP Data also available

ISBN 0–7102–0793–X (c)
       0–7102–1416–2 (pbk)

To my mother
in loving memory

# Contents

# Preface

Artificial Intelligence (AI), the science of thinking machines, is once again a subject of public interest. It has attracted particular attention – and funding – in the United States, but interest has also revived, albeit to a lesser extent, in Britain and the rest of Europe. To make a machine that can 'think', one must have ideas about what thinking is. These ideas provide insights into the way the human mind works. It is, therefore, difficult for psychologists, who have a professional interest in mental phenomena, to ignore AI research. It would, in any case, be wrong for them to do so.

Many psychologists recognise the importance of AI for their own discipline. Its influence is reflected in both research and in teaching. Ideas from AI have had a profound impact on psychological theories, and undergraduate courses in the psychology of vision, thinking and reasoning, and language have included an AI component for some time. Moreover, in recent years the AI content of such courses has increased considerably.

There are several reasons for teaching AI to psychology students in a separate course. I will mention just two. First, AI raises general questions about the explanation of mental phenomena that all psychologists should consider. It is not always appropriate to discuss such questions in specialist courses on, say, vision or psycholinguistics. In any case, it can be difficult to find time. Second, a background in AI, particularly if it is combined with some experience of programming, opens up a range of employment opportunities for psychology graduates. Programming is usually only taught in specialist AI courses. Some departments, among them the Laboratory of Experimental Psychology at Sussex University, have been teaching AI courses for several years. However, they remain in a minority.

There are two approaches to writing a comparatively short textbook. One is to provide a detailed account of a small number of studies, and to assume that a wider range of topics will be discussed in lectures and tutorials. The other is to cover more material in the book, and to allow lecturers and tutors to expand the explanations, where necessary. I have tended to the latter course, so the density of the information in this book is rather high.

When I started writing, my plan – insofar as I had one – was to provide an account of the most important AI programs. As soon as I became conscious of this intention I realised that I did not approve of it. Simply to say 'there is one machine that can do so-and-so and another that can do such-and-such' is of little interest, except to fact collectors. It is not the existence of 'clever' machines that is important to psychologists, but an understanding of how they work and, hence, of the insights into the nature of intelligence that they provide.

I have not, of course, abandoned the idea of an overview of AI. Indeed, since the AI research community is much smaller than that of psychology, and since AI has a shorter history, it is possible for a fairly small book to be relatively comprehensive. Most undergraduate AI courses for computer scientists are taught from a single text, usually called *Artificial Intelligence*. Specialist texts, like specialist courses, remain a rarity. Although this situation is beginning to change, psychology undergraduates, assuming that they will also be referred to the primary literature, are unlikely to need more than a single text.

My misgivings about a simple overview have had three consequences. First, I have tried to emphasise those areas in which AI research has led to general principles for explaining intelligent behaviour in both man and machine. Second, I have given some space to the broader philosophical issues raised by the possibility of intelligent machines, more to stimulate thought than to say the last word on them. Third, I have attempted to give the reader some feel for AI research. For example, chapter 2 contains what some might see as an overelaborate account of the unification and resolution algorithms. In this particular case the intention was to give some idea of the 'nuts and bolts' of AI programs. AI should show that the mind is not inherently mysterious, but if someone cannot see how an idea – in this case the resolution rule for theorem proving – can be incorporated into a program, then the mind will remain a mystery to them.

I have not, however, tried to provided instruction in programming, for two reasons. First, I am not competent to do so. Second, this book is intended for psychologists, and many psychology departments cannot, and will not for some time be able to, teach AI programming. Furthermore, when they are able to, they may not all teach the same language, and it is virtually impossible to provide a programming course that is not language-specific.

The book is part of the series *Introduction to Modern Psychology*. However, I hope that its usefulness will not be restricted to psychologists. It does have a 'psychological' slant, but only insofar as I have emphasised research that is particularly relevant to psychologists. However, I have tried to provide a reasonably fair overview of AI, and one that is accessible to anyone – including 'the educated layman' – who requires an introduction to that discipline. In particular, it may be suitable for those who find books written by computer scientists for computer scientists daunting. The book is intended as a text for the kind of AI course that I expect to become increasingly popular in psychology departments. It could also serve as reading material for AI sections of more traditional courses on vision, thinking and reasoning, language and learning. I hope it will also be of use to psychologists who cannot attend taught courses, but who want a background in AI, be they undergraduates, postgraduates or more senior people.

A number of people have helped make this a better book than I could have produced on my own. Two of them deserve special thanks. The first is Steve Isard, whose knowledge of AI is much broader than mine, and who spent many hours explaining its complexities to me. I often felt that he should have been the author. He also read through drafts of all the chapters and corrected some of the errors that remained, despite his patient explanations. The second is Jane Oakhill, who also read a complete draft, from the perspective of a potential reader. She helped eliminate many unclarities and stopped me from taking things for granted that I shouldn't have.

Some of the work on chapter 8 was carried out while I was a Visiting Fellow at the Max-Planck-Institüt für Psycholinguistik, at Nijmegen in The Netherlands. I would like to thank the staff there for making my stay a pleasant one and for providing a congenial working environment.

Sussex, January 1987

# 1 Introduction

*Artificial intelligence* (AI) is an approach to understanding behaviour based on the assumption that intelligence can best be analysed by trying to reproduce it. In practice, reproduction means simulation by computer. AI is, therefore, part of computer science. Its history is a relatively short one – as an independent field of study it dates back to the mid-1950s. The AI approach contrasts with an older method of studying cognition, that of experimental psychology. Psychology has long had intelligence among its central concerns, intelligence not just as measured in IQ tests, but in the broader sense in which it is required for thinking, reasoning and learning, and in their prerequisites – high-level perceptual skills, the mental representation of information and the ability to use language.

AI and psychology have inevitably interacted with each other. Psychologists have borrowed concepts from AI, and AI workers have taken an interest in psychological findings. Nevertheless, there has been a certain amount of antagonism between the two approaches, with proponents of each pointing out the strengths of their own methodology and the weaknesses of their opponents'. This uneasy relationship lasted until the late 1970s, when many people on both sides felt the need for a more constructive amalgam of these different approaches to the same problems. A new discipline, *cognitive science*, came into being, combining the strengths of psychology, AI and other subjects, in particular linguistics, formal logic and philosophy. Cognitive science attempts to answer some of the unsolved problems about intelligent behaviour, in the widest sense of that term. The importance of its interdisciplinary approach is reflected in the fact that it is now difficult for psychologists to understand new work in perception and cognition if they are ignorant of AI.

This book is an introduction to AI. It describes research in AI, and discusses the strengths and weaknesses of the AI approach to cognition. Only by familiarising themselves with AI can psychologists, and others, judge for themselves what contribution it can make to the study of mental functioning, and in what way it complements and reinforces more traditional psychological techniques.

The present chapter provides a general introduction to AI, its history, its tools and research methods, and its relation to psychology. Chapters 2 to 6 describe AI research in five major areas: knowledge representation, vision, thinking and reasoning, language, and learning. The more important applications of AI are described in chapter 7, and some of its wider implications for a theory of mind are discussed in chapter 8. The final chapter speculates about future research in cognitive science.

## What is 'artificial intelligence'?

*Artificial intelligence* is the study of intelligent behaviour. One of its goals is to understand human intelligence. Another is to produce useful machines. In some ways the term *artificial intelligence* is an unfortunate one. Both parts of it are misleading. On the one hand, as many people have pointed out, *artificial* implies not real. Although many critics of AI have claimed that artificial intelligences are not really intelligent (see chapter 8), most AI researchers disagree with them. On the other hand, the word *intelligence* suggests that AI is restricted to the study of behaviour that is indicative of intelligence, in the everyday sense of that term – behaviour such as solving problems, playing chess and proving theorems in geometry and predicate calculus. These kinds of behaviour are the ones that particularly interested the AI pioneers of the mid-1950s. However, in writing programs to simulate these skills, they developed a battery of programming techniques that could be applied to aspects of behaviour not normally thought of as requiring any great intelligence – recognising objects and understanding simple text, for example. More recently, particularly in the study of visual perception and speech recognition, programming techniques have been introduced that are not immediately applicable to the simulation of problem solving. Nevertheless, it is usual to extend the term *artificial intelligence* to include this work.

Even when AI research aims to reproduce human behaviour, it need not necessarily attempt to reproduce the mechanisms underlying it. AI is more immediately relevant to psychology when it does try to model those mechanisms, but other types of AI research may be of psychological interest if they suggest general principles for describing or modelling cognitive functions. Therefore, although this book is addressed primarily to psychologists, the term *artificial intelligence* will be taken in its most general sense, and the full range of AI research will be discussed.

## Artificial intelligence – a brief history

The term *artificial intelligence* was first used in print by John McCarthy, in a proposal for a conference at Dartmouth College, New Hampshire, to discuss the simulation of intelligent behaviour by machines. As an academic discipline, AI had its origins in the mid-1950s, at about the time of the Dartmouth conference. Its history is, therefore, comparatively short. However, AI did not emerge from a theoretical vacuum. Before that time there had been many investigations of the nature of intelligence. However, until the advent of the digital computer, most of this effort was directed towards understanding intelligence as manifested by people.

It is possible, and in many ways useful, to view current AI research as a continuation of previous work in philosophy, science, and technology. Two authors who explore this idea in detail are McCorduck (1979) and Gregory (1981), who lays particular emphasis on the role of technological advances in understanding the human mind.

Perhaps the principal line of development that led to AI was the attempt to produce machines that took the drudgery out of human intellectual endeavour and, at the same time, eliminated some of the errors to which it is prone. Gregory (1981) describes an ancient Greek device, the so-called *Antikythera Mechanism* (c. 80 BC) which models the movements of heavenly bodies. Its discovery shows that the Greeks were more technologically advanced than has often been assumed. However, the gap between ancient Greek culture and our own is comparatively wide. It is difficult to be sure what the existence of such mechanisms meant to the Greeks, or how they shaped ideas about the mind.

The Antikythera Mechanism is the ancestor of medieval orreries and Renaissance clocks. It is not on the direct line to the digital computer. That device, as its name suggests, developed from aids to numerical calculation, which can be traced back through the abacus to groups of pebbles. Calculating *machines*, whose principal components were cogwheels, were first constructed by the philosophers Pascal (1623–1662) and Leibniz (1646–1716). However, the capabilities of these machines were severely limited (by today's standards) by the fact that their parts were mechanical. These same limitations thwarted the ambitions of Charles Babbage (1792–1871) to produce a much more powerful machine. Babbage's first project, the *Difference Engine*, was designed to perform the relatively modest task of compiling tables of logarithms, whose principle use was in nautical computations. In the early nineteenth century these tables were produced by teams of human computers and were often error-ridden, sometimes with fatal results. In the early 1830s, when its construction was almost finished, Babbage lost interest in the Difference Engine, because he had conceived the much more ambitious *Analytical Engine*, which never came close to realisation. The Analytical Engine was intended to compute any mathematical function, not just logarithms. It was to be programmable by punched cards, in much the same way as the recently invented Jacquard loom. As well as performing mathematical computations, Babbage realised that the Analytical Engine would be able to play games such as noughts-and-crosses (tic-tac-toe) and chess, and at one time he proposed to build a game-playing version of the machine to raise funds.

In the event, the all-purpose computer, such as the Analytical Engine was intended to be, did not become a reality until mass-produced electronic components were available. Even then the earliest machines, conceived during the Second World War and constructed shortly afterwards, were unreliable and difficult to operate. The real breakthrough came with the discovery of semi-conductors and the development of the transistor as a replacement for the vacuum-tube diode.

The first programmable computer was constructed in Germany by Konrad Zuse before the war was over (see McCorduck, 1979, p. 50). However, Zuse was not taken seriously by the German authorities, and Germany's defeat meant that his efforts came to nothing. In Britain and the USA, on the other hand, special purpose computing machines had contributed to the war effort and, when the war was over, funding was made available for further development. In the USA, scientists at the Moore School of the University of Pennsylvania had developed the ENIAC, a machine for calculating bombing tables. After the war, they explored its use as a general purpose computer. In Britain, Alan Turing and a team of cryptanalysts at Bletchley Park had used electromagnetic computing machines for code breaking. Only recently has it become public knowledge how crucial this work was in avoiding defeat in the early years of the war. Turing, also, obtained funds for the design of general purpose electronic computers after the war (see Hodges, 1983, for an account of his work).

The first electronic computers, although physically very large, were severely limited in their capabilities compared with even a modest home microcomputer of the late 1980s. Several developments, in addition to the change from valves to transistors, were needed before AI programming became a reality. Two of these were particularly important. The first was the idea of storing a program, rather than just data, in the computer's memory. The second was that of a high-level programming language, from which programs could be translated automatically into a form that the machine could use. This process of translation is called *compilation*.

The first programs that could be called AI programs,

though that term had not yet been invented, were game players. Turing in Britain and Shannon (1950) in the USA, like Babbage before them, explored the idea of a chess-playing computer, and Turing had simulated the performance of such a machine by hand before he could program a real computer to play. However, these early projects were hampered by the lack of high-level programming languages. Programming a machine to perform any task was extremely laborious before the invention of such languages.

1956 is a crucial date in the history of AI. That was the year of the conference at Dartmouth College, which its organisers, in particular John McCarthy, hoped would give a large and immediate impetus to AI research. If the effects of the conference were not as dramatic as had been anticipated, with hindsight they still appear highly significant. If nothing else, the use of the term *artificial intelligence* in the proposal for the conference was instrumental in its gaining currency.

Although McCarthy was disappointed that the conference did not produce more immediate results, it brought together many of those who became prominent in the early days of AI, and laid the foundations for work that was very soon underway. Among the people at Dartmouth were Allen Newell and Herbert Simon, who had already implemented a high-level programming language designed for AI research. Using this language they had written a program, called the Logic Theory Machine, which could prove theorems of formal logic (see chapter 4).

In developing this program, Newell and Simon, together with their colleague Shaw, had largely ignored two lines of research that many of the other delegates at the conference considered important. The first was neural nets (McCulloch and Pitts, 1943). Neural nets are models of the logical properties of interconnected sets of nerve cells. By investigating the properties of such nets, neural net theorists hoped to show how the brain could mediate intelligent behaviour. However, this research was based on what later turned out to be a simplistic view of the properties of neurons, and AI researchers soon lost interest in it. Newell, Shaw and Simon emphasised the importance of studying intelligence at a *functional*, rather than a physiological, level, and it is only recently that ideas similar to those of McCulloch and Pitts have been revived in connectionist and parallel distributed processing (PDP) models.

The second idea that Newell, Shaw and Simon repudiated was that programs should work according to the *principles* of formal logic (rather than prove theorems in it). Their claim that people do not reason using logical rules but use *heuristics*, or rules of thumb, remains important to this day.

Although the implications of Newell, Shaw and Simon's work had not become fully apparent by the end of the Dartmouth conference, their ideas became the dominant influence in the early years of AI, as is evidenced by Feigenbaum and Feldman's (1963) *Computers and Thought*, the first collected volume of AI papers, and one which gives a good overview of the early work.

In the early 1960s the Massachusetts Institute of Technology (MIT) became the leading centre for AI research. This period is often referred to as the era of *semantic information processing*, a name taken from a book summarising its most important work (Minsky, 1968). The term *semantic information processing* indicates that the meaning of the information being processed, and not just its structure, is important for the task in hand. For example, in language processing, interest shifted from the syntax-based attempts at machine translation of the 1950s to meaning-based language-understanding systems.

The work of the early 1960s retained the assumption, made by Newell, Shaw and Simon, that AI research should result in general models of intelligent behaviour. Later in the 1960s it was realised that such behaviour requires large amounts of background knowledge, often knowledge that is specific to a particular task. This observation led to the writing of programs that worked in restricted domains, most notably the MIT BLOCKSWORLD, which comprised prismatic blocks on a table top. However, many people continued to believe that principles discovered by solving problems in one domain would carry over to others. This era produced some programs that performed impressively, though it later turned out that they often depended on domain-specific tricks, and that the ideas on which they were based could not, after all, be generalised to other domains.

Another set of programs on which work began in the 1960s were unashamed specialists, whose performance was deliberately restricted to a single type of problem, such as diagnosing a particular class of diseases. These programs, which were intended to be used in the real world, initially met with some hostility – they were not regarded as genuine AI. Now renamed *expert systems*, they form one of the central areas of AI research (see chapter 7).

The 1960s also saw a revival of interest in formal logic as a tool in problem solving. The principal reason for this revival was the invention by Alan Robinson of the resolution method for deriving conclusions from premises stated in predicate calculus (see chapter 4).

The early 1970s was a comparatively quiet period. Although detailed accounts of some of the most impressive semantic information-processing systems were published (e.g. Winograd, 1972) and work on expert systems continued, there was little sense of progress. In Britain, the Lighthill report concluded that AI was not a priority area for research. However, the late 1970s saw a renaissance. After a lengthy period of evolution, the first expert systems were put into everyday use, working out the structure of organic molecules, configuring computer systems and diagnosing diseases. This development signalled that AI had potentially lucrative applications, and was partly responsible for an upsurge in funding. On the theoretical side, much of the work of the preceding twenty-five years was systematised, and a welcome attempt was made to identify underlying principles, and to dispense with *ad hoc* solutions to problems.

Because AI is a young discipline, the age of a piece of research is a poor guide to its current relevance. This book will, therefore, describe some of the earliest work in AI, as well as more recent studies. There will, however, be an emphasis on later work.

## The goals of AI research

AI researchers try both to understand intelligent behaviour and to build clever machines. Indeed, a single AI project may have both of these goals. The fact that many projects aim to produce a specific product – a machine that is, or could be, used in the real world – suggests that AI is more like engineering than physics, that it is more of an applied than a pure science (see e.g. Feigenbaum, 1977). The truth is rather that it is more difficult to distinguish between pure and applied AI than between physics and engineering. In some AI projects the primary goal is to produce an intelligent artefact. The principles underlying its behaviour are of secondary importance, and there is no intention to search for new principles. However, in other projects, perhaps the majority, the aim is to understand the mechanisms underlying behaviour, to make general statements about knowledge representation, vision, thinking, language use or learning. In particular, AI programs that try to simulate human behaviour are often written in an attempt to give a principled account of that behaviour.

AI is most akin to engineering when the goal is to produce a program with a specific application, and when there is little or no concern with whether the program solves the problem in the way that a person would. In such cases the existence of a satisfactory working program indicates the successful completion of the project. The distinction between pure and applied AI is blurred by the fact that many AI workers have used this criterion for success even when they were not trying to produce programs with applications in the real world. AI workers write programs that embody general principles, and consider their projects complete when they have a satisfactory program. However, if one's goal is to understand some aspect of language understanding, say, or vision, then the existence of a working program is important only in so far as it illustrates how a set of ideas works in practice. In such a case, the theory of language understanding or vision is embodied in the principles that underlie the construction of the program. Typically these principles will not be sufficient to produce a complete specification for a language-understanding program or a vision program. To make the program work it will be necessary to add components that are of no theoretical interest. It may even be necessary to *patch* the program – to add bits whose sole purpose is to eliminate unforeseen problems and to allow the program to run. Such programming is only useful in so far as it allows a test of whether the rest of the program is consistent and whether it behaves as predicted. It is particularly important that patches should not be allowed to hide problems in underlying principles.

Closely related to the aim of having a complete working program is that of producing an overall model of a cognitive system. One reason for adopting this goal has been the assumption that cognitive systems comprise sets of interactive subsystems, and that this interaction is a major hindrance to testing theories of individual subsystems. If the behaviour of a subsystem depends on that of the rest of the system, then what it does when working alone may give a misleading impression of what it does in the system as a whole. The fallacy in this argument is that even if a subprocessor's operation depends on what is happening elsewhere, it is not necessary to have a complete model of the rest of the system, but only an account of the input/output functions of the other subprocessors. Even if, say, language processing is interactive, a more orthodox scientific approach can be adopted. Tractable subproblems can be identified and solved. Confronting edifices such as the whole of language understanding is not to be recommended.

The goals of having a working program and of modelling a complete cognitive system, when taken together, suggest that an AI program should be a working model of, say, the language-understanding system, and that the program should produce *realistic outputs*. Many AI researchers have deliberately aimed for programs that produce realistic outputs, and they have tried to validate their programs by investigating the range of inputs for which they produce such outputs. This approach can be attacked on two fronts. First, a program that produces realistic outputs may not be a good model of a cognitive system. This problem might be dubbed the ELIZA problem, after Weizenbaum's (1966) program that engages in realistic dialogues with its user (see chapter 5). The program cannot be said to understand what is said to it in any interesting sense. The fact that simulation does not necessarily imply explanation is also reflected in the fact that extremely accurate mechanical clockworks simulating planetary motion were constructed on the basis of the discredited epicyclic theory of that motion. Second, the outputs that a subprocessor should produce can often be specified independently of its role in the system. For example, a parser should output (partial) syntactic analyses. A model of the parser can, therefore, be tested without embedding it in an overall model of the language processor. Hence, realistic outputs are neither necessary nor sufficient for testing hypotheses about the way language is understood.

AI is most directly relevant to psychology when it aims to discover general explanatory principles. Nevertheless, AI applications may shed indirect light on psychological problems, and complete working programs are useful as testbeds for sets of ideas. All these types of research will therefore, be described in this book.

## AI and psychology

There are two main reasons why psychologists should study AI. First, and most important, psychology and AI share an interest in the scientific understanding of cognitive abilities such as reasoning, object recognition and language understanding. Psychologists and AI researchers should work together, as cognitive scientists, towards an understanding of human cognition, using whatever techniques are most appropriate. They should not see themselves as being in opposition to each other. Second, in this age of high technology, we make increasing use of intelligent and less intelligent computers in our everyday lives. If our interactions with these machines are to be fruitful, rather than frustrating, system designers must take account of the assumptions people make about how to use computers.

Some AI projects address specifically psychological problems about the way people (or minds, or brains) behave intelligently. Other projects aim to produce clever machines, but do not try to make those machines behave like people. Nevertheless, there is much that psychologists can learn from such research. In many areas of psychology detailed theories have yet to be produced, and any well-specified account of how a complex task can be performed – an account such as might be implicit in a computer program that performs the task – could be a useful source of psychological ideas.

The way people interact with machines, and the assumptions they make about them, are legitimate areas of psychological study. But if psychologists are to contribute to the study of the interaction of people and computers, they have to understand what computers can do. Only on the basis of such understanding can they make sensible suggestions about how computer systems should be designed and how they can be used most effectively. Increasingly, knowing about computers that people have to interact with will mean knowing about AI. So psychologists will need to study AI if they are to contribute to the study of human-computer interaction.

## AI as a source of psychological theories

AI had its origins in computer science. Its founders were not inspired by psychological research but by the idea that computers and computer programs might provide an appropriate metaphor for understanding mental processes. However, psychology and AI remained independent of each other for only a short period. In the 1960s the human experimental branch of psychology, at least, was strongly influenced by the computer metaphor for mind, and *information-processing* theories of cognitive functions became the norm. These theories emphasised the role of internal representations and processes in the causation of behaviour, and provided a sharp contrast with previous behaviourist approaches that focused on input and output, and that regarded the 'organism' as a black box whose inner workings were irrelevant to psychological theorising. By the end of the 1960s the term *cognitive psychology* was virtually synonymous with human experimental psychology. This change in approach brought human experimental psychology much closer to AI, whose pioneers had stressed the digital computer's role as a general *information-processing device*, as opposed to a mere number cruncher.

The proliferation of information-processing models in cognitive psychology reflected a very general influence of AI and the computational metaphor on psychological theorising.

The 1960s also saw an attempt to integrate computer modelling much more directly with the experimental study of human behaviour. Newell and Simon (1963) claimed that they could explain the steps that people went through in solving a problem by comparing what they said as they worked on it with how a program, the General Problem Solver (or GPS, see chapter 4), solved the same problem.

Newell and Simon distinguished between the broad field of artificial intelligence and a particular part of it, the computer simulation of human behaviour. AI was the attempt to make machines behave intelligently, by whatever means. *Computer simulation* was a particular method for producing intelligent machines – making them reproduce human behaviour. Computer simulation, therefore, had the specific goal of providing a model of human cognitive functioning. Although the distinction between computer simulation and the rest of AI remains clear in principle, most contemporary AI projects are influenced to a greater or lesser extent by considerations of how people behave. Very few researchers simply attempt to build clever machines. On the other hand, many still have the explicit goal of writing a program that works the way people do. However, the term computer simulation of behaviour is rarely used these days.

To test their computer simulations Newell and Simon introduced a new research methodology – protocol analysis. A protocol is a record, either written or tape-recorded, of what a person is thinking as he or she carries out some experimental task – usually solving a problem. For example, a person working on a geometry proof might say, 'I'm going to drop a perpendicular from point A to line BC, and see if that helps.' Protocols were assumed to be a direct indication of the way people attempted to solve those problems. They were compared with so-called *traces* of a computer program trying to solve the same problem, and an attempt was made to match what the program did with the operations that people said they were performing.

There are two main problems with this technique. First, it is difficult to measure the goodness of fit between a protocol and a trace of a computer program. Second, it is unclear how people's commentary on what they are doing relates to the mental operations that contribute to the solution to a problem. Furthermore, in some cognitive domains, such as object recognition and language understanding, none of the mental operations that underlie our abilities is available to consciousness. In studying these abilities the technique of protocol analysis is inappropriate. However, interest in protocol analysis has recently revived, particularly in so-called naive physics research, which attempts to model the way scientifically unsophisticated people, and scientists in their more relaxed moments, think about the workings of the physical world (see, for example, some of the papers in Gentner and Stevens, 1983).

Work on the computer simulation of behaviour in the 1960s could be regarded as a (failed) attempt by AI researchers to take over cognitive psychology. At the same time psychologists started to take a greater interest in AI research and to import its ideas into their own theories. Despite the slight antagonism between the two disciplines, which arose mainly from a disagreement about how cognitive functions should be studied, the flow of ideas steadily increased. In the late 1960s and early 1970s concepts such as *semantic network, production system* and *frame* made their way from AI into psychology. Furthermore, a small but increasing number of psychologists began to express their theories in the form of computer programs (e.g. Norman, Rumelhart and the LNR Research Group, 1975).

A different attempt to link experimental and programming techniques is found in Marr's research on vision (see chapter 3, and Marr, 1982). Marr's work, which in some ways lies outside mainstream AI, shows how psychology and AI might contribute jointly to a science of perceptual and cognitive functioning. One of Marr's most important contributions is his somewhat misleading named concept of a *computational theory* of a psychological process. A computational theory is *not* a theory in the form of a computer program. It is an account at a more abstract level of an information-processing device. It states what function (in the mathematical sense) that device computes, and why it computes that function. Below the computational theory is an algorithmic description of how the function is computed, usually couched in the form of a computer program, and below that details of the hardware on which the program runs. A computational theory is a set of general principles that help to explain a psychological process. Marr, unlike many AI researchers before him, explicitly demands that general principles be formulated. For him a working program does not, by itself, explain psychological functioning.

### Cognitive science

By the late 1970s, cognitive psychologists had more in common with AI researchers than with other psychologists, and AI researchers had more in common with cognitive psychologists than with other computer scientists. In recognition of this fact, the term *cognitive science* was coined, and an attempt was made to initiate more interdisciplinary research that combined the strengths of the two approaches.

## Interactions between people and artificial intelligences

More and more, computers are becoming part of our everyday lives. Many of these computers, such as those used by utility companies, we do not interact with directly. Others we do, for example those that dispense cash or provide information services over telephone lines. As yet few of these computers show much intelligence. One of the goals of applied AI research is to make them more intelligent so that they are easier to use and so that they can perform more complex tasks than they do at present. For example, a computer that allows access to a large database of information would be simpler to use if it understood questions in ordinary English – if it had an intelligent *natural language front-end*.

To design computers that people can interact with easily it is necessary to know both something about computers and something about human behaviour. Psychologists with a knowledge of AI are, therefore, ideally qualified to provide specifications for such machines. On the one hand, their knowledge of AI indicates to them what such machines are capable of. On the other hand, their psychological background should provide two things; first, a stock of information about typical reactions to machines, and second, a set of techniques for deciding objectively whether a machine is easy to use. It is easy to convince oneself that a machine will be simple to operate, but less sophisticated users may have unanticipated problems.

## AI research tools

Controlled experiments play a major role in psychological research on knowledge representation, vision, thinking, language and learning. In these experiments 'stimuli' are presented to human, or sometimes animal, subjects and some aspect of their 'response', either immediate or delayed, to those stimuli is recorded. Such experiments are not conducted in a theoretical vacuum, but are, or at least should be, designed to test predictions derived from theories about the psychological mechanisms underlying our cognitive abilities. Computers play a role in this research, often providing on-line experimental control. However, these computers are comparatively modest – nowadays they are often microcomputers, and their programs only record behaviour. They do not simulate it.

AI research is very different. Part of the difference can be attributed to the applied nature of many AI projects, which aim to produce machines that work in the real world. Nevertheless, pure AI research, as well as applied, contrasts sharply with work in experimental psychology. The most obvious difference is that AI's principal research tool is the digital computer. Furthermore, AI programs are large. Mainframe computers, not micros, are required, so AI research can be very expensive. Such research requires substantial financial backing. In the United States, where most AI research has been carried out, the majority of AI projects have been supported from Defence funds.

Computers

AI is, in principle, possible without digital computers. As Turing demonstrated, the steps that a program goes through can be worked out by hand. However, for all but the simplest of AI programs, such hand simulation is too time-consuming and too error-prone to be useful. In practice, modern AI research, with its complex programs, is impossible without sophisticated hardware. AI workers have always tended to demand the largest available machines, since their programs are both large and take a long time to run. Part of the explanation of this latter fact is the extensive use of recursive functions – functions that in the course of their execution may call themselves over and over again.

Some of the earliest AI programs ran on IBM computers. However, DEC machines have been favoured since the late 1960s, originally DEC-10s (and DEC-20s) and more recently VAXs. It is now also possible to install AI programming languages on home and business microcomputers, and to learn the rudiments of these languages on such machines. However, microcomputers are not suitable for writing and running large-scale programs.

A recent trend is to replace mainframe computers with personal workstations, with a large permanent memory shared between several of them. People with such workstations have, for most purposes, machines dedicated to them, and need not worry about what other users of the system are doing, as they must on a traditional timesharing system. One of the most useful features of a workstation is a large high-resolution graphics screen, on which it is possible to maintain multiple 'windows', so that the programmer can look at several parts of a program at once. This facility is made possible by the powerful processor dedicated to the workstation. A lot of computer power is needed to maintain the complex displays that workstations make available.

Another development is that of special machines on which AI programs run more efficiently, enabling larger projects to be undertaken. *LISP machines* are specially designed to run the programming language LISP. Many of the features of LISP are reflected in the hardware of these machines. There is no need to have programs for converting commands in LISP into statements that the machine understands directly. Most LISP machines are spin-offs from the MIT MACLISP project, which has always emphasised speed and efficiency.

## Programming languages

A computer is of little use without programs to run on it, and the writing of programs requires a programming language. Such languages are, therefore, another important tool in AI research.

In one sense all high-level programming languages are equivalent. A mathematical theory – the theory of computability – shows that if a programming language has certain basic features it can perform any computation that can be carried out on any machine (barring limits on the memory of the computer it is running on). However, different high-level programming languages make different types of computation easy, both to think about and to carry out.

Many people regard computers primarily as machines for numerical computations. For these computations languages such as FORTRAN and ALGOL, in scientific applications, and COBOL in business applications, are particularly suitable. However, most of the computations required in modelling intelligent behaviour are *non-numerical* – they require the manipulation of abstract symbols standing not for numbers, but for such things as people, places, words and sentences, and the relations between them. A special class of programming languages has been developed that are particularly suitable for non-numerical computations. They are called *list-processing languages*.

List-processing languages are distinguished from other languages by their use of *list structure*. List structure was first described by Newell, Shaw and Simon (see e.g. Newell and Shaw, 1957), who developed a series of languages called Information-Processing Languages (IPL-I to IPL-V). It is based on the psychological concept of an *association* between two arbitrary objects. A *list* itself is any sequence of elements, some or all of which may themselves be lists. Examples are:

[6 3 7 3 7 4]
[4 5 [5 8 9] [3 4] 3]
[d n e s i f]
[boy girl fish priest]
[2 d 4 r same [x 5] are]
[[the boy] [saw [the girl]]]

The term *list structure* refers to the way lists are represented inside the computer. A *cell* encodes a single association between the first element of a list (called its CAR, in LISP or HEAD, in POP-11) and the rest of it (its CDR or TAIL), which is also a list. Another cell encodes the association between that list's HEAD and TAIL. The list [2 4 6] is, therefore, represented as three cells. The first associates 2 with the list [4 6]. The second associates 4 with [6] (the list containing the single element 6). The final cell associates the element 6 with [] (the empty list).

In the 1960s the IPLs were replaced by LISP (LISP-Processing language), which had been invented by McCarthy in 1958, and which rapidly became the most important AI language, at least in the USA.

LISP has a number of features that make it particularly suitable for AI programming. First, like the versions of BASIC that run on home micros, LISP is primarily an *interpretive language*. There is no need to go through an intermediate process of compilation between typing the text of the program and getting it to run. LISP programs can be compiled, and they usually are once they have been written and debugged, but only because compiled programs run faster than interpreted ones. Second, because LISP is interpretive it allows interactive programming. A programmer can type a statement that will be interpreted straight away, or define a procedure and try that out immediately. Third, a LISP program comprises a large number of separate procedures, each of which can be written and debugged on its own. This feature further enhances the value of interactive programming. Fourth, defining recursive procedures – procedures that call themselves – is straightforward in LISP. Recursive procedures play a crucial role in AI programs. A very simple recursive procedure is one for calculating factorial n (i.e. n × n -1 × n-2 × . . . × 3 × 2 × 1). Informally this procedure is:

to find factorial n
  if n = 1 then the answer is 1
  otherwise to get the answer
          multiply the factorial of n−1 by n.

In computing, say, factorial 4, this procedure will call itself to calculate factorial 3, factorial 2 and factorial 1. Only when it calculates factorial 1 will it get a definite result (1), which is then fed back into the other calculations, whose results are still pending.

Another distinctive feature of LISP is that LISP programs are themselves lists, so the syntax of LISP is simple. However, this simplicity does not mean that LISP programs are readily comprehensible. Indeed, one frequent complaint is that they are hard to understand. Another is that there has never been a standard for LISP in the way that there has been for languages such as FORTRAN and ALGOL, so it may be difficult to transfer a LISP program from one machine to another. However, two dialects of LISP are more important than any others – MACLISP, developed at MIT, and INTERLISP, developed at BBN (Bolt, Berenek & Newman) and Xerox. Each of these is far more than a language, it is also a programming environment. The differences between the two are not so much in the language itself, though that does differ, but in the additional facilities provided. A recent attempt to provide a subset of LISP in which programs can be written that run on any LISP system has resulted in the language COMMON LISP.

LISP interpreters (and compilers) are usually written in LISP, so a LISP statement or procedure will typically be interpreted by another LISP procedure. LISP, therefore, lends itself to having additional facilities designed to run 'on top of' it, because a LISP programmer can write a procedure to interpret a new command. These additional facilities sometimes become so complex that they are best thought of as new languages. The most important are PLANNER and CONNIVER (see chapter 4).

In Britain the language POP-2 (Burstall, Collins and Popplestone, 1971) was developed as an alternative to LISP. In later versions it is known as POP-11 (Barrett, Ramsay and Sloman, 1985). POP has all of the advantages of LISP, except that it sacrifices simplicity of syntax for readability. Its syntax is modelled on that of ALGOL, and POP programs are not lists. POP programs are easier to read than equivalent LISP programs. In many cases they are quite close to English. The dialect of POP-11 that runs in the POPLOG programming environment is likely to become a standard.

Another language that is now popular for some AI applications is PROLOG (Clocksin and Mellish, 1981). Considerable attention has focused on this language since the announcement that the Japanese intended to write intelligent knowledge-based systems in PROLOG as part of their fifth-generation project. PROLOG is based on a subset of the logical language predicate calculus, and its use is sometimes referred to as *logic programming*. In a logic programming language, a program is a set of logical formulae and the result of running the program is a deductive consequence of those formulae. A logic programming language, therefore, requires a built-in theorem prover to deduce the consequences of its programs. PROLOG provides only an approximation to true logic programming, because the behaviour of a PROLOG program cannot be completely predicted from the corresponding set of logical formulae. Part of the reason is that PROLOG's theorem prover is comparatively simple. While it is adequate for some applications, it has to be programmed around in others.

## Programming environments

Present-day computer programmers, particularly those who produce large programs, are not satisfied with a language for writing their programs and a computer to run them on. They want a range of other facilities for editing and debugging programs, and for recompiling the relevant parts of a program when small changes are made. Since AI programs have always been among the largest and most complex that have been written, the demand for such advanced facilities has come mainly from the AI community. They are provided in the MACLISP, INTERLISP and POPLOG *programming environments* already mentioned. The range of such facilities has increased considerably since the early days of AI research, and modern programming environments remove many of the chores from computer programming. AI research has not suddenly become easy, but the amount of time spent on menial tasks has been dramatically reduced. A good programming environment is now one of the standard tools of AI research.

One of the most important facilities in an AI programming environment is an editor specially suited to LISP or POP-11. The best known of these is the EMACS editor developed at MIT for MACLISP. The POPLOG POP editor is called VED. Such an editor knows the names of the built-in functions of the language and its syntax. It can, therefore, detect possible spelling and syntax errors. Other facilities include on-line documentation and help in keeping track of all the procedures in a large program.

## Summary

AI represents a comparatively recent approach to the study of cognition. It is part of computer science, and aims to simulate intelligent behaviour, in a very broad sense of that term, using computer programs. The approach of AI can be contrasted with that of psychology, which proceeds via the experimental testing of predictions derived from theories.

AI has many intellectual antecedents, in particular the work of Babbage, but real progress was impossible before the advent of the digital computer. Such machines were developed in the years after the Second World War, and by the mid-1950s AI had become an actuality with Newell, Shaw and Simon's Logic Theory Machine. Newell *et al.* emphasised functional, as opposed to physiological, models in AI, and introduced the concept of heuristics, or rules of thumb, for solving problems. In the 1960s the range of AI projects increased, the idea of semantic information processing was introduced, and work began on expert systems. More recently, attempts have been made to combine the advantages of AI and psychology in cognitive science.

Pure and applied AI research have not always been easy to disentangle, partly because many AI projects adopt the goal of a working program with realistic outputs. However, in the absence of underlying principles, such programs may make little contribution to the understanding of intelligent behaviour. A recent trend in AI is to place more emphasis on such principles.

Psychologists should study AI for two reasons. First, and most important, AI is a source of psychological theories. Concepts from AI have regularly been imported into psychology, but AI also shows how precise and detailed models of cognitive functioning can be formulated. Second, psychologists who know about AI are uniquely placed to make decisions about the deployment of information technology, because they know both what computers are capable of and how people will react to them.

The mainstay of AI research is the writing of computer programs. Its principal research tools are, therefore, large computers, special list-processing computer languages – primarily LISP, POP-11 and PROLOG – and programming environments designed to make the routine parts of programming easier and less time-consuming.

# 2 Knowledge representation

Both AI and cognitive psychology seek to explain mental functioning in information-processing terms. They claim that cognitive abilities should be explained with reference to what happens in the mind when those abilities are exercised. Behaviour results from the interaction of information currently available from the environment ('stimulus information') and information stored in the mind ('knowledge'). AI and cognitive psychology must, therefore, provide an account of how information is mentally represented, an account that can be applied to both sensory information and stored information. Such theories are, of course, free to claim that different types of representation are used for different purposes.

This chapter surveys the main ideas about the mental representation of information that have been developed in AI. It begins by pointing out that both implicit and explicit knowledge are important in cognitive tasks, and argues that these two types of knowledge can be represented in the same way. The distinction between procedural and declarative representations is also discussed, but deemed problematic. Predicate calculus, a language in which any information can be represented in a uniform way, is described, and the limitations of uniform representations pointed out. Non-uniform representations – semantic networks, frames, scripts, and production systems – are then introduced, and their uses outlined. The chapter closes with discussions of the primitives required in a knowledge representation language, and knowledge representation in computers with parallel architecture.

## Explicit and implicit knowledge

Each of us has in long-term memory a vast store of knowledge about the world, information about both specific events (what psychologists call *episodic* memory) and generalities (what they call *semantic memory*). In everyday parlance things in memory are things that can, though often not very readily, be brought into consciousness. In AI and cognitive psychology it is assumed that skills such as object recognition, language understanding and reasoning depend on information stored in memory, information that it may be impossible to make explicit – to remember in the everyday sense of that term.

This information is often referred to, perhaps misleadingly, as *knowledge* – knowledge, for example, of how to derive a valid conclusion from a set of statements, or of the fact that a sentence can be made up of a noun phrase followed by a verb phrase. However, this way of talking is not intended to suggest that people can formulate such knowledge verbally. If this information is rightly referred to as knowledge it is more akin to Gilbert Ryle's (1949) *knowing how*, the 'knowledge' that underlies skills such as swimming and bicycle riding, than his *knowing that*, the possession of information.

One reason for using the term knowledge is that the 'implicit knowledge' underlying a skill such as language understanding can be represented in much the same way as my (explicit) knowledge that I had cheese and pickle sandwiches for lunch, or that most cheddar cheese is not made in Somerset. The techniques for describing the encoding, storage and retrieval of information that can be brought into consciousness, therefore, carry over to the description of how other information is used in cognitive processing, even if people never become aware of this information. So, although the study of what is usually called memory might constitute a legitimate research project in cognitive psychology or AI, that project would not require very many special information-processing concepts.

All cognitive processing makes use of either explicit knowledge or implicit knowledge or both. Theories about such processing must, therefore, include a description of how knowledge is organised in memory, and of how it is accessed in the course of, for example, object recognition or language understanding. The development of methods for representing knowledge and for accessing and manipulating it efficiently is, therefore, one of the most fundamental aspects of AI research. Indeed, in the absence of an appropriate method of representation even the most trivial problem can be difficult to solve. To take an example from outside AI, multiplication and division of two numbers is very much more difficult if those numbers are represented by roman, rather than arabic, numerals.

In the tasks studied in AI and psychology the relative contribution of knowledge open to introspection and knowledge that is not varies widely. Although, as has already been indicated, the distinction is unimportant for how information is represented, it does bear on how easy a skill is to model. The reason is that knowledge that we cannot become aware of tends to form self-contained systems, relevant to only one task or a limited range of tasks. People are not aware of the processes underlying such skills as low-level visual processing (see chapter 3), or recognising words and the structural relations between them in sentences (or chapter 5). However, these skills are relatively self-contained and comparatively easy to model.

In the majority of cases, the kind of intelligent behaviour studied in AI is only possible if an open-ended amount of knowledge about *the world* is available to the person or system that is behaving intelligently – the kind of knowledge that people can usually, but not always, make explicit. It was only by incorporating such knowledge into AI programs that progress was made in the study of, for example, language understanding, object recognition, and 'real-world' problem solving. To take language processing as an example, in the 1950s and early 1960s attempts were made to use computers to translate from one language to another. These attempts are generally regarded as almost complete failures. An only slightly far-fetched story has it that the sentence 'the spirit is willing, but the flesh is weak' was translated into Russian and then back into English. The result was 'the vodka is good, but the meat is rotten'. These programs were unable to use either knowledge of the world or knowledge of linguistic context to select the correct interpretation of the words in a sentence. However, the open-ended nature of knowledge about the world makes these skills difficult to model.

It might be objected that people are not aware of facts going through their minds as they take part in conversations or read books and magazines. However, the claim about world knowledge is not that we become aware of it every time we use it, but that we *can* become aware of it. In understanding the sentence:

The teacher cut into the juicy steak.

the language processing system may use the information that a sentence can be made up of a noun phrase followed by a verb phrase, a fact that people only find out if they study linguistics. Similarly, the information that steaks are usually cut with knives may be accessed in the course of comprehension, without that information entering consciousness.

## Methods of representing knowledge

The distinction between explicit and implicit knowledge is not important for how information is represented, and knowledge that can be made explicit need not come into consciousness every time it is used. These two points should be borne in mind throughout the following discussion of specific methods of knowledge representation used in AI.

### Programming languages

AI programming languages were briefly described in chapter 1. These languages are used to encode information into a computer's memory. The form of programming languages has, therefore, a pervasive, but rather non-specific, effect on the way in which AI programs represent knowledge. The most important structure for encoding information in AI languages is the list, a sequence of elements with the property that its length need not be specified in advance. List structure is important because it make some ways of doing things easy and others hard.

Lists have many uses. They can express facts about the world – [elephant clyde] might mean that Clyde is an elephant. They can encode information about sentence structure – [s np vp] represents the fact that a sentence can be made up of a noun phrase followed by a verb phrase. They can be descriptions of parts of an image. This use is illustrated in a more complex example taken from Marr (1982, p. 73), which also shows that one list can be contained within another, as an *element* of it. The list:

[blob [position 146 21] [orientation 105] [contrast 76]
[length 16] [width 6]]

indicates that there is a blob with certain properties at a certain position in a representation of a visual field (the primal sketch, see chapter 3).

There are indefinitely many ways that lists can be interpreted. Programmers must be clear about what the lists, and larger data structures, in their programs are supposed to represent.

## Procedural vs. declarative representations of knowledge

In the 1970s there was a lengthy debate about the circumstances under which knowledge should be represented procedurally and those under which it should be represented declaratively (see especially Winograd, 1975). The distinction between declarative and procedural knowledge corresponds to the distinction between a database and a program that acts on a database. Declarative representations seem more natural than procedural representations to non-programmers because they are like statements of facts – knowing a fact (such as: Paris is the capital of France) is a paradigmatic case of having a piece of information. Procedural representations are best explained by an example. To represent the fact that all cats have whiskers procedurally, it can be embodied in a piece of program, called a *demon*, or in a rule of inference. The demon watches for new cats to appear in the database and, for each of these cats, it adds to the database the information that the cat has whiskers. For any particular cat, the fact that it has whiskers is represented *declaratively* in the database. Only the generalisation that all cats have whiskers is represented procedurally. A rule of inference encoding the same information would be: if you want to prove that something has whiskers, it is sufficient to prove that it is a cat.

For two reasons the distinction between procedural and declarative representations is neither as clear nor as important as it at first appears. First, any piece of information can be represented in either way. How a given item is best encoded depends on the overall structure of the system that it is part of. Second, in AI programming languages a section of code may be used sometimes as a procedure and sometimes as a declarative representation. On the one hand, one procedure can treat another as data. On the other, data can be incorporated into one procedure to produce another, more specific one. To take a trivial example, the procedure times(x,y) for multiplying two numbers can be combined with the datum 3 to produce the more specific procedure times 3 (x,3) which multiplies one number, x, by 3. The same applies to knowing how, even though it might appear more natural to encode this type of knowledge procedurally. Because of these complex interactions between procedures and data, it is hard for an observer who cannot look inside a system, for example a psychologist studying human behaviour, to determine whether a particular piece of information is represented procedurally or declaratively.

## Predicate calculus

Predicate calculus is a logical system invented by the German mathematician and logician Gottlob Frege (1879/1972). It was designed to formalise arguments in which the premises can contain more than one instance of the quantifiers *every* and *some*. An example of such an argument is:

> Every man loves every woman.
> Some women love no men.
> so, Some men love some women that do not love them.

There are many different, but equivalent, ways of writing down predicate calculus. The reader should, therefore, be aware that there are variations on the one used here. In particular, when predicate calculus is used in AI, it must be modified to suit the list notation of languages such as LISP and POP-11.

Predicate calculus is a language in which states of affairs can be described. Sentences, or *well-formed formulae*, of this language are made up from predicates, constant terms, variables, logical connectives, and quantifiers. Predicates take one or more *arguments*. For example, the predicates *blue* and *sleeps* take one argument each. So, the well-formed formula *blue*(*block-32*) means that some particular block, which has been given the label block-32, is blue. Similarly *sleeps*(*john*) means that a person called John is asleep. Examples of predicates taking more than one argument (with glosses on the right) are:

sees(mary, john)              Mary sees John.
put(man-3, book-58, table-31) A man puts a book on a table.

It is sometimes useful to think of propositions (the meanings of sentences) as predicates that take no arguments.

In the examples above the arguments of the predicates were constant terms, which correspond roughly to (both proper and arbitrary) names. Predicates can also have *variables* and *function applications* as arguments.

left-of(x,table-22)          Something is to the left
                                 of a table.
sees(mary,brother(john))     Mary sees John's brother.

In the second example *brother* is a function that can be applied to a person to give the brother of that person. So brother(john) − a function application − means John's brother.

The connectives of predicate calculus are the one-place connective ~, which corresponds to *not*, and which can be placed in front of a well-formed formula to produce its negation:

~loves(john,mary)            John does not love Mary.

and the two-place connectives &, v, → (*and, or, if . . . then*), which stand between two well-formed formulae.

made-of(moon,green-cheese) If the moon is made of green
   → edible(moon)      cheese then it is edible.

The two quantifiers are the universal *for all* and the existential *for some*. A quantifier is always associated with a variable (for all x; for some y, etc.). The quantifier and its variable stand in front of an expression containing instances of that variable, which they are said to *bind*:

(for all x)(man(x))→    For all x, if x is a man
(for some y)(woman(y)  then there is some woman y,
  & loves (x,y))      such that x loves y.
                  i.e. every man loves some woman.

As with any other language, there are rules specifying how the vocabulary items of predicate calculus can be put together to form meaningful sentences. The most important of these rules are implicit in the examples above.

As well as *formation rules*, specifying which strings of symbols are well-formed formulae, predicate calculus also has *inference rules*, which show how one formula can be derived from others. One example of such a rule – the rule of *modus ponens* – is that from two formulae of the form P and P → Q, the formula Q can be deduced. Another is that from a formula of the form (for all x) (. . .Fx. . .), the formula . . .Fa. . . can be deduced, where a is an arbitrary name. These rules are set up so that, given true formulae as a starting point, only true formulae can be derived from them.

It is usual to supplement the system described so far with a special identity predicate (=) to give *first order predicate calculus with identity* (FOPC). The term *first order* indicates that quantification is allowed only over objects. There is no quantification over predicates, which are said to be *second order* because a predicate characterises a set of objects. So, although predicate calculus allows statements about, for example, all women, it does not allow talk about all properties that women have (i.e. all one-place predicates that apply to women). FOPC contains only *constant* predicate terms, no variable predicates.

FOPC is a useful language for reasoning because it is both

*consistent* and *complete*. A consistent system is one in which no contradiction can be derived from a set of non-contradictory premises. A complete system is one in which, from such a set of premises, every other well-formed formula that follows from them can be derived mechanically. Many formal languages other than predicate calculus are not complete in this sense.

There are two possible misinterpretations of the claim that FOPC is complete. First, it does not mean that the consequences of a set of assertions are always easy to derive in FOPC. Anyone who has taken a course in introductory formal logic will know that finding proofs can be very hard for people as well as for machines. Second, FOPC is *not* complete in the sense that it can be used to formalise any inference. There are many types of inference that it cannot show to be valid, for which other logical languages have been invented. FOPC cannot capture arguments that depend on quantifiers such as *most*, or *more than half*. Neither can it accommodate the *modal* concepts of possibility, belief and obligation.

Predicate calculus has, nevertheless, been used to represent and manipulate information in many AI projects, particularly in domains where there are no modal concepts. A modified notation has been devised that allows its formulae to be represented in list form in a straightforward way. The completeness result guarantees that any (logical) consequence of the information can, in principle, be derived. A method of deriving such consequences, *resolution*, will be discussed in chapter 4.

## The indexing problem

FOPC provides a way of representing facts declaratively. A collection of predicate calculus assertions can, therefore, be treated as a database. In a psychological system the point of maintaining a database is to use the information in it, in conjunction with incoming information, in the performance of cognitive tasks. For example, to answer the question (incoming information) 'What is the capital of France?' it is necessary to find a database item of the form (capital France x), where x is a variable. If the database is large, the efficient location of relevant items in it may be a problem. Of course, it is possible to check every fact in the database to see if it is about, say,

France or Paris, but such a procedure is very time-consuming. Search would be easier if some organisation could be imposed on the database. The question of how to retrieve pertinent facts from a database gives rise to the *indexing problem*: how should database items be labelled, or *indexed*, so that they can be found rapidly when they are wanted? Part of the answer is that a single fact needs to be indexed in several ways. For example, 'Paris is the capital of France' is for some purposes a fact about France, for others a fact about Paris, and for others still a fact about capital cities.

POP-11, the British AI language, has a built-in database facility. The database itself is simply a list of assertions, which in any interesting application will be very long. There are also pattern-matching procedures for finding items in the database, given a pattern such as (capital, France, x). POP-11 users need only worry about how the pattern matching works if they find it too slow, and wish to replace it with a more efficient procedure (it is comparatively simple and does not provide fast access from large databases). Most versions of LISP, the US standard, do not have built-in database and pattern-matching facilities and many different suggestions have been made for how database search should be implemented in LISP. A common element in many of these ideas is the use of three-element indexes for predicate calculus formulae. The three items in each index are a (constant) expression in the formula (the item, such as France or Paris, about which information may be sought), the position of that element in the (list representation of the) formula, and the formula's predicate. The predicate can be used as part of an index because it is always a constant – variable predicates are not allowed in FOPC. It is never necessary to match a predicate in a database entry to a variable in a question. Other constants in database entries may, however, be matched to variables in queries. This matching is achieved by the unification procedure described in chapter 4. *See.*

## Non-monotonic logics

FOPC and other traditional logics are *monotonic*. If a new fact is added to a FOPC database, all the facts already in that database, and any others that follow from them, remain true. Problems can only arise if the new fact contradicts one of the original facts. Some types of human reasoning *appear* to be *non-monotonic*. When new facts are discovered, conclusions may no longer hold. However, there is some controversy over whether *non-monotonic logics* (e.g. McDermott and Doyle, 1980; Moore, 1985) are needed to model these types of reasoning. One type of inference that is often taken to be non-monotonic is the use of *default values*. If a database contains facts about (typical) elephants, and information comes to light about an elephant called Clyde, it can be inferred that Clyde has four legs. However, if it is subsequently learned that Clyde lost a leg in an accident, the original conclusion no longer holds. A new fact has falsified a conclusion derived from what was known before that fact was learned. McCarthy's (1980, 1986) *principle of circumspection* makes explicit the idea underlying default reasoning. It holds that all *qualifications* must be explicitly stated. In the absence of qualifications, it can be assumed that things conform to expectations – that Clyde, for example, has four legs. However, not all facts about Clyde are learned at the same time. A qualification may only be discovered after facts have been deduced on the assumption that there are no qualifications.

There are several ways in which the conclusion that some types of deductive reasoning are non-monotonic can be avoided. One is to claim that Clyde's four-leggedness cannot be deduced at all, but merely inferred probabilistically. Another is to say that it can be deduced, but only on the basis of a hidden premise. This premise states that there is no evidence that Clyde has an unusual number of legs. On this view the new information about Clyde falsifies a *premise* used in a previous argument, and holds that the new conclusion follows from a new set of premises.

Default reasoning and other types of apparently non-monotonic reasoning are common. So, regardless of whether non-monotonic logics are required to describe them, AI must show how they can be formalised. One approach to default reasoning is to use memory representations such as frames and scripts, described below. A more general solution is to introduce *data dependencies* (Doyle, 1979). A data dependency links two facts in a database. It indicates that one of the facts is justified by, or believed on the basis of, the other. In general, one datum depends on several others. Data dependencies are particularly useful when a database represents a collection of interdependent beliefs, some of which may be discovered to be false, or discarded for some other reason. The most important rule for data dependencies is that if all the reasons for believing a fact are deleted from the database, then that fact should be deleted, too. Doyle calls a system for keeping a database with dependencies up to date a *truth maintenance system*.

## Semantic networks

Predicate calculus provides a uniform method for representing facts in a database – all facts are treated in the same way. However, uniform representations are not always the most useful. Because they treat all facts in the same way, such representations favour general procedures for inferring new information. When using such procedures, the ease of making an inference does not depend on the conclusion to be drawn, but only on such factors as the number of inferential steps from the premises to the conclusion. Any set of premises gives rise to indefinitely many inferences, and the larger the set the more conclusions there are that can be reached in a given number of steps. So, with a large database, a uniform proof procedure can be very inefficient. It has difficulty finding the required conclusion among all possible conclusions.

Predicate calculus databases do not readily support the *domain-specific* methods of inference making that can be exploited if non-uniform methods of representation are used. Domain-specific methods assume that only some types of conclusion should be drawn. They never consider others. A good domain-specific method is, therefore, one that produces just those conclusions that are required in the domain that it is intended for. Such methods have been widely used in AI, and it is to them that discussion now turns.

One of the earliest methods used to represent the information needed in a high-level cognitive task was *semantic networks* (Quillian, 1968). The networks were called *semantic* because they encoded information about meaning. When similar networks are used for other purposes they are referred to as *associative* networks.

The utility of semantic networks is reflected by the fact that they are still widely used in AI research, in language understanding and in other fields. However, their continued success has depended on the theoretical basis of network theory being made more secure. Early work using semantic networks was criticised by Woods (1975), among others. The most important problem was that no formal account was provided of what networks represented. The interpretation of a piece of network was left largely to the intuitions of people reading about it. Furthermore, in some cases, the same piece of network was effectively interpreted in different ways by different parts of the same program.

A semantic network is an example of the kind of structure that mathematicians called a (labelled) graph. It consists of a set of *nodes* connected by *links*. In the earliest networks the nodes stood for concepts – roughly, word meanings – and the links for relations between them. The most important links were *class inclusion* links and *feature specification* links. These links connected, for example, the dog node to the animal node and the barking node, respectively. A complete network modelled a person's knowledge about the meaning of words. In subsequent research, networks were used to represent facts about the world conveyed in dialogues and text. These networks contained nodes standing for individuals, such as Fifi the spaniel, and for the meanings of sentences. Additional types of link were also introduced, to represent the relations between individuals and between sentence meanings.

Semantic networks provide a non-uniform way of representing information, because the relations represented by links are treated differently from other relations. In predicate calculus these relations would simply be two-place predicates. In a semantic network, the inference:

          All dogs are mammals
          All mammals are animals
     So,  All dogs are animals

is made by following the class-inclusion links from dog to mammal to animal. The rules of predicate calculus are not used. Since inference making in semantic networks is essentially a process of link following, it can be carried out by special graph-searching algorithms. Such algorithms make only a subset of the inferences that would be made by a uniform proof procedure. However, the inferences that they do make are produced very quickly. The degree of non-uniformity, and hence of domain-specificity, that can be provided by a network representation depends on what relations are encoded by links. In any particular application, an attempt must be made to choose a representation and an algorithm that can produce just the required inferences.

### Quillian's nets

Quillian (1968) developed semantic networks as a model of semantic memory. He later (1969) incorporated them into a program called the Teachable Language Comprehender (TLC). TLC used a semantic network memory structure in an attempt to understand text. It was described as teachable because it could add new concepts from a text to its network.

The success of TLC as a comprehension system was very limited. However, in developing TLC, Quillian rationalised the organisation of his nets. It was these revised nets that formed the basis of the network model of semantic memory that was tested experimentally by Quillian and Allan Collins (Collins and Quillian, 1969, 1972). Two main ideas inspired these experimental studies. The first was that of an *intersecting search* through a network. Intersecting search is a method of finding a connection between two concepts. It can be used, for example, to decide whether *spaniel* and *animal* are related in such a way as to make the sentence *a spaniel is an animal* true. In an intersecting search, activation starts at the nodes representing each of the concepts, and spreads first to the nodes directly connected to them, then to those two links away, and so on. When activation from the two sources meets, the path between them is tested to see if it verifies the putative relation between them. These ideas were refined by Collins and Loftus (1975) under the name of *spreading activation*.

The second idea was that of an *inheritance hierarchy*. It played a crucial role in checking the kind of relation supported by a path between two nodes. The hierarchy part of an inheritance hierarchy is a taxonomy of the concepts denoted by common nouns. Normally, it is that of the layman rather than the expert. For example, the concepts *spaniel, dog,* and *animal* will be found at successively higher levels of the hierarchy. The links that encode the relation between nodes at adjacent levels of the hierarchy are often referred to as ISA links. Thus, *spaniel* ISA *dog* and *dog* ISA *animal*. This series of links supports the claim that a spaniel is an animal. The direction of the links is important. It is not true that an (arbitrarily chosen) animal is a spaniel.

The hierarchies are called *inheritance* hierarchies because nodes inherit properties from those above them in the hierarchy. Animals have the property of breathing, so there is no need for an explicit representation of the fact that spaniels breathe. They breathe by virtue of the fact that they are animals. Similarly they bark because they are dogs. Only properties specific to spaniels (e.g. having long floppy ears) need to be linked directly to the spaniel node. Thus, an appropriate combination of ISA links and feature-specification links along a path found by spreading activation can verify a claim such as 'spaniels breathe'.

### Representing facts about the world

Semantic networks can be used to represent not only relations between concepts, but also relations between individuals, and hence facts about the world. To extend networks in this way, nodes corresponding to people, places and things must be introduced, and links corresponding to the relations between them. Since individuals inherit properties from the classes to which they belong, they can be included in inheritance hierarchies. Such hierarchies then contain two types of links – set membership links and subclass links. However, the inclusion of individuals in inheritance hierarchies raises a number of problems. If Fifi is my pet spaniel, she will have long floppy ears in virtue of being a spaniel, and she will bark in virtue of being a dog. However, she will not be numerous even if spaniels, or dogs, are. To put this another way, individual dogs should inherit properties that each dog has individually, but not properties that dogs have only when they are considered as a class. In fact, this problem is not limited to individual dogs. The typical spaniel inherits properties from the typical dog, but spaniels may be a rare breed, even if dogs are common.

One way of making sure that only the right properties are inherited is to have two nodes, one representing the class of dogs (which may be numerous), and one representing the prototypical dog. Properties are then inherited only among prototypes. However, this solution introduces a further complication. On the most natural interpretation of *prototype*, the prototypical dog has properties that not all dogs have. The prototypical dog frisks about, for example, but bull mastiffs do not. Individual dogs should not inherit all properties from the prototypical dog, but only properties that do not conflict with information stored at a node lower in the hierarchy.

The multiplicity of types of relation between individuals presents another problem in representing facts about the world. The simplest solution is to introduce links corresponding to each verb, SEE links, LIKE links, BUILD links and so on. However, there are two problems with this solution. First, each type of link requires a graph-searching algorithm for generating the inferences it supports. A proliferation of such algorithms will detract from the efficiency of inference making that semantic networks provide. Second, many verbs, such as *put* (X put Y on Z), relate more than two individuals. Links can only connect two nodes.

The usual solution to this problem is to introduce nodes standing for *propositions*, the meanings of simple sentences. A proposition node represents the event, state or process described by the sentence to which it corresponds. There is a link from the proposition node to a node standing for the verb of the sentence. This link is usually called a VERB link. In addition, each individual that plays a role in the event, state or process is linked to the proposition node. The required links are drawn from a small set, and represent *case relations* that the individuals and the verb can stand in. These relations have names such as AGENT, PATIENT, BENEFACTIVE and INSTRUMENT. Unfortunately there is no general agreement about how many case relations are required or what those relations are (see Bruce, 1975, for a survey of the use of case relations in AI).

### Brachman's KL-ONE

The use of semantic networks to represent information about the world and the proliferation of case systems made it difficult to state clearly what a given piece of network was supposed to represent (Woods, 1975). This problem suggested that assumptions about knowledge representation should be made more explicit and that more thought should be given to the *primitives* out of which networks are built. Brachman (1979) argued that more than one set of primitives is required, and that the different sets correspond to different levels at which networks can be described. In addition to the implementational level of description, with which AI programmers need not concern themselves, and the logical level, where logical operators and the concepts of proposition and predication are defined, Brachman argued for an *epistemological* level of description. *Epistemology* is the theory of knowledge. Epistemological primitives describe the internal structure of concepts and explain how information is inherited. The levels of descriptions above the epistemological level are the conceptual and linguistic levels. At the conceptual level the primitives are case relations and (a subset of) concepts. The linguistic level provides an interface between the conceptual level and natural language. The choice of primitives at any level is independent of the choice at lower levels. In particular the epistemological primitives do not restrict the concepts that can be made available at the next level up.

Having put semantic network theory on a more secure footing, Brachman proposed a language for describing networks, KL-ONE, which provides a set of epistemological primitives. These primitives describe relations between KL-ONE concepts, of which there are two types, *generic concepts*, representing classes of object, and *individual concepts*, representing individual objects. An individual concept is represented by a single node that denotes a real-world object. The complex internal structure of that object is represented by further pieces of network constructed from the epistemological primitives and linked to the individual concept node. *Roles,* and their *filler descriptions*, correspond to the parts of the object. Restrictions can be placed on the kind of thing that can fill a role. The relations among parts of an object are encoded in *structural descriptions*. Special epistemological primitives account for inheritance.

KL-ONE, like Fahlman's NETL, described below, is a *knowledge representation language*, which should not be confused with a programming language. It is implemented in INTER-LISP, and requires standard LISP facilities if it is to be used by a computer system to represent knowledge.

### Fahlman's NETL

If all of a person's knowledge were encoded in a single semantic network, that network would be very large, and it might be difficult to find a particular piece of information in it. In particular, a node standing for an individual, such as Fifi the spaniel, could inherit properties from nodes an arbitrary distance away in the network. So, verifying that Fifi has a certain property (that she breathes, for example) might require an extensive search. This problem is made worse by the fact that information in a realistic memory system does not have the simple hierarchical structure of the networks described so far. Rather, it forms a *tangled hierarchy*, in which each element can belong to several more general categories. As well as being a dog, Fifi might be a pet and a companion, and she inherits different properties by virtue of belonging to each of these classes.

Fahlman (1979) addressed the question of how search in such a network could be made efficient. His most important idea, which subsumes that of an inheritance hierarchy, was that of a *virtual copy* of part of a network. Since Fifi has all the properties of a typical spaniel (except those that she is specifically known to lack), the part of the network representing Fifi should behave as if it contained a copy of the part representing the typical spaniel. That part, in turn, should behave as if it contained the part representing a typical dog, and so on. However, the copies cannot really be there. The network is already large and its size would rapidly get out of hand if copies within copies were actually present.

Fahlman devised a representational system, which he called

NETL, that behaves as though it contains virtual copies. It also allows specific facts about an individual to override information from a virtual copy of a typical member of a class to which it belongs. However, despite the rationalisation of information in NETL, searching a large NETL network remains time-consuming, particularly if it is implemented on an ordinary serial computer. By contrast, people are very quick at making inferences that depend on the classes to which people and things belong. They can rapidly decide, for example, that Fifi has four legs, even though they haven't been told. If she didn't have four legs, that fact would surely have been mentioned. In fact, making these inferences is so natural that people do not always realise that any mental work has been expended.

Fahlman proposed that a semantic network should be implemented not on an ordinary (serial) computer, but on specially built parallel hardware that directly reflects the structure of the network. Specifically, he suggested that each element (node or link) in the network should be a simple processor, capable of performing a few operations on its own. Retrieval of information is guided by a separate *controller*, which is an ordinary serial computer. The controller broadcasts messages to the network, saying, for example that all nodes of a certain type are to propagate activation to nodes immediately above and/or below them in the hierarchy, or that all links with a certain type of activation at each end are to report their identities. Thus, the controller initiates a search, the search is carried out by the parallel hardware, and the controller then asks for the results of the search.

The essence of Fahlman's proposal is that, if the network is implemented on parallel hardware, then activation can genuinely spread from one node to several others at the same time. On a serial machine such parallel spreading of activation can only be simulated. Such simulation may take many machine cycles, particularly if there is a lot of branching in the network. In the kind of machine that Fahlman envisages, the time taken for activation to spread through the entire net depends only on the length of the longest path.

Fahlman did not attempt to simulate brain processes directly. However, he points out that the analogy between the brain and his proposed parallel hardware is much closer than that between the brain and a serial computer. Ironically, in 1979 it was not feasible for Fahlman to implement his ideas. He was forced to simulate the parallel hardware on a serial computer! Technological developments since 1979 have brought a genuine parallel machine closer to reality. Parallel models of memory are discussed further at the end of this chapter.

### Hendrix's partitioned networks

The discussion so far has shown how semantic networks can be used to represent relations between classes and their members and subclasses, and between objects and their properties. These networks encode simple generalities. A feature link between the SPANIEL node and the FLOPPY EARS node, for example, represents the fact that all spaniels have floppy ears. However, such networks have no means of representing the multiple generalities of FOPC. Hendrix (e.g. 1979) was one of the first to show how networks could be extended to represent statements of multiple generality, and hence how they could be made equivalent in expressive power to FOPC.

Hendrix's basic idea was to *partition* associative nets. As the term suggests, partitioning a net means dividing it into smaller parts. These parts are called *spaces*. Just as there are links that relate nodes, there are relations between spaces. Hendrix makes use of just one such relation, that of *viewing capability*. Within any space it is only possible to access and manipulate information in spaces that can be viewed from it. A simple example of the use of this idea is in the encoding of (the meaning of) a statement. The statement has its own space from which its *background space* can be viewed, but which is not visible from that background space. The background space represents the part of the world that the statement is about. It must be visible from the statement space, since the statement (e.g. 'John sees Mary') makes reference to objects in that space. However, the statement itself is isolated from the background, because it may be false. Each space is represented by a corresponding *supernode*, which can be linked to other nodes by the usual types of arc. The supernode corresponding to the 'John saw Mary' space will be connected by an ISA link to the set of statements. Another important use of spaces is to represent, for example, a person's beliefs or wants. The supernode corresponding to such a space will be linked to, among other things, the node representing the person who has those beliefs or desires.

Since Hendrix's partitioned networks are equivalent to FOPC, they can represent the existential and universal quantifiers of that calculus. Existential quantifiers are not represented by additional pieces of network structure. The fact that a node representing, say, a man is in the network is taken to be an implicit assertion that a man exists in the domain corresponding to the space in which the node occurs. A universal statement about a particular class of things, for example 'All spaniels have floppy ears', is represented as a type of implication (*if* . . . *then* statement). In general an implication links separate antecedent and consequent spaces. However, in an implication corresponding to a universal statement the same variable occurs in both the antecedent and consequent spaces (for all x, if x is a spaniel then x has floppy ears), which therefore overlap. Every implication of this form is taken to represent a universally quantified statement. More complex statements of FOPC, and in particular those with more than one quantifier, can be represented using a combination of these devices.

Partitioned networks can be used to represent any fact that can be expressed by a set of FOPC formulae. Earlier networks did not have this power of expression. However, partitioned nets retain the graph structure of simple semantic nets, and hence they share the advantages of the networks over a more straightforward FOPC representation. In particular, special graph-searching algorithms can be used to perform a limited class of inferences highly efficiently.

### Other approaches to semantic networks

Semantic networks have been very popular and the work described above represents only a small fraction of the research using such networks. However, the most important ideas have been covered. A good summary of the main themes of semantic network research is the collection edited by Findler (1979), which includes papers by Brachman and

Hendrix. Other important papers in the collection are those by Schubert, Goebel and Cercone (1979), which provides an alternative way of establishing a correspondence between networks and predicate calculus, and by Levesque and Mylopoulos (1979), which further emphasises the need for an unequivocal account of how network structures should be interpreted.

## Schemata, frames, scripts

In an ordinary semantic network there is no intermediate level of structure between that of links and nodes and that of the whole network. Hendrix's method of partitioning divides a network into spaces, for example by grouping together those nodes and links that represent a particular person's beliefs, but it does not introduce any additional structure. Many people have argued that information in long-term memory is organised in ways that cannot be captured by the network formalism. However, as will become apparent, many of the problems that led to proposals for specific long-term memory structures are the same as those that Brachman and Fahlman addressed in their revisions of network theory.

The psychologist Bartlett put forward the idea that our interactions with the world are mediated by large-scale memory structures, which he called *schemata* (Bartlett, 1932). However, although Bartlett's ideas are often cited as an inspiration for recent AI research on memory organisation, they are not formulated in a way that can be directly translated into programming terms.

Since the mid-1970s a number of proposals have been made in AI about large-scale memory structures required for cognitive tasks. The earliest of these proposals to have a widespread influence was Minksy's (1975) *frame-system theory*. This theory was originally applied to the problem of how the same object can be recognised from different viewpoints. Minsky proposed that there should be a different but related description of the object for each point of view. However, Minksy always intended his theory to have more general applications and, indeed, he discussed some of these in his 1975 paper.

A *frame* is a knowledge structure that represents some aspect of the world, which might be, for example, an object (or a view of an object), an event, or a sequence of events. A frame can represent either a specific object or a type of object. A frame representing a specific object is derived from one representing the corresponding type of object by making a copy of it and filling in information that is 'missing' – information that is true of the specific object, but not necessarily of the type of object. This information goes into *terminals* or *slots* in the frame, and there may be constraints on the values that the *fillers* for these slots can have. For example, an elephant frame will have, among others, slots for the elephant's COLOUR, its NUMBER-OF-LEGS, and its TYPE – whether it is INDIAN or AFRICAN. The COLOUR slot must, of, course be filled by a colour, the NUMBER-OF-LEGS slot by a (small) number, and so on. Some terminals have associated *default values*, values that can be assumed in the absence of information to the contrary. Elephants are usually grey, and they usually have four legs. However, without any contextual information it is not safe to guess whether an elephant is Indian or African. That terminal can only be filled by specific information or by a context-dependent default. The structure of a frame is intended to mirror the important aspects of the structure of an object, and frames themselves are organised into systems that are intended to reflect higher-order structures in the world.

One way that frames are organised is into an inheritance hierarchy of the kind found in semantic networks. The fact that a frame representing a specific elephant is derived from a generic elephant frame can be stated another way by saying that a representation of Clyde is joined by an ISA link to the prototypical elephant frame. That frame is, in turn, joined to the prototypical animal frame and so on.

Frames provide a declarative method of representing knowledge, but a system that uses frames usually has other information represented procedurally. In particular, procedures can become associated with slots by a process called *procedural attachment*. Such procedures have two main purposes. First, they find values to fill the slots when those values are needed. A slot can have *if-needed conditions*, which specify when it is necessary to fill the slot. It is the procedure's job to find out whether the if-needed conditions are satisfied and, if they are, to find a value. Second, attached procedures may produce further inferences once a slot has been filled. Bobrow *et al*'s (1977) GUS, a natural language system that simulates an airline reservations clerk, uses frame-driven reasoning in this way.

Schank and Abelson (1977) developed the concept of a *script*, which is an application of Minksy's frame idea to one aspect of language understanding. A script encodes information about a stereotypical sequence of events, such as a visit to the doctor's or a trip to a restaurant. When such sequences of events form the basis of a narrative, some of the events in the sequence may not be mentioned. For example, in a description of a meal out there need be no mention of the participants being shown to a table, ordering the food, eating it and paying the bill. Indeed, if everything that typically happens in a visit to a restaurant were described, the text would be extremely boring. But in the absence of information about these events, people assume that they have happened. If asked whether the bill was paid, they say 'yes'. Schank and Abelson explain this ability to fill in missing information by assuming that scripts are used in the interpretation and encoding of information in a text. They further assume that the occurrence of the events in a script, rather than their non-occurrence, is the default. Schank and Abelson's computer program for understanding text uses scripts in this way, and is able to confirm, for example, that the bill was paid at the end of a meal, even if it has not been explicitly told so.

Some psychological experiments (e.g. Bower, Black and Turner, 1979; Graesser, Gordon and Sawyer, 1979) have attempted to investigate the psychological reality of scripts. However, while the results are broadly consistent with Schank and Abelson's proposal, they are consistent with a wide range of other similar hypotheses. Indeed, Schank (see e.g. 1982) has revised his ideas about scripts quite radically. He no longer regards them as basic structures in memory, but takes them to be built up from units called Memory Organisation

Packets (MOPs). This idea derives from the fact that many scripts, such as visit to doctor and visit to lawyer, have elements in common. It is unparsimonious to propose that the same information is repeated in many scripts without any indication that it is shared.

As well as scripts (and MOPs), Schank and his colleagues have described several other memory structures that they believe are implicated in language understanding. The more important of these are sketchy scripts, plans, TOPs, points, plot units and affects. *Sketchy scripts* are used in a system called FRUMP (the Fast Reading Understanding and Memory Program, de Jong, 1982), which produces summaries of news stories. Since they are used as the basis for summaries, sketchy scripts contain less information than scripts. In fact each sketchy script only contains information about the main points of the type of story that it represents. FRUMP decides, from a rather crude preliminary analysis, which sketchy script best applies to the story it is trying to summarise. It then forces the story to fit the script, filling in details such as dates from information in the text.

Detailed understanding of texts about people's actions, as opposed to summarising them, is notoriously difficult to simulate, despite the ease with which skilled readers perform this task. *Plans* (see Wilensky, 1983), TOPs (thematic organisation points, Schank, 1982), *points* (Wilensky, 1982), *plot units* (Lehnert, 1982) and *affects* (Dyer, 1983) all represent attempts to encode information about the structure of such texts. The theory of plans, for example, is an attempt to codify the sorts of plans people have, how those plans can be fulfilled and the role that beliefs play in putting plans into action. Another important factor in understanding longer stories, as Rieger (1979) has emphasised, is the construction of personality models of the characters, and models of the relationships between pairs of characters.

## Production systems

Knowledge representation systems such as semantic nets, frames and scripts encode information in an essentially declarative form. However, some types of knowledge are more naturally thought of as sets of rules. A *production system* is a set of rules, called *productions*, that embodies knowledge about a particular domain, and which can be used for making inferences in that domain. In AI, production systems are also known as *rule-based systems*.

A production states that if a certain set of conditions holds then a certain set of actions can be performed. The terms *condition* and *action* are interpreted broadly. In some applications they refer to states of the world and actions to be performed on them, respectively, but in others the 'conditions' are facts known to be true, and the 'actions' deductions of further facts. A production of the first type would be:

If (1) the room temperature is below 15 degrees Centigrade.
(2) someone wants to use the room for more than 20 minutes
Then turn on the central heating

Production systems are modular. New productions, corresponding to new bits of knowledge, can be added to them without affecting the way the production system works. Productions may share conditions, so it may happen that, when an action is to be performed, more than one production is applicable. To handle such cases a *conflict resolution strategy* is needed. A production whose conditions are satisfied in the current state of the world is said to have been *triggered*. One selected by the conflict resolution strategy is said to have *fired*.

Several conflict resolution strategies have been proposed. One is to use the most specific production – the one with the greatest number of conditions satisfied. If this strategy is adopted, the production system might include odd-looking productions of the following kind:

If you are painting the door
Then stop painting the door

This production would be part of a system with productions such as:

If (1) you are painting the door
(2) the frame is painted

(3) the panels are not painted
Then  paint the panels

The very general production will only be invoked when the door is completely painted. It might be elaborated as:

If      you are painting the door
        (and no part of the door is unpainted)
Then  stop painting the door
        start painting the wainscotting

This production initiates the next stage of a task when the present one is finished.

Another control strategy is to divide the productions into sets, and to mark each set with the contexts in which it is applicable. Within a set each production should have different conditions, so that no conflict ever arises within that set. Marcus's parser PARSIFAL, discussed in chapter 5, represents knowledge about the structure of sentences in the form of productions. It uses this conflict-resolution strategy.

The point of representing knowledge is always so that it can be used for some purpose. Although the need for conflict-resolution strategies complicates the question of when a production will fire, the form of a production makes it relatively clear when and how the information in it can be used. Production systems can, therefore, be contrasted with systems such as predicate calculus, for which a separate procedure (resolution, see chapter 4) is needed to make use of knowledge in a database. A predicate calculus representation does not itself indicate how the information in it can be used.

The most natural way of using productions to make inferences is *foward chaining*. Forward chaining starts from a set of initial conditions and performs the actions that they warrant. This step creates a new set of conditions in which further productions are triggered. The process continues until the required conclusion is reached. Productions can also be used for *backward chaining*. In backward chaining the goal to be achieved or the statement to be proved is taken as the starting point. It is matched against the *actions* in the set of productions to find out what conditions would have to hold for the goal to be achieved or for the statement to be true. These conditions are in turn matched against the actions of the productions to see how they can be achieved. Matching continues until the starting conditions are reached.

Production systems have been proposed as psychological models of human cognition by a number of authors (e.g. Newell and Simon, 1972). In their application to human cognition additional assumptions about production systems must be made. In particular, it is assumed that productions are held in long-term memory, as part of our stored knowledge about the world, but that they are triggered by, and operate on, items in short-term memory. Since short-term memory is a store of limited capacity, there are limitations on the operations that can be performed on items in it.

## Knowledge representation languages

In the mid- to late 1970s some of the emerging ideas about knowledge representation were incorporated into new programming languages for AI. As was mentioned above, semantic networks can be thought of as a language for representing knowledge. Both Brachman (1979) and Fahlman (1979) emphasise this aspect of their work.

KL-ONE and NETL provide ways of representing the structural relations between parts of objects that are also made explicit in frame representations. Two other languages, also developed as additions to LISP systems, are more closely related to Minsky's frame-system theory than to semantic networks. These are FRL (Frame Representation Language, Roberts and Goldstein, 1977) and KRL (Knowledge Representation Language, Bobrow and Winograd, 1977). KRL and FRL give their users more choice about how to represent information, and how to access it, than network-based languages. FRL and KRL focus on the structure of representations of particular objects, their relation to other representations of the same object, and their relation to representations of prototypical objects of the same category.

None of these languages has been widely used, though their development has brought a number of issues into sharper focus. The main reason for their lack of impact is that the facilities one person builds into a language are likely to be different from those required by someone else. The current trend is for programmers to construct their own facilities piecemeal within a LISP (or POP) system. These facilities are not developed into languages, though, of course, they are often made available to other researchers, to avoid duplication of programming effort.

## Two general issues

This chapter ends with a discussion of two general issues that must be faced in any system of knowledge representation. The first concerns the vocabulary needed to express the information stored in memory. The second is the question of whether parallel, as opposed to serial, computers can provide better information stores and more appropriate models of human memory.

### Semantic primitives

Brachman (1979) distinguished five levels of description needed in a theory of knowledge representation. He focused on the epistemological level, which he felt had been neglected in previous work. The next level up, the semantic or conceptual level, is more difficult to overlook. It is the level at which specific items of information are encoded. However, reasoned decisions about the vocabulary required at that level are not always easy to make. Sometimes they are difficult because people have poor intuitions about the concepts required. An example of a domain in which this problem arises is low-level vision (see chapter 3). Other domains produce stronger intuitions though they are not necessarily correct. For example, in many natural-language and semantic-memory systems the primitives for encoding meaning correspond, more or less, to (say, English) words. However, it has often been suggested that a smaller set of meaning primitives will suffice, most notably by Wilks (e.g. 1975) and Schank (e.g. 1972).

Wilks used over eighty primitives to construct definitions of words for his machine translation system. Earlier machine translation programs had difficulty selecting the intended meaning of ambiguous words. Wilks's goal was to provide representations of their meanings that would enable his program to choose the correct one. His basic idea was that word senses provide a set of constraints that 'ought' to be fulfilled. For example, the verb *break* specifies that its subject – the thing that does the breaking – ought to be human. The intended sense of a word is the one with most constraints satisfied. Wilks's system, which he calls *preference semantics*, does not require that all the constraints should be fulfilled. It is satisfied with the best fit.

Schank's goals are more ambitious. He seeks to provide a language-neutral representation of the information content of sentences. This representation will be used for paraphrase, inference and question answering, as well as for translation. He calls his system of representation *conceptual dependency*, because it comprises a set of relations (or dependencies) between concepts. Schank concentrates on representing the information carried by verbs. He claims that the meaning of each verb can be represented in terms of about a dozen primitive ACTs, such as MOVE, PROPEL, EXPEL, PTRANS (physical transfer), and MTRANS (mental transfer, or transfer of information). Like Wilks, Schank takes a pragmatic view of how the set of primitives should be chosen, but Schank's chief criterion is that each primitive ACT should support its own set of inferences. The higher-level Schankian constructs, such as scripts, plans, and goals, were designed to overcome some of the obvious inadequacies of conceptual dependency representations, such as their inability to represent the purpose behind an action.

## Parallel architecture

Fahlman (1979) proposed to implement a semantic network on purpose-built parallel hardware, so that inferences could be made in a reasonable amount of time. Another reason for investigating parallel implementations of knowledge representation systems is that the human brain is a parallel system. Such implementations may, therefore, provide pointers to the way knowledge is represented in the human mind.

A serial machine can only perform one operation at a time, whereas a parallel machine can carry out as many operations as it has independent processors. The human brain resembles Fahlman's proposed implementation of his NETL system in that it comprises a large number of simple processors. The brain, however, has many more processors than Fahlman envisaged for NETL – about 10–100 million neurons, and even more glial cells. It is, therefore, a *massively parallel* system. Feldman and Ballard (1982) argue from neural firing rates and typical reaction times in psychological experiments that complex problems are solved in the brain in the time that any one neuron can perform about one hundred operations. The basic components of serial computers already operate millions of times faster than neurons, and there are prospects of still faster operation. An AI program may, therefore, take hundreds of millions of machine cycles to solve even a comparatively simple problem. However, on each cycle only one operation is performed. In the brain there may be millions of operations per cycle.

It has always been possible to formulate models of cognitive tasks in terms of massively parallel architecture, but in the absence of parallel hardware to test them on there has been little motivation to produce such models. New Very Large Scale Integration (VLSI) techniques should allow the construction of parallel machines that run at a reasonable speed and that are not prohibitively costly. The essence of VLSI is putting more and more electronic components on smaller and smaller pieces of silicon (chips). Each processor in a parallel machine contains at least one component – in practice more. So millions of components must be put on to one chip to produce a reasonably powerful single-chip parallel machine. Hillis (1985) describes a prototype of such a machine, which he calls the *connection machine*.

*Connectionism* is an approach to knowledge representation in which information is stored as a set of connections or associations (of varying strength) between simple neuron-like elements. Some connectionist proposals, like Fahlman's, retain a localised representation of information. Each concept in the NETL system has its own node. Another example is McClelland and Rumelhart's (1981) *interactive activation* model of letter and word detection, which has localised feature, letter and word detectors. Other connectionist models employ *distributed* memories. In these systems a single item of information is represented as a pattern of connections between a number of units. Furthermore, each unit contributes to a large number of memories. Hinton (1981) describes a distributed representation of semantic nets – a parallel implementation that is radically different from Fahlman's. Techniques for extracting of information from distributed memories are available. They are error-prone, but so is human memory.

Connectionist models are easiest to formulate for relatively low-level processes. A difficult, and largely unsolved, problem is how to bridge the gap between the conceptual apparatus of connectionist models and the types of representation that are used in traditional AI models of higher-level processes, in particular rule-like representations of generalities. How can parsing (chapter 5) be carried out by a connection machine, for example, or mathematical problem solving (chapter 4)?

Rule-governed behaviour can be an *emergent property* of a connectionist model. A connection machine can behave as if it knows a set of rules, even though it has no explicit representation of those rules. For example, an extended version of McClelland and Rumelhart's model predicts experimental results on the pronunciation of letter strings. An alternative explanation of these results is that people apply spelling-to-sound conversion rules, which are explicitly stored in their minds. An optimistic view is that there are no problems in principle in using connectionist models to simulate rule-governed behaviour. However, this view leads to the accusation that connectionist models are simply arcane implementations of standard ideas from AI and cognitive psychology (cf. Broadbent, 1985). However, as well as being biologically more plausible, connection machines might be distinguished from serial machines in the way that they learn. Learning algorithms for connection machines may have no counterpart for serial machines, yet they may closely reflect the way that people learn.

*Cognitive Science* (vol. 9, no. 1) contains a collection of papers on connectionist models of high-level processes.

## Summary

Cognition results from an interaction between incoming sensory information and information stored more permanently in memory. One of the most fundamental aspects of AI research is, therefore, the development of methods for representing and manipulating information. Some stored information is accessible to consciousness – it can be remembered in the everyday sense of that term – but the rest we cannot become aware of. However, there is no reason to believe that this distinction has implications for *how* information is represented.

AI programming languages have a very general influence on the representation of information, particularly via the concept of list structure, which is based on the psychological notion of association. However, the distinction between procedural and declarative representations, which is suggested by programming considerations, is neither as important nor as clear-cut as it first appears.

Predicate calculus provides a uniform method of representing a variety of facts, one that has been widely used in AI. However, in putting knowledge to use, predicate calculus has two disadvantages. First, there are some types of inference that it cannot account for, for example, those associated with modal concepts, such as possibility and obligation. To model some types of human inference making it is, therefore, necessary to use different types of representation. Another type of inference that lies outside the scope of predicate calculus is non-monotonic reasoning. In a non-monotonic logic a new fact can make old conclusions untrue. There is as yet no agreement about whether human reasoning is genuinely non-monotonic.

The second disadvantage of predicate calculus is that inferences from a large predicate calculus database tend to be inefficient. Indexing schemes can help to make facts easier to find, but they produce only modest improvements. An alternative solution is to use non-uniform methods of representation together with domain-specific inference methods. These methods include semantic networks, frames and scripts. In developing semantic networks to encode both conceptual knowledge and facts about the world, a number of problems were encountered. These problems have led to more explicit accounts of what a particular piece of network represents. One way of achieving this explicitness is to regard knowledge representation systems as languages. This approach has been taken in both network-based systems (KL-ONE and NETL) and frame-based systems (KRL and FRL).

Predicate calculus, networks, frames and scripts are primarily declarative methods of representing knowledge. Production systems are procedural representations. They represent knowledge as sets of rules, called productions, that can be applied when certain conditions are met. Representing a piece of information as a production makes it easy to see when and how it can be used.

Two general issues in the theory of knowledge representation are what primitives representations should be built out of, and whether parallel models of memory are better than serial ones. Many people assume that the appropriate primitives for high-level tasks, such as language understanding and problem solving, correspond to words. However, both Wilks and Schank have argued for much smaller sets.

Since the brain is a massively parallel device, parallel models of memory might seem more appropriate for those trying to analyse human cognitive functions. Computer technology is only just reaching the stage where genuine parallel hardware is available for the development of such models. However, they can be simulated on serial machines. There is some debate over whether parallel models are interestingly different from serial models, or whether they are simply outlandish implementations of traditional ideas. One way in which parallel machines might be distinguished from serial machines is in how they learn. Parallel machines may learn in a way that is much more akin to the way people do.

# 3 Vision

The ability to see, which is the topic of this chapter, is not usually thought of as a manifestation of intelligence, in the everyday sense of that term. However, it is mediated by complex information processing of a kind that can readily be modelled using computational techniques, and vision is now a major topic in AI research.

The bulk of this chapter is devoted to the work of David Marr (1945–1980) and his associates. This program of research represents a radical departure from earlier AI work on vision. The earlier research, which is described towards the end of the chapter, investigated the recognition of simple 3-D objects – prismatic solids – from line drawings. Marr's work is emphasised here for two reasons. First, Marr attempts to model in detail the human visual system, taking into account experimental evidence from psychology and neurophysiology. Second, Marr stresses the importance of general explanatory principles of the type found in other scientific theories. Earlier AI researchers often failed to provide explicit formulations of such principles.

The chapter begins with a general account of Marr's work, which is followed by a more detailed discussion of his theory of 'low-level' vision. Low-level (or early) visual processing culminates in the production of a viewer-centred description of the surfaces in the visual world, which Marr calls the 2½-D sketch. The later part of the chapter provides a discussion of the higher-level processes that recognise the objects in a scene. The early research on the identification of prismatic solids is described first. Marr's more general approach to the problem of object recognition is then outlined.

## Marr

In the past decade or so the study of vision, both in AI and in experimental psychology, has been transformed by the work of David Marr and his associates. It is now hardly possible to talk about vision without mentioning Marr's name. His work is widely believed to represent one of the most important recent advances in any branch of psychology. It is particularly important because it demonstrates how computational, psychological and neurophysiological ideas can be combined within a single coherent framework. A fuller, very readable, account of Marr's work can be found in his book, *Vision* (Marr, 1982). His ideas are presented in more detail, and in a more technical manner, in the papers cited throughout this chapter.

Most of Marr's work was carried out at the AI laboratory of the Massachusetts Institute of Technology (MIT). It certainly deserves discussion in a text on AI, particularly one with a psychological bias. However, Marr's approach differs, in many respects, from that of previous AI researchers. In particular it differs from the earlier AI approaches to vision that will be discussed later in this chapter. Indeed, Marr criticises this work for its failure to make distinctions that he regards as crucial for any explanatory account of how information-processing tasks are performed.

One obvious difference between Marr's work and earlier AI vision research lies in the kinds of computations that his programs perform. Marr places comparatively little emphasis on list processing and relies more on mathematical techniques, such as differentiation and convolution. For this reason Marr's work is sometimes said to be applied mathematics, though there is, of course, no reason why mathematics should not be applied in AI as it is in other sciences. However, the difference between the two approaches is not confined to computational details and, in any case, the computations performed by an AI program have to be tailored to the domain in which it operates.

Marr brought to AI a new view of the form that its theories should take – a view that was sketched briefly in chapter 1. He believed that vision could only be understood by considering it as an *information-processing problem*. He argued that explanations of how information-processing problems are solved must be couched at several levels. Writing a computer program that solves the problem is not enough. Programs are too detailed, in irrelevant ways, to be theories of visual processing.

In AI, attention *has* focused on programs, though it has only rarely been claimed that a computer program is itself a theory of how an information-processing task is performed. More usually programs are said to be *models* of theories. However, the theoretical principles that underlie AI programs are often not explicitly formulated. Neither is it always clear from examining a program what principles it embodies.

Marr held that a proper explanation of the workings of the visual system requires the formulation of principles governing its operation. He argued that these principles must be made explicit not only before any programming is done, but before, or at least independently of, any consideration of how the program is to be written or what machine it is to run on.

Marr's theory is mathematical in nature. At the most abstract level he proposes to describe the visual system in terms of the mathematical *functions* that it computes. A function is a way of stating the relation between the input and the output of a system – for every possible input, it says what the output will be. A function may simply be a list of inputs, together with the output that each one produces. However, interesting functions – those used to describe the visual system, for example – can be expressed in a more informative way – in the form of mathematical equations.

Marr called a description of part of the visual system in terms of the function(s) that it computes a *computational theory* of that part of the system. There are two aspects of a computational theory: a specification of *what* function is computed, and an explanation of *why* that function is computed. The 'why' part of the computational theory can be stated in terms of the uses that animals make of their visual systems. For animals with relatively simple nervous systems this part of the computational theory may be quite specific. One function of the frog's visual system, for example, is to detect moving blobs that are probably flies (Lettvin *et al.*,

1959). When a hungry frog thinks it has seen a fly, it shoots out its tongue to catch it. The reason why blobs are computed from the visual image is so that the frog can decide when to shoot out its tongue and where to aim it. In general, however, the 'why' part of the computational theory is not so specific. It might, for example, be couched in terms of the construction of a 3-D representation that can be used to guide movement through the world.

Marr's term *computational theory* is, in some ways, misleading, since a mathematical function simply relates inputs to outputs. It gives no details of *how* the output is derived from the input, no information about the way the computation is performed. A computational theory is about computations in the abstract mathematical sense, not in the sense of operations performed by a real computer, as the name might suggest.

A computational theory is only one part of an information-processing account of a psychological process. According to Marr, two other levels of explanation are required. Most obviously, the machinery that does the computing must be described in a way that makes it clear how the computations are performed. In the case of vision the structure and function of neurons in the visual system have to be described. These neurons are found in the retina, lateral geniculate nuclei, visual cortex and other parts of the brain. However, it is not immediately apparent how a computational theory and a neurophysiological description of the visual system relate to each other. Marr argued that the gap between them should be bridged by a third level of explanation, that of algorithm and representation.

These terms can be explained by way of examples. Even at an abstract level of description – one that makes no reference to computational machinery – there are many different ways in which a function can be computed. To take a very simple example, the value of the function (i.e. its output):

$$z = 3(x + y)$$

can be computed for given values of x and y (inputs) either by adding those values together and multiplying the result by 3, or by multiplying each of them separately by 3 and adding those results together. Different ways of computing a function that can be described independently of machinery for carrying out the computation are called different *algorithms* for computing the function.

The idea of a (system of) representation should also be familiar from arithmetic. Numbers can be represented in the usual arabic (decimal) notation, in similar systems with different bases, such as the binary system that is now commonly taught in schools, or using roman numerals. We use the arabic notation because it is more convenient than the roman for carrying out the basic arithmetical operations of addition, subtraction, multiplication and division. We use the decimal system at least partly because we have ten fingers. Similarly, there are more or less convenient ways for visual systems to represent (aspects of) the external world, given the uses to which they put that information. However, it is not easy to determine which system of representation the visual system uses.

Marr's use of the term *representation* is different from one that is current in other branches of AI and in psychology. For him a representation is a *system* of encoding information, and not something that stands for a particular object. When a representation is applied to a particular entity, a *description* of that entity is produced. For Marr, the most important aspects of a representation are the kinds of information that it makes explicit and those that it leaves implicit. Experiments often suggest what kinds of information people have readily, and hence presumably explicitly, available to them. They, therefore, provide clues to the representational system being used.

To summarise: in Marr's view a theory of vision has three parts. The computational theory specifies, in the most general terms, what the system does, and why it does it. The algorithm and system of representation provide a detailed description of how information is encoded and transformed – of the steps that the computation is broken down into. The description of the implementation shows how the computations are actually carried out.

The separation of the implementational level from the other two is Marr's version of the view that there should be a purely psychological level of description of visual processes. He rejects the idea that vision could be explained neurophysiologically. For example, some cells in the lateral geniculate nuclei respond strongly to oriented edges but not to other stimuli. These cells are sometimes described as edge detectors. Marr argues that the response of these cells does not mean that they *detect* edges. Their *function*, as opposed to their *properties*, only becomes apparent in the context of a theory of the (computational) system of which they are part. Marr's view is that they are part of a system one of whose functions may be to detect edges. However, without considering the information-processing problems that the visual system is trying to solve, it is impossible to explain why neurons have the receptive fields and sensitivities that they do.

Four principles

The ideas presented so far represent Marr's general thoughts about the form that AI theories should take. His theories of visual processing embodied further general principles, which he did not necessarily expect to apply in other branches of AI. Though Marr regarded these principles as important, they have not been universally accepted. The four most important of them will be discussed, before Marr's theory is described in more detail.

The first principle is that, as far as possible, visual analysis should be characterised as a data-driven (or bottom-up) process, rather than as a hypothesis-driven (or top-down) process. In particular Marr avoided, wherever possible, the use of *specific* knowledge about the current state of the world in his account of low-level processes. Such knowledge can only come from high-level analysis of the current scene. Marr thought that this knowledge was not passed back to low-level processors.

The kind of theory that Marr disliked can be illustrated using one of the early processes in visual perception, edge detection. Edges *could* be detected in a hypothesis-driven manner. If the visual system knew, or could guess, what objects were in the visual field and where they were, it could use this knowledge to predict where edges should be found. Such predictions could then guide an edge finder.

Marr argued against theories of this kind. He pointed to psychophysical evidence showing that, for example, edges can be detected when no top-down information can be obtained. The process that finds edges in these cases can be used even when top-down information is available. The top-down information would simply be ignored. However, Marr's claim that top-down information is never used by low-level processes is not universally accepted. In particular, it is possible that preliminary identification of objects might be used to guide edge finding (cf. Shirai, 1973).

Marr's second principle is that, although *specific* knowledge about the world is not used in visual processing, general assumptions about what the world is usually like play an essential role in vision algorithms. Unless such assumptions are made, the information in the retinal image is highly ambiguous, and grossly underdetermines the situation in the world that produces it. Examples of these general assumptions are: that most of the things we see are rigid objects and that most of the visual field is made up of smooth surfaces – only small sections correspond to abrupt changes in depth. Marr argued that the success of his programs depended critically on these general constraints. To give just one example, the assumption about continuity of surfaces ensures that a patch of uniform intensity in the image is almost always interpreted as a single surface. Without these assumptions such a patch could be a collection of smaller surfaces at different distances, differently lit.

The third principle was adopted by Marr to account for the speed of visual analysis, which has to be rapid if animals are to survive in an often hostile environment. This principle discourages the use of *iterative* algorithms in models of visual processing. An iterative algorithm is one that runs repeatedly through a cycle of steps, with the output from one cycle providing the input for the next. Each cycle produces a closer approximation to the desired result, but it may take many cycles before a satisfactory approximation is obtained.

Finally, Marr proscribed computational theories or algorithms whose sole motivation was to provide an account for neurophysiological or psychological data. He always looked for an independent justification for the form of his theories.

An outline of Marr's theory

To conform with his own ideas about how visual processing should be explained, Marr had to specify a computational theory of the visual system – to say what function it computes. The specification of the input to the system is relatively straightforward. The first representation of the light falling on the retina is a *grey-level description*, which encodes the intensity of light at each point in the image. Marr took this description to be the input to the visual system. (In most of his work Marr was able to ignore colour, though he endorsed a version of the retinex theory of colour vision proposed by Land and McCann, 1971.) For the purposes of processing by digital computer, both intensity and spatial location in grey-level descriptions are digitised. Spatial location is digitised by dividing the image into a number of picture elements or *pixels*, each of which has a single intensity value.

The question of how to characterise the output of the visual system is a more difficult one. Marr (1982, pp. 31–6) describes how he came to realise that, at least in the higher mammals, the main purpose of vision is 'building a description of the shapes and positions of things from images' (1982, p. 36). So the output of the visual system must be encoded in a (system of) representation that makes explicit what objects are present, where they are and what shapes they have. The 'what' part of the computation theory is, therefore, a function from grey-level descriptions to what Marr calls *3-D model descriptions*.

Marr did not consider it possible to compute 3-D models directly from grey-level descriptions. He proposed that the computation is carried out in three main stages, in which grey-level descriptions are transformed into more abstract descriptions 'not cluttered with irrelevant information' (1982, p. 31). He made specific proposals about the information made explicit in the intermediate representations, and gave detailed arguments for the choices he made.

The first transformation – of grey-level description into *primal sketch* – takes place in two substages, with the *raw primal sketch* as an intermediate level of representation. The raw primal sketch encodes the location and orientation of edge segments, blobs and bars in the image. Unlike the grey-level description, the raw primal sketch is a *symbolic* representation. It contains tokens, to which Marr gives the not very mnemonic name *place tokens*, that stand for things in the world. The *full primal sketch* contains, in addition, tokens standing for regions and their boundaries, features that are generally larger than those represented only in the raw sketch. The full sketch is computed from the raw sketch by grouping procedures, some of which have their origins in the laws of perception formulated by the Gestalt psychologists.

The orientation and approximate distance from the viewer of surfaces are computed in the second of Marr's three stages and are represented in the *2½-D sketch*. The 2½-D sketch is a (very short-term) memory store into which information is written by a number of independent processes that provide information about surfaces. These processes may operate on slightly different time scales. A memory store is essential if their results are to be brought together. The processes include stereopsis, structure from motion, and shape from shading.

The 2½-D sketch is a *viewer-centred* representation. It represents the world as it appears from a particular viewpoint, but does not indicate what would happen if the viewpoint changed. That information is contained in Marr's third level of representation, *the 3-D model*. This *object-centred* representation describes the three-dimensional shapes of objects. Marr showed that the construction of 3-D model descriptions does not require specific knowledge about the world from long-term memory. However, if such descriptions are used to recognise, and hence label, objects in the world, knowledge about the shapes of particular kinds of object must be used.

## Low-level visual processes

In AI, low-level visual processes have been studied chiefly within Marr's framework. By early (low-level) processes Marr meant those that culminate in the construction of the 2½-D sketch. The principal problem in deriving a 2½-D sketch from a grey-level description is separating changes in intensity that can be attributed to the geometry of the scene from those produced by three other factors: the way the scene is lit; the position that it is viewed from; and how the surfaces reflect light – Marr assumes that complex textures, such as a cornfield viewed from afar, can be treated as surfaces. Marr's account of how this separation is achieved is presented in the following sections.

## The primal sketch

Marr divides low-level visual processing into two main stages. In the first a representation of the important features of the image – the primal sketch – is computed, and in the second a viewer-centred description of the visual surfaces – the 2½-D sketch – is derived.

Marr based his theory of the way that the primal sketch is computed, and of the information it encodes, on a number of general assumptions about the world and about the purposes of early visual processing. The first of these assumptions is that the visual world is made up primarily of smooth surfaces. Surface discontinuities, though they occur at sharp edges and at the boundaries of objects, account for only a small part of most retinal images. The second assumption is that images need to be described at different levels of detail and that the description at one level is relatively independent of that at other levels. At a fine level of detail the image of a cat can be described in terms of the individual hairs that make up its coat. At a coarser level the cat's surface markings have shapes and orientations that do not depend on those of the individual hairs. Finally, the shape and orientation of the cat itself is (almost) independent of those of its surface markings.

The remaining assumptions relate to the grouping of elements in the image. The first is that elements at one level of description (hairs, surface markings or cats) are more similar to one another than they are to elements at other levels. Groupings processes should, therefore, operate within levels rather than across them. The second assumption is that elements lying along straight lines or simple curves are likely to form significant groups. The third is that discontinuities can also be expected to lie along simple curves, for example those corresponding to object boundaries.

On the basis of these assumptions, Marr argued that the primitive elements of the primal sketch are zero-crossings, which are discussed in more detail below – blobs, terminations, edge segments, virtual lines, groups, and boundaries. Zero-crossings are computed first. Next blobs, terminations, and edges, are derived from zero-crossings to produce the raw primal sketch. Finally, higher-order groupings and boundaries are added to produce the full primal sketch.

*From grey-level representation to raw primal sketch*

An algorithm for constructing the raw primal sketch was described by Marr (1976) and modified by Marr and Hildreth (1980). The primary function of the algorithm is to locate edges in the image. An edge usually corresponds to a (fairly) sharp change in intensity (or grey-level), but not all intensity changes correspond to edges. Furthermore, not all edges are associated with changes in intensity, because of factors such as lighting. The edge-detecting algorithm, therefore, begins to separate information about surface geometry from intensity variation produced in other ways.

Marr noted that the intensity changes corresponding to edges may be more or less rapid. This fact poses a problem because of an additional assumption that Marr makes – that the early stages of visual analysis require only relatively local processing and do not combine information from distant parts of the image. In particular, Marr assumes that changes in intensity are computed locally, with no account taken of global changes that may be caused, for example, by the way the scene is lit. This assumption is compatible with what is known about the structure of the retina and the lower levels of the visual system. However, it means that only comparatively large changes in intensity can be identified as edges, otherwise every intensity gradient, including those caused by the distance from the source of lighting, would be interpreted as an edge. This fact may have one of two consequences, depending on how the edges are detected. With a very local process, edges that are fuzzy in the image will be missed, because they will not produce sufficiently large local changes in intensity. With a less local process sharp edges will be inaccurately located, because information about where within the region of the computation an intensity change occurs is inevitably lost.

Marr and Hildreth (1980) solve this problem by searching for both large and small intensity gradients at the same time. They detect steep gradients using computations that are more local than those that find less steep gradients. Their algorithm, therefore, requires several copies of the grey-level image – they use four – for different ranges of intensity gradient. A further complication is that to find the less steep gradients it is necessary to ignore the steeper ones. Each copy of the image is, therefore, blurred by a different amount. Blurring eliminates rapid changes in intensity without affecting the less rapid ones. So the shallower the gradients to be detected, the greater the blur needs to be.

Once the images have been blurred, the edges are found by applying the mathematical operation of differentiation to them. Differentiation determines the rate at which intensity is changing at each point in the image. For those interested in technical details, differentiation is, in fact, applied twice. The reason is that at points where intensity is changing most rapidly (i.e. at edges in the image) *the second derivative* of the intensity (the result of differentiating it twice) will be zero. A *zero-crossing* in the second derivative (i.e. a point at which its value changes from positive to negative or vice versa) may, therefore, correspond to (part of) a boundary in the image.

According to Marr and Hildreth, the blurring and differentiation are produced by a series of filters, called *del-squared G* filters, one for each range of intensity gradients. There are, therefore, four such filters in Marr and Hildreth's model. Blurring simply means replacing each point in the image by the weighted average of it and the points around it. The G indicates that the weighting function is a two-dimensional Gaussian function – the two-dimensional version of the familiar bell-shaped normal distribution. The standard deviation of this normal distribution corresponds to the degree of blurring, and so varies from filter to filter. It determines how local the computations are. Del-squared is the *Laplacian* operator, which is a symmetrical two-dimensional second derivative – one that detects intensity changes in the up-and-down direction just as well as in the left-to-right direction. Each del-squared G filter is referred to as a *channel* through which visual information is processed. A channel comprises an array of local processors, one for each part of the image. Detailed mathematical justification for the choice of these operators is given by Marr and Hildreth (1980).

When the image has been filtered through the four channels, information from those channels must be combined to detect boundaries in the image. There are several rules that apply to this combination of information. Two of them are particularly important. First, if a zero-crossing in the broadest channel is matched by single zero-crossings in all narrower channels, then an edge segment should be inserted into the raw primal sketch. The second is that if such a zero-crossing is matched by two parallel zero-crossings in the narrower channels, a segment of a bar should be put into the sketch. Once again these rules derive from facts about the physical world. For example, since an edge occupies a fixed point in space, it should produce a zero-crossing at the same place in each channel.

The ends of bars are called *terminations*. They are explicitly represented in the raw primal sketch. Closed loops of edge segments form *blobs*. Edges, bars, terminations and blobs form the principal elements of the raw sketch. They have the attributes of orientation, contrast, length, width and position.

It was in his analysis of the earliest stages of visual processing that Marr was most successful in relating his three levels of explanation both to one another and to experimental work in psychology and physiology. Marr and Hildreth suggest that the X cells in the retina and the lateral geniculate nuclei compute del-squared G functions. These cells have simple centre-surround receptive fields, which respond to changes in intensity in small regions of the retinal image. Their responses can be modelled by so-called DOG (difference of Gaussians) functions. Given certain physiologically plausible assumptions, Marr and Hildreth argue that processing an image with an array of cells that compute DOG functions is equivalent to passing it through a del-squared G filter. They argue that X cells with different sizes of receptive field, which have been identified physiologically, correspond to different del-squared G channels. The existence of both on-centre and off-centre X cells is explained by the fact that del-squared G can have both positive and negative values, but neurons cannot fire at negative rates. One type of cell encodes positive values and the other negative values. The physiological basis of the combination of information from the separate del-squared G channels has not yet been identified.

The existence of del-squared G channels is also supported by psychophysical evidence. The detectability of gradually varying patterns of light and dark stripes (sinusoidal gratings) is decreased by prior exposure to gratings with stripes of a similar width, but not to ones with much wider or much narrower stripes. The width of the stripes in a sinusoidal grating is related to how quickly intensity changes across the grating and, hence, to how sharp the edges in it are. These findings provide evidence for the existence of channels sensitive to a range of intensity gradients by suggesting that they can be selectively habituated.

*From raw primal sketch to full primal sketch*
The second part of the program described by Marr (1976) converts a raw primal sketch into a full primal sketch. In other words, the computational theory that it embodies is a function from raw primal sketches to full primal sketches. The full primal sketch contains information about outlines and occluding contours and about features internal to the shapes delineated by those contours.

Edge segments in the raw primal sketch may correspond to (parts of) edges in the world, though there are usually more possible edges in the raw sketch than there are real edges in the object(s) it represents. Furthermore, the raw sketch contains no explicit representation of 'large'-scale features, such as the eyes, nose and mouth of the teddy bear in one famous example of an image processed by the program. The *full* primal sketch is a representation in which such features are explicitly represented, by further place tokens, and in which boundaries between sets of similar tokens are also made explicit. The identification of these features and boundaries continues to operate at a number of different scales.

The new tokens in the full sketch represent collections of lower-level tokens. Despite Marr's general ban on iteration, they are produced by the repeated application of grouping procedures. These procedures operate *locally* on the following properties of the tokens in the raw sketch: average intensity, average size, density, orientation of items, orientations of clusters of items (which may be different from the orientation of the items themselves, as in a herringbone pattern) and distances within clusters. The description of these last two properties requires a new type of primitive element – the *virtual line*. Virtual lines join similar tokens that are close to one another. They are not physically present in the image, but otherwise they have the properties, such as length and orientation, of real lines. Distances within clusters and orientations of clusters can be described in terms of lengths and orientations of virtual lines.

After grouping is completed, and place tokens representing features of various sizes are present in the primal sketch, boundaries can be identified. A boundary may simply be a set of place tokens lying on a straight line or a simple curve, representing a discontinuity of some kind. However, boundaries can also be indicated by a change in some property of place tokens, such as their density or orientation. In this case new tokens are added to the primal sketch to represent the boundary.

### Identifying surfaces: from primal sketch to 2½-D sketch

The final stage of what Marr calls early visual processing is the construction of the 2½-D sketch from the full primal sketch and the information from which that sketch is derived. According to Marr, a number of relatively independent processes write their results into the 2½-D sketch. These processes include stereopsis, structure from motion and shape from shading. The input to some of these processes is the full primal sketch itself, but others may work from the raw sketch, or even from zero-crossings alone. The 2½-D sketch acts as a memory. It holds the results of the various processes until they can be brought together to produce a representation of the orientation and (approximate) distance from the viewer of surfaces in the visual world. Marr described this sketch as having 2½ dimensions, because he believed that, although it represents relative depth at surface boundaries and relative orientation fairly accurately, it provides only a very rough indication of absolute depth. Since most of the processes that contribute to the 2½-D sketch identify discontinuities in the image, details of large uniform surfaces have to be filled in by interpolation procedures. Marr describes the operation of these procedures as conservative. Once the 2½-D sketch has been constructed, further computations are performed to confirm that it represents a possible scene.

The 2½-D sketch is similar to what Barrow and Tenenbaum (e.g. 1978) call an *intrinsic image set*. An intrinsic image is a representation in which some intrinsic property of a scene is represented, rather than a property of the grey-level image. Each process that contributes to the 2½-D sketch can, therefore, be thought of as constructing a single intrinsic image. The sketch itself is a set of such images.

Marr (1982, chapter 3) describes some of the processes that contribute to the 2½-D sketch. He gives most space to those for which he has some well-formulated ideas relating to at least one of his levels of explanation. The topics he covers are stereopsis, directional selectivity, structure from motion, depth from optical flow, surface orientation from shape contours, surface texture, shape from shading, lightness and colour. He also discusses photometric stereo, which is not used by the human visual system. He allows that there may be other inputs to the 2½-D sketch. Three processes that Marr treats extensively, stereopsis, structure from motion and shape from shading, are described in the following sections.

*Stereopsis*
The two eyes have different views of the world. In some animals, such as the rabbit, these views are largely non-overlapping. However, in species such as the primates, in which the two eyes see the same things, the slightly different views contain information about the distance from the observer of objects in the visual field. The difference, or *disparity*, between the two views of an object is related to its

distance from the eyes, though it also depends on where the viewer is looking. A theory of stereopsis is a theory of how information about distance is extracted from the two images. For a person with normal sight, stereopsis provides depth information for objects up to about 135 metres away. Beyond this distance the differences between the images is too small to be useful.

The first stage in extracting depth information from the two images is to solve the so-called *correspondence problem*. (Almost) every point in the visual world stimulates one point on the left retina and one on the right. However, the two images are initially separate. To compute the differences between them the points in the two images must be paired up on the basis of which point in the visual world gave rise to them. How to pair them up is the correspondence problem.

One solution to the correspondence problem immediately suggests itself. If the objects in each image could be recognised independently, the points in the images could be matched using those objects as a guide. However, random dot stereograms, invented by Julesz, show that stereopsis does not *require* monocular object recognition (see Julesz, 1971, for a summary and many examples that prove this point). In a random dot stereogram related patterns of random dots are presented, one to each eye. The two patterns are derived from a single original. In one of them a section is shifted and the gaps filled by a new random pattern. Viewed by itself each pattern looks flat. In particular, the shifted section cannot be seen. But in a stereoscope that section floats either above or below the rest, depending on the direction of shift. Stereopsis has, therefore, been produced when neither eye alone can see the two 'objects' – the shifted section and the surround – that seem to be at different depths.

Random dot stereograms also illustrate, in a particularly clear way, the problem of false matches in stereopsis. Considered by itself, any black dot in one image could, in principle, be matched with any one in the other. However, for any particular dot only one of those matches is the true one. The possibility of false matches make the correspondence problem difficult to solve.

The idea that stereoscopic fusion does not depend on object

recognition is consistent with Marr's assumption that early visual processing is data-driven rather than hypothesis-driven. Marr and Poggio (1976, 1979) produced two different algorithms for stereo matching, both based on a single computational theory that does not assume monocular object recognition. However, the question of whether the human visual system uses information about objects to solve the correspondence problem remains open.

Marr and Poggio's computational theory incorporates three general principles, derived from properties of the physical world, that constrain the set of possible solutions to the correspondence problem. Marr and Poggio call these principles the *compatibility, uniqueness*, and *continuity constraints*. The compatibility constraint requires that matching points have similar properties, since they are representations of the same thing in the visual world. The uniqueness constraint states that a point in one image should match only one point in the other. The continuity constraint, which reflects the fact the visual world is made up primarily of (fairly) smooth surfaces, says that distance from the observer should vary smoothly almost everywhere (i.e. except at boundaries between surfaces). Marr and Poggio proved that, given a sufficiently detailed image, these constraints guarantee a unique solution to the correspondence problem.

Marr and Poggio's first algorithm can best be described in terms of the way it solves random dot stereograms. Each dot in the stereogram can be represented by one place token with a single binary feature: black or white. Features from the left and right images are fed into a network of elements, one corresponding to each possible pairing of tokens in the two images. So if each image is made up of 10,000 dots, then the network has 100,000,000 (= 10,000 × 10,000) elements.

In the first stage of the computation those elements corresponding to possible matches become active. The compatibility constraint restricts this set to elements that have either two black inputs or two white inputs. The other two constraints are represented by excitatory and inhibitory connections between the elements. Uniqueness is encoded by inhibitory connections between elements along the same line of sight. Since the lines of sight are different for the two eyes there are two sets of these connections. If one element in the array along a line of sight in, say, the right eye represents a true match, no other element along that line of sight can be a true match. There cannot be visible surface features at different depths along the same line of sight. Continuity is encoded by excitatory connections between elements corresponding to a single depth plane. If surfaces tend to vary smoothly, nearby points will usually be the same distance from the viewer.

These last two constraints guide the operation of an iterative procedure of the kind that Marr was later to argue against. Its first input is the initial state of the network as determined by the compatibility constraint. On each cycle, the activity of the elements changes as a function of the activity around them. Excitation tends to increase their activity, inhibition tends to decrease it. For simplicity, each element can only be either active or inactive. When the surrounding activity is summed, a threshold is used to decide whether the element is active or inactive. Eventually the network reaches a steady state in which (apparent) depth is correctly represented. The computation uses only local information – it takes no account of the global features of the stereogram. Marr calls this feature of the algorithm *co-operativity*.

Marr and Poggio's (1979) second algorithm is a non-iterative one. It was designed to be compatible with psychophysical evidence about how people achieve stereoscopic fusion. As described above, at an early stage in visual processing del-squared G filters, working at several levels of resolution, detect zero-crossings in the second derivative of the intensity map (grey-level description). The second algorithm uses the zero-crossings detected by these filters.

The algorithm relies on a mathematical theorem that relates degree of blurring to the probability of matching a feature in one image with one in a given region of the other. The more blurred an image, the coarser the features it contains. Therefore, the more blurred it is, the larger the area in which there is likely to be only one feature and, hence, only one possible match for a feature in the other image. The algorithm looks for a match in an area in which there is a probability of, say, 95 per cent of finding only one. If a false match happens to be made, as it will occasionally be, then the overall success rate of the matching process in the vicinity of that match drops. The algorithm, therefore, checks that, close to any putative match, its success rate is about 95 per cent. This check makes use of the continuity constraint – it assumes that most regions of the image will correspond to parts of continuous surfaces.

The algorithm begins by looking for matches between zero-crossings in the most blurred channel. Blurring eliminates fine details, so only fairly coarse features can be matched at this stage. However, the area that must be searched for each match is comparatively large. It corresponds to a fairly wide range of possible image *disparities*, and, hence, of possible distances from the viewer of the feature corresponding to the zero-crossing.

Once the zero-crossings in the most blurred channel have been matched, a rough estimate of the depth of the features in the image can be made. Zero-crossings can then be matched in the second coarsest channel, using the approximate depth map from the first channel as a guide. In the second channel finer details are represented, but features can only be matched within smaller areas, which correspond to a more restricted range of disparities (and depths). To decide which restricted range of disparities to consider, the algorithm uses, at each point in the image, the estimate from the widest channel as the centre of the range. So the full range of possible disparities is never considered. This process of moving from broader to narrower channels continues until a disparity map is produced in the narrowest channel.

Marr and Poggio claim that their second algorithm models fairly closely the way that people achieve stereo fusion. They claim that, at each stage, information from the narrowest channel in which matching has so far been achieved drives *vergence* eye movements. These movements turn the eyes either inwards or outwards, so that their lines of sight meet at a given distance from the viewer. Any object at this point produces zero disparity in the retinal images. As the eyes move over a scene, these movements, therefore, ensure that the range of disparities to be considered by the next narrower channel are always centred around zero.

The narrowest channel, which produces the finest resolution of the image, is available only in foveal vision – the central few degrees of the visual field. However, we build up an impression of depth over the whole visual field. Marr and Poggio suggest that this impression comes about because depth information from each part of the visual field is stored in the 2½-D sketch.

Mayhew and Frisby (1981; Frisby and Mayhew, 1980) have proposed a third algorithm for stereoscopic fusion. They suggest that there is a close connection between stereoscopic fusion and the computation of the raw primal sketch. Indeed they propose that stereoscopic fusion is linked to the production of a *binocular raw primal sketch*. Any principle that is used to construct the raw primal sketch can, therefore, be used to aid stereoscopic matching. In particular Mayhew and Frisby identify two principles that they claim are used to solve the correspondence problem: figural continuity and the relation between the outputs of the del-squared G filters that is used to identify edge segments and bar segments (see above). Mayhew and Frisby present psychophysical evidence that is compatible with their algorithm, but not with Marr and Poggio's.

The algorithms described so far compute only the disparity between the two images for each point in the visual field. Disparity is expressed in terms of the difference in the angle between the line of sight and the line to the object for the two eyes. A further computation is required to convert disparity into distance from the viewer. However, this conversion is straightforward. Marr (1982, pp. 155–9) provides the computational theory, which is based on simple trigonometry.

### Structure from motion

The problem of recovering structure from motion is similar to that of stereopsis, at least when the moving bodies are rigid and the extent of the motion is small compared with the distance from the viewer. In stereopsis, two views of the same scene from different positions produce information about distance. In structure from motion *three* views of the same scene at different *times* generate this information. The reason why three views are needed is explained below. Stereopsis presents two subproblems: establishing correspondences between the two views and using these correspondences to compute depth. Similarly, there are two problems in recovering depth from motion. Ullman (1979), who was a student of Marr's, called these problems the *correspondence problem* and the *structure from motion problem*, respectively.

Ullman assumes that correspondences are established between temporally distinct views of the same scene. His theory therefore describes the recovery of structure from apparent as well as from real motion. In fact he obtained much of the empirical evidence in support of his theory from the study of apparent motion. In particular he showed that, as in stereopsis, recovery of structure from motion does not depend on prior identification of shape. Just as random dot stereograms can be fused to produce an illusion of depth, a film of related random dot patterns is seen as depicting objects in motion, even though no shape is visible in any one frame of the film.

In any solution to the correspondence problem for motion, the elements between which correspondences are established should be physically meaningful. Ullman argued, on the basis of psychophysical evidence, that those elements are the blobs, edges, bars and terminations of the raw primal sketch. He derived a measure, which he called an *affinity measure*, for the goodness of a match between elements in successive views of a scene. This measure depends both on spatial proximity and on similarity. Ullman worked out, experimentally, trade-offs between proximity and similarity and between different dimensions of similarity, such as size and orientation. He also demonstrated that, in calculating proximity, two-dimensional distance in the image is important, and not three-dimensional distance in the scene depicted. The correspondence problem can, therefore, be solved before any objects have been recognised.

After the affinity measures have been calculated for each possible match, they are adjusted to take account of the values for nearby matches. In the final solution to the correspondence problem a particular token in the first view may not be matched with the token in the second with which it has the highest affinity. A compromise may be reached so that, for example, all the tokens in a neighbourhood can be paired one-to-one. Ullman showed that, given certain assumptions, in particular about the range of velocities and, hence, displacements in the image, there was a maximum likelihood solution to the correspondence problem based only on locally adjusted affinities. As in stereopsis, the correspondence problem in structure from motion can be solved on the basis of local computations.

Marr (1982, pp. 202–5) argues that motion perception differs from stereopsis in that it presents two correspondence problems, not one. In stereopsis an object has the same shape in the two views, but objects in motion can change shape, either because they are not rigid, or because they are jointed, but too far away to be resolved into rigid parts. The first problem is, therefore, to establish what in a second view corresponds to a (possibly non-rigid) object in the first. Marr describes this problem as one of *object constancy*. The second problem – Ullman's – is to determine the more exact correspondences needed to recover shape from motion. Ullman showed that the solution to this problem depends on the assumption of rigidity. However, once the correspondences have been established the rigidity assumption can be checked internally. The more exact correspondences that generate shape information probably take longer to establish than the rough ones that provide evidence for an object's continuing existence.

As in stereopsis, once correspondences between views of objects in motion have been established, a further computation is required to extract depth information. Ullman provided a computational theory for the structure from motion problem by establishing a previously unknown theorem of 3-D geometry. He showed that if a body is rigid, three views of four non-coplanar points on it are sufficient to establish the 3-D arrangement of those points. On the assumption that a body is rigid, its shape can, therefore, be recovered by applying the theorem repeatedly to sets of four points on its surface.

### Shape from shading
The way the visual system recovers shape from shading is less well understood than the way it recovers shape from the two

retinal images or from successive views. Furthermore, Marr believed that, in the human visual system, shading by itself is 'only a weak determiner of shape' (1982, p. 239). However, he cites the effectiveness of make-up, especially in the theatre, as evidence that shading cues are used.

In the general case, the shape from shading problem is difficult to solve. The reason is that the intensity of light at any point in an image depends on both the way the scene is illuminated and the way the surfaces reflect the light falling on them. Both of these factors can vary in complex ways. Horn (1975, 1977) produced an analytical solution to the shape from shading problem for one special case: a single distant point source of illumination falling on uniform matte surfaces. A matte surface is one that scatters light equally in all directions, so the amount of light it reflects depends only on the angle at which the light falls on it and not on the angle from which the surface is viewed.

To solve the shape from shading problem in this special case, Horn had to make only one additional assumption – a general assumption of the kind that Marr thought essential in computational theories of visual processing. Horn's assumption was one that Marr also made – surfaces change smoothly at almost all points in the visual field.

Marr argues that Horn's solution to the shape from shading problem, although elegant, is biologically implausible, in terms both of the computations that it requires and the precision of its results. He does not, however, have an alternative theory of how shading information is used, either for the simple case that Horn analysed or for the general case. More recent work on shape from shading (e.g. Woodham, 1981; Ikeuchi and Horn, 1981) is directed to special applications and is not intended as part of a theory of human vision.

## Higher-level visual processes: object recognition

When we look around, we see *objects*, not surfaces. However, the processes described so far – in Marr's terminology, the early processes – produce information only about surfaces and their orientations. How does the visual system go beyond surfaces and recognise objects? This section begins with a discussion of object recognition in the BLOCKSWORLD. BLOCKSWORLD vision programs analyse photos, TV pictures or line drawings of piles of blocks. They try, in some sense, to recognise the objects depicted in those images. It had been hoped that the techniques used to recognise objects in the BLOCKSWORLD would generalise to other domains. It now appears that they will not. Marr attempted to produce a more general theory of how objects are recognised. The section closes with an account of his theory.

## Recognising prismatic solids – the BLOCKSWORLD

Object recognition was investigated in AI before early visual processing, partly because it is a problem that can be addressed using techniques more like those used in the early AI research on problem solving. Since the problem of object recognition is a difficult one, the approach taken was to try to solve the problem in a simple domain. It was hoped that the solution in this domain could be extended to the general case. The chosen domain was the MIT BLOCKSWORLD of matte white blocks (prisms or prismatic solids) standing on a flat table top and set against a black background. Initially the problem was further simplified by having the blocks uniformly lit so that there were no shadows.

An image of a BLOCKSWORLD scene comprises a set of bounded regions. These regions correspond to surfaces of various objects. The problem of deciding which regions go together is called the *segmentation problem*. A solution to the segmentation problem provides a basis for recognising the objects in a scene.

Part of the segmentation problem is to find the lines in the image that correspond to edges of objects. This problem was addressed in some projects, though many of the programs required line drawings as their inputs. The problem of detecting edges in images has already been discussed. Marr solved this problem in his theory of the primal sketch. His technique is more general than those used in the BLOCKS-WORLD programs. In particular, line finders such as those of

Roberts (1965), Horn (1973), Shirai (1973), Falk (1972) and Grape (1969) are restricted to detecting straight edges.

Roberts's (1965) line finder was comparatively unsophisticated. It worked prior to, and separate from, his segmentation and object identification program. It located points in the image at which intensity was changing rapidly, and fitted straight lines through them by a least-squares similar to that used, for example, in simple linear regression.

Shirai's line finder and those of Falk and Grape represent two different solutions to the problem of detecting lines in complex, noisy images. Shirai's (1973) program was based on the earlier Binford-Horn (Horn, 1973) line finder. It was more general than Roberts's system and could analyse any convex polyhedron. Unlike Roberts, Shirai did not separate line finding and segmentation. His program first produced an incomplete line drawing from the image. This drawing suggested tentative identities for the blocks. The hypothesised blocks were used to predict the locations of more lines. Certain parts of the image were then reprocessed, with a lower threshold for detecting edges, to see if there was any evidence for the predicted lines. The program starts by looking for the easiest lines to detect, which, in the BLOCKSWORLD, are those at the boundary between the white blocks and the black background. Shirai called these lines *contour lines*. Having located the contour lines the program predicts the location of, first, lines corresponding to boundaries between objects, and then lines internal to a single object. Shirai, therefore, attempts to overcome the problem of noise in the image by using top-down information to select certain parts of the image for more extensive processing.

Falk's (1972, but written much earlier) program, INTERPRET, constructs line drawings from images produced by a TV camera. It picks out all the lines it can from the image and then, effectively, hallucinates both extensions of those lines and lines that it has not seen at all. Unlike Shirai's program, INTERPRET does not go back to the image. It tries to complete the line drawing using general principles about what such drawings look like. One such principle is: if three lines can be extended so that they meet in a single point, they should be so extended. Once the line drawing has been completed, INTERPRET tries to identify the blocks in it with nine specific shapes that it knows about. It then generates a line drawing corresponding to the scene it thinks it is looking at, and compares that to the drawing it has derived from the image. If the fit is poor the scene is reanalysed.

Falk's work was developed by Grape (1969). Grape's program uses more sophisticated knowledge about configurations of lines and ends of lines in BLOCKSWORLD scenes. It has both general knowledge that is true of all types of block and knowledge that is specific to blocks such as cubes and wedges. This knowledge is used to interpret locally ambiguous line segments, to ignore lines that do not fit with the preferred interpretation of a scene, and to fill in lines that cannot be detected in the image, but which are required by the preferred interpretation.

Most BLOCKSWORLD vision research was directed towards a solution of the segmentation problem. Roberts (1965) further simplified this problem by restricting the set of blocks to those that could be made up of cuboids, rectangular wedges, and hexagonal prisms. His program had stored models of those three shapes, which it projected on to the picture it was analysing. When it had found the best fit from among its models, the program used its knowledge of projective geometry to determine the position in space of the objects it had recognised. Its computations were based on the assumption that every prism was supported either by the table top or by another prism.

Guzman's (1968) SEE was the first of several programs that only addressed the segmentation problem. SEE required line drawings as input and did not go beyond segmentation to compute a 3-D description of the objects in a scene. Like Roberts's program, SEE could cope with partly occluded objects, but it was able to segment more complex scenes. Guzman's major innovation was the idea that a taxonomy of vertex types and their possible interpretations could be used to solve the segmentation problem, without the aid of stored models. Guzman's taxonomy was intuitive. Some examples of the rules used by SEE are (1) the three surfaces that meet at a FORK (or Y-shaped vertex) are part of the same object; (2) of the three surfaces that meet at an ARROW ($\rightarrow$) the two bounded by acute angles are part of the same object, but the third is not. This intuitive taxonomy was reasonably successful, but the rules required to combine information from different vertices and, thereby, solve the segmentation problem became more and more complex and *ad hoc* as more complicated scenes were considered.

Clowes (1971) and Huffman (1971) independently attempted to give a more systematic account of how information about vertices and edges could be used to solve the segmentation problem. The following discussion is based on Huffman's terminology. Clowes and Huffman emphasised the distinction between descriptions in the (3-D) *scene domain* and those in the (2-D) *image domain*. They also stressed the need for a systematic mapping between features in an image and those in the scene that it depicted. Edges, vertices and surfaces are features of scenes. They are represented in images by lines, line junctions and regions, respectively. In scenes containing only uniformly lit *trihedral polyhdra* – blocks in which three surfaces meet at any vertex – there are four types of vertex, corresponding to different types of corner, and three types of edge: convex, concave or occluding. The three types of edge can be represented by three labels for lines in an image (+, −, and →). There are four basic junction types: Ls, FORKs, ARROWs and Ts. Ts do not correspond to vertices, but to cases in which an edge of one body abuts on to or crosses that of another. These basic junction types give rise to many more derived junction types, since each line at a junction can be labelled in three ways. For example, a FORK, at which three edges meet, has 27 (3 × 3 × 3) possible labellings of its edges. However, only three describe possible views of vertices. The others are either physically impossible, or rotations of one of the three legitimate ones. Altogether there are only sixteen legitimate junction types – six Ls, three FORKS, and three ARROWS – corresponding to possible views of the four types of vertex – and four Ts. Clowes and Huffman showed that, when the junctions in an image have been labelled with their type (L, FORK, ARROW or T) and the kinds of lines that *might* meet at them, only one global constraint – the consistency constraint – is needed to interpret images. This constraint states that an edge must be of the same type along the whole of its length. A line in an image should, therefore, have the same label at its two ends. This constraint allows some of the possible labellings of junctions to be eliminated. It can be used by a search procedure (see chapter 4) that finds all possible interpretations of a scene.

The work of Clowes and Huffman was extended by Waltz (1975), who generalised their ideas to objects with cracks and, more importantly, to scenes with shadows. Shadows had previously been avoided in AI vision research. However, Waltz discovered scenes that, when uniformly lit, could not be unambiguously segmented, but that had only a single interpretation when there were shadows. To extend the domain of his program Waltz increased the number of line labels from three to fifty-three. He also expanded the set of basic junction types to include all four-line junctions and some with five lines. Finally, he introduced three labels for regions in an image: directly illuminated, self-shadowed (i.e. turned away from the light), and shaded (i.e. in the shadow cast by another surface). With this expanded set of labels there are about 800 million derived junction types! Fortunately, fewer than 3000 of these correspond to possible configurations in the scenes that Waltz's program could analyse.

Although Waltz had to consider many more possible interpretations of each junction than Clowes and Huffman, his program worked relatively efficiently by exploiting constraints that Clowes and Huffman had ignored. In particular, his program did not exhaustively search all possible ways of labelling the junctions in an image. It started from junctions that could be unambiguously labelled and eliminated inconsistent labellings of neighbouring junctions. To find a suitable starting point, Waltz used the fact that some types of edge and vertex are easier to recognise than others. Like Shirai's program, Waltz's begins its interpretation at the boundary between scene and background. Waltz's program can analyse a wider range of images than its predecessors. Furthermore, it usually converges rapidly on a unique solution. When it does not, it finds a comparatively small number of possible solutions, among which it is fairly easy to make a choice.

Waltz's method of choosing among the possible labels for junctions is known as *Waltz filtering*. It is an example of a more general technique known as *relaxation*. Another name for relaxation is co-operativity (cf. Marr and Poggio's stereo algorithms). A relaxation (or co-operative) algorithm first assigns all possible labels to every item in an image (or, more generally, to items in an input array). In Waltz filtering the labels are the possible configurations of lines at each junction (e.g. FORK with three lines marked +). The labels can be interpreted as follows: given the processing so far, each of these labels is a possible interpretation of this item in the array. A set of constraints – in Waltz filtering just one, the consistency constraint – is then used to adjust each set of labels using information about the labels of *neighbouring* items. Relaxation algorithms are usually iterative. The process is repeated with the adjusted sets of labels as input. Waltz filtering is so called because of the way the sets of labels are revised. At each iteration, some labels are discarded or 'filtered out'.

In *probabilistic relaxation* labels are not filtered out unless their probability reaches zero. Their probabilities are adjusted at each iteration. Probabilistic relaxation algorithms are common in models of low-level vision, because of the uncertainty of interpretations at that stage of processing. As with iterative algorithms in general, relaxation procedures terminate when the values are steady, according to some set criterion. In simple relaxation a desirable criterion – one which is not always attainable – is that each item should have only one label.

Despite the success of Waltz's program in analysing BLOCKSWORLD scenes, there are two reasons for thinking that it bears little relation to human vision. First, in the line drawing that it works from no distinction is made between shadow edges and object edges. The program has to decide which lines correspond to which type of edge. In real images the two types of edge have different properties. In particular, shadow edges tend to be more blurred. If Waltz's program were part of a vision system it would in effect, be, throwing away this information only to recover it later, a procedure that seems highly inefficient. Second, there are a number of types of image that the program mislabels. Most importantly, it produces impossible labellings (in addition to the correct ones) for simple images, such as those of single cubes, and it produces legal labellings for impossible figures, such as the Penrose triangle, that have no consistent 3-D interpretation. The reason for this mislabelling is that there are constraints on relations between surfaces that the program cannot make use of, because its representation of edges and vertices (and that of Huffman and Clowes on which it is based) does not capture all the information in the image. For example, by representing the top, front edge of a cube simply as convex, the program loses the information that the top and front surfaces meet at a right angle. The program cannot distinguish a cube from any other six-sided convex prism.

One way around this problem is to abandon junction labels and use the idea of *gradient space*, introduced by Huffman (1971), to segment line drawings. Gradient space provides a way of representing the orientation of the surface at each point in the visual world and, hence, at least implicitly, the angles between surfaces. Mackworth (1973) used this idea in his program POLY. POLY tries to find a consistent assignment of points in gradient space (orientations) to the surfaces it identifies in a line drawing. It starts by assuming that all edges are either convex or concave – what Mackworth called *connect* edges – rather than occluding. Using constraints on the relations between surfaces of the same object, POLY checks whether its interpretation is possible. If not, it assumes one edge is occluding and tries again. It continues until it finds a consistent interpretation with the fewest possible occluding edges. This consistent interpretation can then be used to decide which of the connect edges are convex and which concave, and which surface is in front of the other at any occluding edge.

Draper (1981) showed that, just as the junction-labelling technique has its limitations, so does the gradient space method. It fails to make use of all the relevant constraints on relations between surfaces and, hence, mislabels some line drawings. To some extent these limitations can be avoided by giving POLY access to depth information – part of the problem with gradient space is that it tries to represent 3-D information using only two dimensions. However, Draper showed that even an extended SUPERPOLY was unsatisfactory. The only way to avoid mislabellings is to abandon gradient space and to reformulate POLY's rules in a geometrically unappealing way in terms of so-called *plane equations*.

Draper proposed an alternative way of analysing line drawings, called *sidedness reasoning*. Sidedness reasoning is reasoning about where a point or plane lies in relation to another plane – whether it is in front of it or behind it. It makes use of the fact that, at least in the BLOCKSWORLD, the relations *in front of* and *behind* are transitive – if A is behind B and B is behind C, then A must be behind C. A major difference between sidedness reasoning and the gradient-space approach is that sidedness reasoning gives information about occluding edges a central role in image analysis. Draper shows that sidedness reasoning is both more powerful than the gradient-space and junction-labelling approaches, and more intuitively appealing than the plane-equation approach. However, while the transitivity constraint eliminates impossible interpretations of line drawings, sidedness reasoning usually leads to multiple interpretations.

Draper argues that sidedness reasoning produces all and only possible analyses of line drawings. However, there are two reasons for not regarding it as a model of human visual perception. First, most of the interpretations of simple scenes it produces are difficult or impossible for people to see. Second, sidedness reasoning only works in scenes in which all the surfaces are flat. The transitivity constraint fails for curved surfaces. However, most everyday scenes contain at least some curved surfaces.

An alternative response to the problems with junction labels and gradient space is to combine the two in the hope that each will compensate for the other's weakness (Kanade, 1980). Kanade's program labels line drawings of objects in the *Origami world*. The Origami world is more complex than the BLOCKSWORLD of Waltz's program. Its objects are made of plane surfaces, so they include open boxes as well as blocks. Kanade's program uses a further-expanded set of junction labels. In the first stage of analysing a scene all possible labels are assigned to each junction and Waltz filtering is applied. Further filtering of the labels is performed by a second relaxation procedure. This procedure uses gradient space constraints on the surfaces that meet at (the vertex corresponding to) each junction.

These two relaxation procedures rarely produce a unique interpretation for an Origami world scene. To eliminate unnatural, but geometrically possible interpretations, and so to model human vision more exactly, Kanade uses two interpretation heuristics. The *parallel-line* heuristic states that parallel lines in an image usually correspond to parallel lines in the world. The *skewed-symmetry* heuristic reflects the fact that objects are often symmetrical, though that symmetry is usually skewed in an image, because of the way the objects are viewed. This heuristic interprets skewed symmetry in an image as representing symmetry in the scene. The interpretation of a scene produced by Kanade's program is more detailed than that produced by Waltz's. It includes information about the angles between surfaces and can be used to predict how the scene will look from different viewpoints.

The original hopes for the study of object recognition in the limited domain of the BLOCKSWORLD proved unfounded. It did not produce a theory that generalised to other domains and it did not suggest an account of how people recognise objects. As Draper's work makes explicit, the techniques used in the BLOCKSWORLD depend crucially on the assumption of plane surfaces. To explain how objects with curved surfaces can be identified a more general theory is required.

Marr's approach

In Marr's framework early visual processing ends with the construction of the 2½-D sketch. That sketch contains information about surfaces, but not about the objects they are part of. However, recognising objects is a part of visual perception, one for which an information-processing theory is required. Marr was not satisfied with solutions to special cases of the object recognition problem, such as those proposed for the BLOCKSWORLD. He thought that BLOCKSWORLD research placed too little emphasis on the general problems of recognising objects and on the constraints imposed by the physical world on solutions to those problems. He did not believe that BLOCKSWORLD techniques could be generalised and therefore he attempted to formulate an alternative solution to the problem of object recognition.

Marr realised that giving an object a label, such as 'table' or 'chair', 'horse' or 'cow', demands the use of stored information about the appearance of objects. Unlike early visual processing, object recognition *cannot* be purely data-driven. However, following one of his general principles, Marr (Marr and Nishihara, 1978) showed that much of the processing needed to recognise objects can be carried out using only general constraints that reflect what the world is usually like.

According to Marr and Nishihara, object recognition requires an object-centred description of the item to be recognised. This description, called a *3-D model description*, is constructed from the 2½-D sketch. A 3-D model description is a hierarchically arranged set of *3-D models*. 3-D models are built from primitive elements called *generalised cones*. A generalised cone is the solid formed when a shape, which may change its size, but not its proportions, is moved along an axis perpendicular to itself. The axis of a generalised cone can form the basis of an object-centred co-ordinate system of the kind needed for object recognition.

A 3-D model has two parts. The first is a single generalised cone that provides a crude description of the object it represents. The second is a decomposition of the object into a set of cones that describe it in more detail. Each of those cones can, in turn, be the single cone in a 3-D model at the next level in the hierarchy. So a 3-D model description of a person might comprise, at the highest level, a single cylinder and an analysis of it into six smaller cylinders – the head, torso and limbs. At the next level each leg might be analysed into upper leg, lower leg and foot, and so on. Introduction of more detail elaborates, rather than invalidates, the simpler descriptions. According to Marr and Nishihara a large class of objects, including most natural objects, can be described in terms of generalised cones. Furthermore, the principal axes of sets of connected generalised cones resemble stick figures. Marr and Nishihara argue that the ease with which stick figures are recognised supports the idea that the visual system recognises objects using an analysis in terms of generalised cones.

Marr and Nishihara's choice of generalised cones as the primitive elements in their descriptions of shape was guided by a mathematical theorem they were were able to prove. Except in cases of gross foreshortening, the shape and principal axis of a generalised cone can be recovered from its two-dimensional projection in the image. Therefore, for scenes that can be analysed into generalised cones, an object-centred co-ordinate system, and hence an object-centred description, can be derived *before* any object has been recognised.

The process that recovers generalised cones from their projections in the image also interprets silhouettes. It is based on three general assumptions, which are most simply stated using the concept of a *contour generator* – the curve on the surface of an object that produces its boundary in the image or the outline of its silhouette. First, each point on the contour generator corresponds to a different point on the boundary line. Second, points close together on the contour generator correspond to nearby points on the boundary line. Third, the contour generator lies in a single plane (Marr, 1982, p. 223).

Since generalised cones can be recovered from an image, 3-D model descriptions of objects made up of generalised cones can be derived from the 2½-D sketch. Depending on viewpoint, such descriptions may be more or less adequate. Marr and Nishihara propose that in object *recognition* 3-D model descriptions derived from the 2½-D sketch interact with information from an indexed catalogue of 3-D models stored in long-term memory. This interaction results in both a better analysis of the image and a set of labels for the objects in it. Marr and Nishihara suggest that the catalogue is arranged hierarchically. At one level there may be, say, a six-cone model of a biped, and at the next level (six-cone) models of a man and of an ape. These more specific models differ from the biped model by stating more exactly the relative sizes of the component cones. Each model also contains labels for its component parts. A biped model, for example, comprises a head model, a torso model, two arm models and two leg models. These models are stored elsewhere in the catalogue. Marr and Nishihara propose that, when a scene is viewed, partial descriptions of the objects in it are first derived using only information in the image and the general constraints governing the projection of generalised cones. These partial descriptions generate a variety of *indices* (see chapter 2) that can be used to access the catalogue. Information from the catalogue improves the analysis of the image by suggesting, for example, what might be foreshortened or occluded in it.

Marr's approach to object recognition is model-based. In this respect it is reminiscent of Roberts's (1965) work. However, it eschews other BLOCKSWORLD techniques, in particular the use of junction dictionaries.

## Summary

Although the ability to see is not a mark of intelligence, in the everyday sense of that term, it is mediated by complex information processing of the kind that lends itself to computational modelling. However, more than in many other fields, the boundary between AI research on vision and other computational approaches to image processing is not a sharp one. Nevertheless, there are many aspects of computer vision that deserve to be treated in a book on AI.

Vision can be divided into two main stages: low-level, or early, processing, and the higher-level processing required to recognise objects. The most important approach to low-level vision is Marr's.

As well as producing specific theories about visual processes, Marr developed a general account of the form that such theories should take. They should provide explanations, at *three* separate levels, of how an information-processing task is carried out. The *computational theory* describes what (mathematical) function a system computes, and why. The *algorithm and representation* specifies how information is encoded and how it is transformed in order to carry out the task. The *description of the implementation* describes the machinery on which the computations are performed. Marr also proposed a number of more specific principles for theories of vision. The most important of these are that visual processing should, as far as possible, be characterised as data-driven, and that it should be shown to be guided by constraints derived from the nature of the physical world.

Marr distinguished three main stages in early visual processing. In the first, the *grey-level description* is converted into the *raw primal sketch*. This sketch is the first symbolic representation of the image. It contains information about edge segments, blobs, bars and their terminations. An important stage in the derivation of the raw primal sketch is the computation of *zero-crossings* in the second derivative of the grey-level representation. Marr claims that zero-crossings are detected by X cells in the retina and lateral geniculate nuclei. The raw primal sketch is converted into the *full primal sketch* by processes that detect larger features and boundaries. Finally, the *2½-D sketch* is derived from the full primal sketch by processes that extract information about the orientation and relative depth of surfaces. These processes include stereopsis, structure from motion and shape from shading.

Object recognition was first studied in the BLOCKS-WORLD. Some BLOCKSWORLD programs derived line drawings from TV images, but many required a line drawing as input. Roberts's line finder simply detected relatively rapid changes in intensity in the image. Two developments extended line finding to poorer quality images of more complex scenes. Shirai's program produced a partial analysis of the scene that guided further examination of the image for fainter lines. Falk and Grape used knowledge of BLOCKSWORLD scenes to hallucinate invisible lines, without reconsulting the image.

Roberts's object recognition program used stored models of cubes, wedges and hexagonal prisms, which it tried to project on to the image. This model-based approach was replaced by *junction labelling*, a technique for *segmenting* an image into sets of regions corresponding to single objects. Junction labelling does not produce an exact description of an object's shape. The technique was originally used by Guzman in his program SEE. It was systematised by Huffman and Clowes, who stressed the need to distinguish between descriptions of the image and descriptions of the scene. Waltz extended junction labelling to scenes with shadows. He used a relaxation algorithm to filter out impossible combinations of junction labels.

Junction labelling fails to analyse some images correctly, because it does not use information about the angles between surfaces. Mackworth suggested an alternative approach, based on *gradient space*. However, Draper showed that that approach, too, mislabelled some scenes. Draper developed a technique for analysing BLOCKSWORLD scenes called *sidedness reasoning*. Sidedness reasoning depends on an assumption about flat surfaces. It therefore makes explicit the fact that a solution to the object recognition problem in the BLOCKSWORLD will not generalise to other domains.

Kanade attempted to overcome the problems of the junction labelling and gradient space approaches by combining the two. He also introduced two heuristics to eliminate physically possible, but unlikely, interpretations of images – interpretations that people have difficulty seeing.

Marr and Nishihara outlined a more general approach to the problem of object recognition. They showed that, if an object is made up of *generalised cones*, an object-centred description of it, *a 3-D model description*, can be constructed from the 2½-D sketch. They claimed that most natural objects are made of generalised cones. The 3-D model description can be used to label objects by referring to a stored catalogue of 3-D models. Marr and Nishihara proposed that information from that catalogue can help to refine the analysis of the image. In particular they suggest that it is used to 'see' details that are occluded or grossly foreshortened.

# 4 Thinking and reasoning

The activities that we usually consider to require intelligence are those that call for thinking and reasoning – solving problems, proving theorems and playing games such as chess and draughts. The skills underlying these activities were the focus of the earliest AI research, a fact that explains the presence of the word *intelligence* in the name *artificial intelligence*.

This chapter surveys AI research on thinking and reasoning. It begins with problem solving, which is first illustrated by ANALOGY, a program that solves geometrical analogy problems. However, this program is atypical because it can only conceive of a small number of possible solutions to each problem it works on. It examines each of these solutions to find out which is best. Most problems require controlled search of a set of possible solutions that cannot possibly be considered one by one. A number of ways in which search can be controlled are described. Problems can be divided into adversary problems (games) and non-adversary problems, of which geometrical analogies are an example. The two types of problem call for slightly different methods of solution. The adversary problems that computers can solve tend to be more interesting than the non-adversary ones. For this reason, the operation of chess-playing programs is described in detail.

The second major topic of the chapter is theorem proving. It is illustrated by the early Logic Theory Machine that proves theorems in propositional calculus. A more general theorem-proving method, resolution, is then described, together with the unification algorithm on which it depends. Resolution is compared with chaining techniques that are sometimes described as non-resolution theorem proving. Non-uniform (domain-specific) methods are then introduced and illustrated by programs that perform mathematical reasoning. The chapter ends with a discussion of planning and its relation to problem solving.

## Problem solving

There are many situations in which people are confronted with problems to solve. Those problems range from puzzles in puzzle books, through the problems we confront in our daily lives, to intellectual problems in the humanities and sciences. To solve a problem is to find a solution, or in some cases the best solution, to it. The goal of AI research on problem solving is, therefore, to describe how solutions are found. The more explicitly a problem can be formulated, the easier this goal is to achieve. So, there are many AI programs that solve puzzles, for example, but none that successfully simulate scientific thinking. Even with a puzzle, finding a solution can be hard, because there are many ways of encoding the given information and, often, a vast number of possible solutions to consider.

The first program to be described in this section solves geometrical analogy problems. The program has a restricted vocabulary for describing the kinds of figures in such problems. This limitation solves by fiat the question of how the figures should be encoded and it reduces the number of possible solutions to proportions that can be managed by brute-force methods.

## The ANALOGY program

If the autobiographical accounts of scientists and mathematicians can be relied on, analogical reasoning plays a crucial part in creative thought. Kekule, for example, claimed that his insight into the ring structure of the benzene molecule was suggested by the idea of a snake that had caught its own tail. Although a long-term goal of AI might be to explain such creative thinking, research on analogical reasoning has focused on a much simpler kind of analogy – one which is, perhaps ironically, required to solve a type of problem found in so-called *intelligence tests*. Evans (1968) describes a program, ANALOGY, for solving such problems.

An intelligence test analogy problem comprises three given geometrical figures, A, B and C, and several possible solution figures. The figures are made up of simple geometrical shapes, such as squares, triangles, circles, semi-circles, dots and lines. B is a (possibly complex) transformation of A. The problem is to determine which of the solution figures is related to C in the way that B is related to A.

ANALOGY starts by analysing each figure into subfigures. Then it derives a rule, or sometimes a set of alternative rules, that describe how A can be converted into B. The detailed shape of each subfigure is not recorded. ANALOGY simply makes sure that subfigures with the same shape are given the same arbitrary label, regardless of their size. ANALOGY has a small, fixed vocabulary to describe the relations between subfigures in a single figure and the transformations that convert subfigures in one figure to those in another. The parts of a single figure can be INSIDE, ABOVE, and LEFT OF one another, with the converses of these relations being implicitly encoded. In the mapping from one figure to another, a subfigure may change SCALE, or be ROTATED or REFLECTED. In addition, a subfigure in one figure may map into a differently shaped subfigure in another, and subfigures may be added or deleted.

As well as finding rules that will change A into B, ANALOGY produces mappings from C to each of the possible solution figures. Again, there may be several ways of transforming C into any one of these. Once these mappings have been derived they can be compared to the rule or rules that change A to B. This comparison generates a set of difference scores. The solution figure is the one produced by the rule with the smallest difference score – the rule that is most like one that relates to A and B.

ANALOGY rejects some solutions out of hand. When comparing two rules it insists that they refer to the same number of subfigures. This constraint is applied separately to the transformations, additions and deletions mentioned in a rule. However, even when solutions that violate this constraint are rejected, there may still be many to consider. How does ANALOGY compute difference scores for those that remain? Not surprisingly, it prefers to match, say, circles in one rule with circles in another, rather than circles with squares. However, some of its other preferences are not so obvious, and could be varied in different versions of the program. For example, ANALOGY considers that an additional rotation makes rules less different than an additional reflection, even though in many cases the way a subfigure changes from one figure to another may be ambiguous between a rotation and a reflection.

Out of twenty problems that Evans presented to it, ANALOGY made a mistake on only one. Evans claims that its level of performance is equivalent to that of a 15-year-old.

In one important respect ANALOGY is not a typical AI problem solver. In its system of representation there are only a comparatively small number of possible solutions to each problem. The number of subfigures in a figure is usually less than ten, and the ways in which figures can change as one figure is transformed into another is limited by the vocabulary that ANALOGY uses to describe such changes. For a difficult problem, ANALOGY might have to compare a few hundred pairs of rules. The speed at which digital computers work, therefore, allows ANALOGY to use a brute-force method to find its preferred solution. It works through all the difference scores and finds the smallest.

For most of the problems that AI problem solvers work on, such brute-force methods for finding solutions are not viable. The number of possible solutions is too large for even the fastest computer to search exhaustively. Some method is needed, therefore, for reducing the number of possibilities that have to be considered. Before these methods for controlling the search for solutions are described, the types of problems they are used for will be introduced.

## Adversary and non-adversary problems

In the problem-solving literature a distinction is made

between adversary and non-adversary problems. An adversary problem is one in which two or more people pit their wits against each other. The prototypical example of an adversary problem is a two-person game, such as chess. Game playing is a special sort of problem solving in which the problem is to find a winning strategy or, more parochially, to find the best current move.

The focus of AI research on game playing has been on games for two players in which each player always has *complete information* about the state of play and in which there is no element of chance. Noughts and crosses (tic-tac-toe), chess, and draughts (checkers) are examples of this type of game. Backgammon is a game of complete information in which chance plays a role. Games with incomplete information include those card games in which the players do not know what cards their opponents have in their hands.

Non-adversary problems are ones that do not involve another person (except in the role of problem setter). Geometrical analogy problems are an example. Non-adversary problems that require more advanced AI problem-solving techniques include:

*The 8-puzzle* – a 3 × 3 square containing the numbers 1 to 8 which must be moved via the vacant square until they are in order.

*Missionaries and cannibals* (also known as *Hobbits and orcs*) – transport three missionaries (hobbits) and three cannibals (orcs) across a river in a boat that can only hold two people, but that needs at least one to get it across the river. Cannibals must never outnumber missionaries on either bank, or the missionaries will be eaten.

*Jugs problems* – example: three jugs, a,b,c can hold 8,5,3 litres respectively. a is full, b,c empty. Find a sequence of pourings that leaves 4 litres in a and 4 litres in b.

*The Tower of Hanoi* – three vertical pegs with four (or more) discs of decreasing size piled on one peg. Transfer the discs to the second peg, moving only one disc at a time, and never placing a larger disc on top of a smaller one.

*Cryptarithmetic* – DONALD + GERALD = ROBERT. Given that D = 5, and that each letter stands for a different digit (from 0 to 9), find the digits that make the sum correct.

*Rubik's cube*

There are two main differences between AI research on non-adversary problem solving and game playing. First, the non-adversary problems themselves tend to be simpler and less interesting than the problems posed by games such as chess. For this reason, the discussion of search strategies for non-adversary problems will make little reference to specific problems. Second, somewhat different methods are required for solving non-adversary and adversary problems. In what follows, general techniques for solving non-adversary problems are described first. Specialised techniques for game playing are then introduced, followed by a more detailed description of chess-playing programs.

Search

In AI, finding a solution, or the best solution, to a problem is conceptualised as a *search* through a space of possibilities. The study of efficient ways of carrying out such searches is, therefore, an important branch of AI research. Usually searches are *directed* and only some possibilities are considered. A program, such as ANALOGY, that evaluates all possible solutions is a rarity.

Searches are directed by *control strategies*. A good control strategy is one that focuses attention on a subset of possible solutions that contains the actual solution (or a solution) to the problem. That solution should, therefore, be found after only a small number of possibilities have been considered. The ideal strategy leads directly to the correct solution, but it is rarely possible to formulate general strategies of this sort.

Techniques for searching sets of possibilities have a wider importance than their use in problem-solving programs might suggest. They are also used in programs that are not usually thought of as solving problems but which, for certain purposes, might be thought of as doing so. One type of program that uses search techniques is the parser (see chapter 5). Parsing can be characterised as a search through a set of possible structural analyses of a sentence for the correct one.

### The size of search spaces

Before control strategies are discussed in detail, a little more will be said about why there might be a *combinatoric explosion* in the number of potential solutions to a problem. The simplest case arises when the problem has to be solved in several stages. If there are N different things that can be done at each stage, then there are N possible one-step solutions, N × N possible two-step solutions, N × N × N possible three-step solutions, and so on. The number of possible solutions is an *exponential* function of the number of steps. So the number of operations carried out by a program systematically working its way through the possible solutions increases exponentially with the number of steps to the solution. Experience in computer science has shown that when the number of operations that a program must perform is an exponential function of some measure of the 'difficulty' of the input – in this case the length of the path to the solution – then the time taken by the program becomes unacceptably large for difficult inputs.

### Representing problems so their solutions can be searched for

There are two prerequisites for a formal description of how a search is carried out. The first is a method of describing those aspects of the world that are relevant to the problem and its solution. This requirement is not specific to problem solving. Methods of representing states of the world were discussed in chapter 2. For the non-adversary problems above, predicate calculus provides an adequate representational system. Among the states of the world that must be described, the most important are the one that poses the problem – the initial or starting state – and the one (or ones) in which the problem has been solved – the goal state(s). The second requirement is a way of specifying what can be done in an attempt to solve the problem. If the problem is soluble, there is (at least) one way of getting from the initial state to the goal state. In the problem-solving literature, possible moves in solving a problem are called *operators*. There are two particularly important types of operator. The first changes one state of the world into another. The second divides a goal into a set of subgoals that are easier to achieve. A solution to a problem is a sequence of operators that provides a path between the initial state and (one of) the goal state(s). To find a solution the operators must be applied to the initial state and/or the goal state according to a set of rules or control strategy, until a path between those two states is discovered.

In everyday problems and problems that require a high degree of creative thinking it is usual for one or more of the initial state, the goal state, and the operators to be ill-specified. For this reason AI programs that solve such programs are difficult to write. In problems such as Missionaries and cannibals or the Tower of Hanoi, all three are clearly specified. AI programs are relatively successful at solving these problems.

In AI there are two main approaches to describing the search for solutions to problems, one tailored to the use of operators that change one state of the world into another, the other particularly suited to operators that divide goals into subgoals. These two approaches use *state-space representations* and *problem-reduction representations*, respectively.

The basic component of a *state-space representation* is a state of the world or, rather, a state of that small part of the world that is relevant to the problem. For example, in the Missionaries and cannibals problem a typical state of the world might be:

| Left Bank | Right Bank |
|---|---|
| 2 missionaries | 1 missionary |
| 2 cannibals | 1 cannibal |
| boat | |

The states of the world are linked by operators that can change one state into another. So, for example, the above state of the world can be linked to:

| Left Bank | Right Bank |
|---|---|
| 1 missionary | 2 missionaries |
| 1 cannibal | 2 cannibals |
| | boat |

by the operator that takes one missionary and one cannibal from the Left Bank to the Right Bank in the boat. From each state it will usually be possible to reach several others, using different operators. A map of all states that can be reached from the initial state by the application of one or more operators is called a *state space*. State spaces can be represented by tree diagrams, with the initial state at the top, and paths to other states branching beneath it. For many problems such tree diagrams can be extended indefinitely. Solutions to a problem, if there are any, are represented by paths through the tree from the initial state to (one of) the goal state(s).

In a tree representation the same state will appear more than once if it can be reached in several ways from the initial state. It is sometimes useful to use state-space representations in which all occurrences of the same state are collapsed. Such representations are called *graphs*, rather than trees (they can be much more difficult to draw!). There are many useful mathematical results that can be applied to such structures.

In a *problem-reduction* representation each operator divides one goal into a set of subgoals that are easier to achieve. Problem reduction depends on the fact that some subgoals are so simple that they can be satisfied directly. The aim of problem reduction is to analyse the main goal into components of this sort. An example of a problem that can be analysed using the problem-reduction technique is the Tower of Hanoi. Let the three sticks be called A,B,C. The overall goal is to move the four discs from A to B, moving only one disc at a time, never placing a larger disc on top of a smaller one. This goal can be divided into three subgoals:

(1) Transfer the three smaller discs from A to C.
(2) Transfer the largest disc from A to B.
(3) Transfer the three smaller discs from C to B.

Of these goals, (1) and (3) can be reduced further, while (2) can be achieved directly, providing that (1) has been achieved. A complete reduction of the Tower of Hanoi problem analyses it into moves of single discs whose preconditions are met. The preconditions for a move of a single disc are, first, that no disc is on top of it before the move, and second, that no smaller disc will be under it after the move.

Almost any problem can be given a state-space representation, but that representation is usually not as useful as one that reduces the problem to simpler subproblems. However, simple problem-reduction representations do not allow for the fact that a subproblem may be solved in more than one way. This possibility is allowed for in AND/OR trees (or graphs), which combine the features of state-space and problem-reduction representations. In AND/OR trees several branches may be ANDed together to indicate that they are subgoals that must *all* be satisfied at a particular stage in solving the problem (problem reduction). Alternative goals are represented by OR branches only one (ANDed set) of which must be satisfied to produce a solution to the problem. An AND/OR tree with no ANDs is a state-space representation. One with no ORs is a problem-reduction representation.

## Control strategies

Now that methods of representing problems have been considered, the question of strategies for controlling the search for a solution can be taken up. Indeed, since questions about representation are not specific to problem solving, the primary question in AI research on problem solving is that of control strategies.

Control strategies may have two different aims. They may either seek any solution to the problem or they may try to find the best solution, usually defined as either the shortest or the least costly path from initial state to goal state.

The need for control strategies arises because AND/OR trees for many problems can be extended indefinitely. In attempting to solve such problems it is not, therefore, possible to construct the entire tree and search every part of it for a (or the best) solution. Furthermore, even 'small' parts of AND/OR trees rapidly become costly to construct and search for a solution. Such trees grow in both *depth* – the number of operators applied – and in *breadth* – both because goals are divided into subgoals and because there may be several ways of achieving each subgoal (the tree branches). The number of states that can be reached in a given number of moves from the initial state is the average number of branches at any point (the *branching factor*) raised to the power of the depth. The size of the tree, therefore, grows exponentially with its depth, and searching large exponential spaces may effectively take forever. Some method is needed for identifying and exploring promising parts of the tree and, hence, of deliberately failing to construct unpromising parts of it.

The most fundamental distinction among control strategies is between *breadth-first* and *depth-first* search. Breadth-first search starts from the initial state, and considers all states that can be reached by the application of a single operator. If any of these is the goal state then the problem is solved, otherwise the states that can be reached by the application of two operators in succession are examined, and so on. For problems in which all operators are equally costly to apply, breadth-first search automatically finds the optimal solution. However, for problems of any complexity, it can be extremely time-consuming. Breadth-first search can be generalised to uniform-cost search. Some operators may be more costly to apply than others. Like simple breadth-first search, uniform-cost search follows many paths at once, but it keeps the costs of all those paths, rather than their lengths, as close as possible.

In depth-first search a single path is followed until it reaches either a goal state or a dead end. If a dead end is reached, the search *backs up* to the last point at which a choice was made, and another path is tried. Providing that it keeps tracks of choice points and the choices it has made at them, depth-first search can, in principle, examine the whole tree. However, it may never terminate even if the problem has a solution – the path chosen first may never end yet it may never reach the goal state. For this reason, depth-first algorithms often incorporate a *depth bound*. If a path fails to produce a solution in a fixed number of operations it is abandoned. Depth-first search may not find the best solution to a problem first. If there is more than one solution a less good one may be found before the optimal one. To guarantee the best solution, depth-first must be allowed to find all solutions and compare them.

For real problems simple breadth-first and depth-first search algorithms are usually impractical, because the search tree is too large and they examine too much of it. Some method must be found for focusing attention on part of the tree in which a solution is likely to be found. Many such methods are *heuristic*, since they cannot be guaranteed to solve the problem. Algorithms do guarantee to find a solution, if there is one, but they do not guarantee to find it in a reasonable time. Another characteristic of many heuristic methods is that they depend on an evaluation of the current state, for example in terms of its 'distance' from the goal state.

Depth-first search can be modified to produce a *hill-climbing* procedure. In hill climbing, as in depth-first search, a single path is followed to either a solution or a dead end. However, the choice of which path to follow at any point is determined by which alternative gets nearest to the solution in one move. Hill climbing, therefore, depends on the existence of an *evaluation function* that estimates the distance of a state from the solution. The name *hill climbing* derives from the fact that the solution to a problem can be thought of as the highest point in a 'landscape', and the distance of any state from the solution as how far downhill it is. To reach the solution from any other state it is always necessary to 'climb'. However, the landscape is blanketed in 'fog'. It is not possible to look around and see where the highest hill is, only to take the path that locally is steepest. If all possible movements are downhill, then a 'peak' has been reached. This peak may or may not be the solution to the problem. If it is not, it is called a *local maximum* – the top of a hill that is not the tallest hill in the landscape. The easiest way to escape from a local maximum is to make a large random movement. Hill climbing can only guarantee to find a solution in landscapes with a single peak. The more 'uneven' the landscape, the less well a hill-climbing procedure will perform.

Breadth-first search can be improved in a variety of ways. One simple heuristic extension is *best-first* search. A best-first procedure uses the same kind of evaluation function as hill climbing. However, to decide which path to pursue it examines all of the tree built so far and selects the path that has produced a state most similar to the goal state. If an initially promising path begins to lead away from the goal state, its value will go down. Eventually it will drop below that of the next best path, which may be anywhere in the tree, and that will be followed instead. The amount of improvement afforded by best-first search over breadth-first search depends on how good the evaluation function is.

Other extensions of breadth-first search lead to more efficient *algorithms* for finding the optimal path from initial state to goal state. The simplest such extension is *branch-and-bound* search, a variant of uniform-cost search. In branch-and-bound search, as in uniform-cost search, the least costly path is extended. Search ends when the shortest incomplete path is longer than the shortest complete one. This complication ensures that there is no incomplete path that can be completed very cheaply after a (comparatively costly) final operator has completed another one.

A further extension of breadth-first search is the A* algorithm of Hart, Nilsson and Raphael (1968). This algorithm takes into account both the cost so far of each path (like branch-and-bound) and the estimated cost of completing the path (like best-first). In addition, A* assumes that the distance of any state from the goal state does not depend on how that state was reached. So, for example, a path of the form (Initial State)-(State1)-(State2) can be ignored if there is a shorter path of the form (Initial State)-(State2). There is no point in going to State2 via State1 if you can go there directly. It can be shown that, provided that the estimates of the distance to the goal state are never overestimates, A* will find the optimal solution to any problem. From a mathematical point of view, *lower-bound* estimates are the safest. Unfortunately there is no simple method for generating these estimates for A*. For each type of problem a new method must be devised.

A different approach to search is found in a relatively early, but influential, AI program, Newell and Simon's (1963) General Problem Solver (GPS). The approach is known as *means-end analysis*. GPS works forward from the initial state towards the goal state, and at each point it chooses an operator that reduces the difference between the current state and the goal state. Sometimes the operator that could best reduce the difference is not applicable, because one of its preconditions is not fulfilled. GPS can try to move to a state in which that precondition is fulfilled. If GPS reaches a dead end – a point at which no operators can be applied – it backs up, otherwises it continues, depth-first, along a single path. GPS only began to live up to its claim to be a *general* problem-solving system when it was extended by Ernst (Ernst and Newell, 1969). Ernst's version of the program solved problems in eleven domains, though not very efficiently. Furthermore, the revised version of the program lost some of the abilities of earlier, simpler versions. GPS is, therefore, more important for its influence than for its abilities.

One problem that is very difficult to solve using techniques described so far is Rubik's cube. Rubik's cube is difficult because there is no simple way of estimating how near any particular state of the cube is to the goal state – in which each face of the large cube is a single colour – and no obvious division of the problem into solvable subproblems. The normal approaches based on state-space representations and problem-reduction representations are, therefore, unhelpful. Brute-force methods might solve a reduced 2 × 2 × 2 Rubik's cube, but not the usual 3 × 3 × 3 cube (or at least not for 700,000 years, see Korf, 1985). Korf presents a method for solving the problem, one that is also useful or problems such as the 8-puzzle and Missionaries and cannibals. In this method *macro-operators* are constructed from sequences of simple operators. For a 3 × 3 × 3 Rubik's cube Korf derives 238 macro-operators. The purpose of a macro-operator is to position and orient one of the small cubes correctly, without *permanently* disturbing the position of other small cubes that are already correctly positioned. What makes Rubik's cube difficult is that other small cubes must be *temporarily* repositioned so that the cube currently being moved can be put into place.

## Game playing

Search trees for games differ in some respects from search trees for non-adversary problems. This section outlines the differences, using chess as an example. Specific chess-playing programs are discussed in more detail below.

Two-person games are best described using state-space representations, with states corresponding to board positions and operators to moves by either player. (N.B. The term *move* is used here informally, *not* in accordance with its use in the chess literature where one move = a turn taken by each of the players.) The search tree has the initial board position at the top. Alternative levels of the tree correspond to moves by each of the players.

In real games of chess, the 'problems' faced by the players are almost always of the form: which is the best move to make at this point in the game? However, from an AI problem-solving point of view the problem that a chess player or a chess-playing program is trying to solve is finding a sequence of moves that will win the game. This problem is complicated by the fact that the opponent's moves cannot be predicted for certain. However, they can be predicted if it is assumed that the opponent is following a rational strategy and is trying to win. A solution to the chess problem is, therefore, a series of moves that leads from the initial board position to a winning position, provided that the opponent behaves rationally. In principle the selection of a winning strategy, and hence the correct move at any point in the game, is a well-defined problem with a definite answer. However, it is impossible to compute a winning strategy in a reasonable amount of time because the search space is very large – there are about $10^{120}$ possible games of chess. This figure compares with, for example, $10^{16}$ microseconds per century.

Chess-playing programs cannot make an exhaustive search for a winning strategy. What they must do, at each point in the game, is choose a reply to their opponent's last move. However, just as it is not possible to compute a winning strategy for the whole game, for most board positions it is not possible to compute the move that is most likely to lead to a win. The number of possible continuations from any board position, except some in the endgame, is too large to make this computation feasible.

A chess-playing program, unless it simply makes moves at random, must use some method for assigning values to the moves available to it, so that it can choose between them. Although moves cannot, in general, be followed up to see if they lead to a win, the further a move can be followed, the better the assessment of its value is likely to be. In practice, all programs have to limit their *lookahead* – the distance that they follow up each move. Some also limit the number of moves they follow up. Limited lookahead means that decisions about which move to make must be based on the values on the positions that can be reached in a limited number of moves. Since very few of these positions will be wins or losses, a way of evaluating such positions is required – a so-called *static evaluation function*. Static evaluations – evaluations of board positions that are not wins or losses – are made in terms of such factors as the numbers of pieces remaining to each player, how centrally they are placed and how well the kings are guarded.

A sensible program cannot simply head for the most highly valued position several moves away. As any chess player knows, its opponent may foil it. Once a program has assigned values to all the positions it is going to consider, it must use a *decision strategy* to choose between the moves available to it. The most common decision strategy is *minimaxing*. A mini-maxing program operates as follows. First, all the positions that can be reached at the end of the fixed lookahead are evaluated by the static evaluation function. Those values are then 'backed up'. When backing up the values of moves, the program treats its own moves and those of its opponent differently. On its own moves, it assumes that, faced with a choice, it will choose the move that has the best outcome for it. Considering its opponent's moves it assumes that the opponent will choose the move that results in the worst possible outcome for it. Backing values up gives a better estimate of the goodness of a move than just the values of positions that might be reached. Highly valued positions might be blocked by the opponent's replies.

Minimaxing is illustrated in the simple tree shown in Figure 4.1. The changing positions on the left of the tree should be read top to bottom, the backing up of values on the right, from bottom to top. The program would ideally like to reach state S7, which has a value to it of 7. However, in backing up from its static evaluation the program argues that its opponent would, in state S3, choose the move that leads to state S6. So

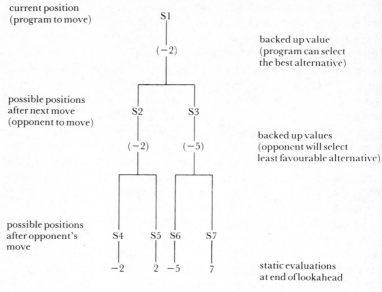

current position
(program to move)                S1

                                    backed up value
                          (−2)      (program can select
                                    the best alternative)

possible positions
after next move          S2      S3
(opponent to move)

                                    backed up values
                      (−2)    (−5)  (opponent will select
                                    least favourable alternative)

possible positions
after opponent's        S4    S5 S6    S7
move

                      −2     2 −5     7   static evaluations
                                          at end of lookahead

Figure 4.1

the value of S3 is only −5. Similarly, the value for S2 is −2. Therefore, at S1 the program chooses the move that leads to S2, because that leads to the best outcome against a minimaxing opponent. If it tried to reach S7, it would be forced to S6, which has a value of only −5. Minimax gets its name from the fact that the program always MINimises its MAXimum loss at the next step.

Minimaxing by enumerating and evaluating all possible outcomes is inefficient because it is often easy to show that some unexplored moves cannot be better than one that has already been evaluated. Those moves can be discarded using the technique of *alpha-beta pruning*. The principle behind alpha-beta pruning is that if an opponent has one reply to a move that makes it bad, then there is no point in finding out about the other replies, provided that a better move is available. A minimaxing opponent will choose what is, from your point of view, the worst possible response to any move.

As well as restricting their lookahead, human chess players follow up only a limited number of moves, further limiting their search. Even the best players usually follow up less than a dozen moves and consider only a few hundred board positions. However, deciding which moves to pursue is a difficult problem, one that has not been satisfactorily solved in computer chess playing. Indeed, with interest focusing on performance rather than the modelling of human chess-playing abilities, the recent trend has been to use the power of modern computers to examine a large number of positions.

Draughts (US checkers) is a simpler game than chess but, from an AI perspective, shares many of its features. It is a competitive two-person game, each player has a definite goal – that of winning – and there are too many possible games for a winning strategy to be selected by exhaustive search. It is easier to make computers play good draughts than to make them play good chess. The most interesting work in computer draughts playing has been on learning. It will be discussed in chapter 6.

*Chess-playing programs*
Perhaps because games like chess appeal to the kind of person that is attracted to AI, AI researchers have always been fascinated by attempts to make machines play chess. Even before computers were available, Turing, Shannon and others considered the possibility of writing chess-playing programs and Turing, in particular, demonstrated how simple programs might work, simulating their operation by hand (see Hodges, 1983).

Some of the first non-numerical computer programs were chess players. Kister *et al.* (1957) wrote a program for the early MANIAC computer that played on a reduced 6 × 6 board. This program was neither very sophisticated nor a very good player. It simply followed up all moves to a fixed depth of two moves (for each player) and backed up its evaluations using a modified minimax procedure. Bernstein *et al.* (1958) progressed to a full-size board and produced a much better chess player by improving the static evaluation function. On the machines available in 1958, following up all moves on a full-size board would have taken a very long time, particularly with a complex evaluation function. Bernstein, therefore, devised a method for choosing seven moves to follow up in more depth, using routines called *plausible move generators*. These move generators considered such factors as which of the program's pieces needed defending and which of the opponent's could be attacked. The use of plausible move generators makes the program's operation more like that of a human chess player. However, Bernstein's program only followed up the chosen moves to the same depth as the MANIAC program followed up every move. It did not look as far ahead as human players do and it, therefore, appeared to have 'blind spots'.

Since 1958, there have been two lines of development in research on chess playing. On the one hand people have continued to write programs that play games of chess. The level of play of such programs has improved dramatically. However, most of this improvement can be attributed to increases in the size and speed of computers. There have been only minor advances in modelling human chess-playing strategies. Until the early 1970s the most successful programs used techniques similar to those in Bernstein's program – following up moves selected in ways that were supposed to reflect the choices of human chess players. The best of these programs was Greenblatt's MACHACK (Greenblatt, Eastlake and Crocker, 1967), which beat Hubert Dreyfus, a notorious critic of AI (see chapter 8), in a much-publicised challenge match.

Work on chess programs was further encouraged by the Association for Computing Machinery's (ACM) computer chess tournaments, which began in 1970, and by other cash prizes that have been offered since. The ACM tournaments soon came to be dominated by programs from Northwestern University, first their Series Three programs CHESS3.0-CHESS3.6, and then their Series Four programs. The Series Three programs were in the Bernstein mould, but Series Four reverted to the brute-force methods used in the MANIAC program. The plausible move generator was discarded and all moves were followed up to a fixed depth. The increase in computer power since the 1950s meant that such brute-force methods were much more successful. CHESS4.6 performed at the level of a chess master, by simply looking ahead for four to five moves and considering about 400,000 positions. CHESS4.6 does not play like a human player. Its limited lookahead means that it cannot develop the kinds of plan that characterise human chess play. Recent ACM winners have also depended on brute force. BELLE, a program from Bell Telephone Labs, had a special opening program, but relied on exhaustive search in its midgame. Its successor as ACM champion, CRAY BLITZ, runs on two Cray 1.0 computers, generally recognised to be the most powerful machines available in the mid-1980s.

The second line of research on chess has focused on simulating the way people play. For two reasons, programs from this tradition have been restricted to parts of the game. They do not play a full game of chess. First, the programs have become highly complex. Second, different skills are required in different parts of the game. This fact is recognised in the chess literature, in which openings, midgames and endgames are analysed separately.

In the midgame, human chess players develop complex plans, which may require a comparatively lengthy sequence of moves for their execution. At each point in the sequence the opponent's reply must also be predicted. A typical plan might have as its goal the safe capture of one of the opponent's pieces. Pitrat (1977) and Wilkins (1979) have developed programs that can generate such plans and execute them. These programs must be given more sophisticated chess concepts than Bernstein's program and its successors. The plans that these programs develop are, in effect, complex control strategies that direct the programs' attention to a very small part of the search tree. The programs can, therefore, pursue ideas to a much greater depth.

Other examples of programs that play only part of the game are the endgame programs described by Bratko, Kopec and Michie (1978; Michie and Bratko, 1978) and by Berliner and Campbell (1984). The first of these programs treats each combination of pieces in the endgame as a separate problem and has a knowledge base of stored advice for each combination. For example, when king and knight play against king and rook, advice used to guide the search for moves includes 'do not loose the knight' and 'keep the king and knight together. The program is much more successful in standard endgames than CHESS4.6.

Berliner and Campbell's program, CHUNKER, analyses king and pawn endgames. It maintains a library of *chunks*, which are functionally related groups of pieces with known properties. Chunks are used both to evaluate positions of which they are part, eliminating much of the search through positions that can be reached from them, and also to select moves, usually in the attempt to force a position with a known (positive) evaluation. CHUNKER has been instrumental in the development of new ways of assessing positions in the literature and it plays 'with a speed and accuracy that no present human or machine can come close to matching' (Berliner and Campbell, 1984, p. 98).

## Theorem proving

People who are good at solving problems are said to be intelligent in a certain sense of that term. Those who are good at proving theorems of logic and mathematics are intelligent in the same sense. Indeed, theorem proving can be regarded as a variety of problem solving – the problem is to find a proof of a theorem from a set of axioms. However, problem solving and theorem proving have been treated rather differently in AI, and it is convenient to discuss theorem proving separately from problem solving. This section begins with a discussion of the first real AI program, Newell, Shaw and Simon's Logic Theory Machine, which used heuristic, rule-of-thumb methods for proving theorems in propositional calculus. It then describes more general inference methods that can be used for theorem proving, before turning to modern heuristic methods.

### The Logic Theory Machine

The earliest working AI program was Newell, Shaw and Simon's (1957) *Logic Theory Machine* (LT), which proves theorems in propositional calculus as formalised by Whitehead and Russell (1910) in *Principia Mathematica*. Propositional calculus is part of predicate calculus (see chapter 2). It formalises inferences that depend only on the connectives $\sim$,

&, v, → (*not, and, or, if . . . then*). Whitehead and Russell formalised propositional calculus as a set of axioms and a set of inference rules that can be used to derive all other theorems from the axioms. Although there are mechanical methods for finding a proof of any given theorem, they are very tedious and do not reflect the way people find proofs. LT's proofs are similar to those produced by people.

In their attempt to simulate theorem-proving abilities, Newell, Shaw and Simon developed the idea of *heuristics* – procedures that can be used to prove theorems, or solve problems, but which cannot be guaranteed to find a solution, even if there is one. Heuristics are contrasted with *algorithms*, which are procedures that do offer such a guarantee. For many problems, such as finding proofs in propositional calculus, or winning in chess, algorithmic procedures can take unrealistic amounts of time. When people solve such problems they must be using heuristic methods.

LT uses a number of heuristics for finding proofs, which, even for simple proofs, speed it up in comparison with an algorithmic procedure it was compared with. The algorithm generates systematically all proofs of a given length from those one step shorter, by applying all possible inference rules. Eventually the required theorem appears. There were many theorems that LT could not prove. For the most part its problems arose from limitations on its memory and on the amount of time it was allowed to run for. However, Newell, Shaw and Simon identified some theorems that LT was in principle unable to prove. Interestingly LT found an elegant proof of a theorem in *Principia Mathematica*, which Whitehead and Russell had apparently overlooked.

In one sense heuristic proof procedures for propositional calculus are uninteresting. Although there is no quick *proof-theoretic* method of deciding whether a propositional calculus formula is a theorem, there are straightforward *model-theoretic* procedures (i.e. procedures that rely on the meaning of the formulae). One such method is the method of truth tables. If truth tables show that a formula is always true whether its components are true or false – that it is true because of what it means – then that formula is a theorem. An example of such a formula is (P v ∼ P). Nevertheless, LT was important because the idea of heuristics dominated research on theorem proving and problem solving in the decade following its publication. Newell, Shaw and Simon incorporated the idea into their GPS program, which was a more direct simulation of human thinking than LT, and into a chess program. Other programs that used heuristics include Gelernter's Geometry Machine, described below, and Slagle's SAINT, a program that performed symbolic integration at the level of a first-year mathematics undergraduate. Symbolic integration later became an important component of the mathematician's aid MACSYMA (see chapter 7), but whereas SAINT took a generalist approach to integration, Moses built specialised mathematical knowledge into the symbolic integration component of MACSYMA.

## Resolution

The Logic Theory Machine was a first attempt at modelling people's theorem-proving abilities. LT's proofs are quite similar to those that beginning logicians produce and, like people, LT often fails to prove theorems that can be proved. However, in designing an intelligent machine it is often better to replace heuristic methods with algorithmic ones, particularly if efficient algorithms can be found. This section introduces the resolution procedure, a comparatively efficient algorithm for deducing the consequences of statements expressed in predicate calculus. Resolution has been used in many theorem-proving applications.

In chapter 2 the use of predicate calculus as a knowledge representation language and its major advantage, that of completeness, was discussed. The completeness of predicate calculus ensures that, if some fact is entailed by a given set of facts (i.e. if it follows from them according to logical principles alone), then that fact can be derived mechanically from them. Unfortunately there is no corresponding guarantee that a fact that does not follow can be shown not to follow. If the completeness result is to be of use in AI, a mechanical procedure must be found that is suitable for use on a computer. The resolution algorithm (Robinson, 1965) is such a procedure. It derives from a method of proving the completeness of predicate calculus devised by the mathematician Herbrand.

The resolution algorithm uses the principle of *reductio ad absurdum*, or proof by refutation. It adds the negation of the fact to be proved to the set of given assertions, and tries to derive a contradiction. A contradiction shows that the negation of the fact to be proved is false, provided that the given set of facts is itself consistent. The principle of excluded middle ($\sim \sim P = P$, i.e. not not P is equivalent to P) converts the falsity of the negation into the truth of the fact itself.

The resolution algorithm converts all formulae, both the ones that are given and the negation of the fact to be proved, into *conjunctive normal form*. In conjunctive normal form a formula is represented as a conjunction (X and Y and Z and . . .) of a series of disjunctions (U or W or V or . . .) of atomic formulae and their negations. An atomic formula is a single predicate followed by constants or variables as its arguments. Examples are sleeps(john), sees(john,mary), falls(x), loves(y,z), eats(john,w). Atomic formulae and their negations are referred to as *literals*. In conjunctive normal form all quantifiers are universal, and occur at the front of the formula. Conversion to conjunctive normal form can be carried out mechanically. The details of the conversion, which makes use of standard equivalences, such as that between $P \rightarrow Q$ and $\sim P$ v Q, are of little interest in themselves.

The existential quantifiers are replaced using a procedure called *Skolemisation*, in which each existentially quantified variable is replaced by a function, called a *Skolem function*, of the universally quantified variables on which it depends. So, for example, in

(for all x)(man(x) → (for some y)(woman(y) & loves(x,y))

the variable y is replaced by a function, say skolem1(x), that maps each man on to the woman he loves. The resulting formula is:

    (for all x)(man(x) → (woman(skolem1(x)) &
            loves(x,skolem1(x)))).

When all the existential quantifiers have been eliminated, the universal ones can be moved to the front of the formula, using another standard equivalence. Finally, the universal quantifiers are dropped and all variables are assumed to be universally quantified. This dropping of quantifiers depends on the fact that when quantifiers at the front of a formula are all universal their order is immaterial. When converting to conjunctive normal form, it is necessary to ensure that variables both within a clause and in different clauses do not accidentally have the same name. The full details of conversion to conjunctive normal form are given by Nilsson (1980) and others. These details are not important here, only the fact that every formula can be mechanically reduced to such a form.

Once a set of well-formed formulae have been converted to their conjunctive normal forms, and the quantifiers have been removed, they can be regarded as a set of *clauses*, each of which is a disjunction of atomic formulae and their negations. The conjunctions (ands) are implicit in the fact that each clause is in the set. For this reason conjunctive normal form is sometimes called *clause form*.

Resolution is an iterative procedure in which two clauses are combined, and pairs of disjuncts of the form P,~P eliminated. The rule that licenses this combination is called the *resolution rule*. It states that Q v R can be concluded from Q v P and ~P v R. That is to say, if at least one of q and p is true and at least one of not p and r is true, then at least one of Q and R must be true, since P and not P cannot both be true together. If two clauses resolve to the empty clause, then a contradiction has been found, and the fact to be proved is true. Otherwise the new clause, *the resolvent*, is added to the set and two more clauses are resolved. Provided that clauses are selected for resolution in a systematic way, the resolution algorithm will eventually prove any theorem of predicate calculus.

The resolution algorithm is complicated by the fact that the atomic formula, P, need not have exactly the same form in the clause that contains P and the one that contains ~P. In particular, if either occurrence contains variables it is sufficient that there is a *uniform substitution* for those variables that makes the two occurrences identical, except for the negation.

The algorithm for determining whether two atomic formulae

can be made identical by a uniform substitution of variables is called the *unification algorithm*. This algorithm is required as a subroutine of the resolution procedure for predicate calculus. A pair of disjuncts is a contradiction if one unifies with the negation of the other. To give the flavour of this procedure, block(x), where x is a variable, contradicts ~block(table21), because block(x) and block(table21) are unifiable under the substitution x = table21. The two are contradictory because, in clause form, the x is implicitly universally quantified. Block(x) means that everything is a block, whereas ~block (table21) says that there is some table that is not a block. When two atomic formulae are eliminated from a resolvent clause, the substitution used to unify them must be used throughout the resolvent.

In general, if two literals can be unified, there are infinitely many substitutions that can be used to unify them. Most of them contain substitutions in addition to those that are necessary for unification. The unification algorithm finds the simplest or *most general* unifier, sometimes abbreviated to MGU.

There are several ways of choosing clauses for resolution that guarantee to find a proof for a theorem, if there is one. One is the *unit preference* strategy, which favours clauses with the smallest number of literals. Another is the *set-of-support* strategy, in which each resolution must include the negation of the statement to be proved. Unfortunately, none of these strategies guarantees a quick solution, because the number of possible paths to the proof grows exponentially with the number of resolutions in the proof.

There are also a variety of ways for making resolution more efficient. However, some of these make it incomplete, in the sense that it will not always infer a true consequence from a set of premises.

## Rule-based inference systems and chaining

In the AI literature on reasoning, the terms *forward chaining* and *backward chaining* are frequently used. These methods of reasoning are commonly used in domains in which predicate calculus is an appropriate representation system. They have much in common with resolution theorem proving. Indeed, some people broaden the definition of resolution so that chaining methods become types of resolution (cf. Bundy, 1983; Charniak and McDermott, 1985, pp. 378ff.). Other authors, however, refer to chaining and related methods as *non-resolution* theorem proving (e.g. Bledsoe, 1977) or *rule-based deduction*.

The main parallels between resolution and chaining are that both use Skolemisation and unification. There are two principal differences. First, chaining is usually considered to be a *direct* method of theorem proving – it does not proceed indirectly via a *reductio ad absurdum*. Second, statements need not be converted to clause form for chaining. The importance of this fact is that a clause such as:

$$(\text{for all } x) \ (\text{block}(x) \ v \ \text{table} \ (x))$$

is logically equivalent to both of the following:

$$(\text{for all } x)(\text{block}(x) \rightarrow \sim\text{table}(x))$$
$$(\text{for all } x)(\text{table}(x) \rightarrow \sim\text{block}(x)).$$

However, in a rule-based system, the first of these statements is a rule for proving that something is not a table, whereas the second would be used to show that something isn't a block. Statements that are logically equivalent may be used in very different ways – ways that are obscured by the conversion to clause form for resolution.

Both forward and backward chaining are based on the logical inference schema of *modus ponens*. Modus ponens states that P and P → Q together imply Q. For predicate calculus, Skolemisation and unification are required, and modus ponens is modified to: from P′ and P → Q infer Q′, where P′ unifies with P, and Q′ is derived from Q by the substitution that unifies P′ with P. In forward chaining, reasoning proceeds from the premises to the desired conclusion, via successive applications of modus ponens in the 'forward' P to Q direction. Forward chaining systems are often implemented so that as soon as a statement is added to the database, the reasoning rules are applied to derive all its consequences.

Backward chaining, or *goal-directed reasoning*, starts from the desired conclusion and works back to the premises. It searches for a rule of the form P → Q that can be used to prove the conclusion, Q. Then it looks to see if the P of that rule is one of the premises. If it is not, it tries to prove it. Backward chaining is typically used to prove things when they are queried.

Forward chaining works forward from premises to conclusion, backward chaining backward from conclusion to premises. Resolution, too, can effectively work in either direction, depending on the strategy for choosing clauses to resolve. A 'forward' resolution strategy is one that starts by resolving (two of the) premises, whereas a 'backward' strategy starts from the negation of the conclusion (and one of the premises).

Two further points should be made about chaining methods. First, rule-directed inference systems are often implemented as production systems (see chapter 2). Second, most expert systems are rule-directed systems. However, expert systems are often complicated by the fact that the rules are regarded as probabilistic or not completely reliable (see chapter 7).

## The relation between resolution and rule-based inference

As should be apparent from the foregoing discussion, the exact relation between resolution theorem provers and rule-based systems is somewhat problematic. The step-by-step operation of rule-based systems does not parallel that of the resolution algorithm, under its most straightforward interpretation. However, from some points of view the two types of theorem proving are equivalent. They produce the same results, often by similar methods.

A useful perspective on this issue is that of Bundy (1983), who argues that non-resolution systems can be reconstructed within a resolution framework. Thus, unity can be imposed retrospectively on theory-proving research – a unity that was not apparent when it was being carried out.

## Non-uniform proof procedures

Resolution and chaining are *uniform* theorem-proving methods in the sense that they are intended to find a proof of any statement that follows logically from a set of premises in FOPC, regardless of its content. The advantages of these methods have already been discussed. Their major disadvantage is that for any but the most trivial of proofs they take too long, because of a *combinatoric explosion* in the number of possibilities that have to be examined. The resolution algorithm, for example, is constantly adding new clauses – the resolvents – to the set that it is working with. These additions cause the number of possible resolutions to increase at an exponential rate.

There have been a number of attempts to improve the efficiency of uniform theorem provers. Those that impose uniform, universally applicable, restrictions on such methods have been of little help, except where they have used what Bundy (1983, pp. 88–9) calls *cheating techniques*. They have neither speeded up uniform proof procedures, nor brought them nearer to discovering interesting theorems. Interestingly, Bundy's main concern is mathematical theorem proving, an area in which the layperson might expect uniform proof procedures to be most likely to succeed.

The only domains in which uniform proof procedures have been successful are relatively new branches of mathematics (Bundy, 1983, p. 258). The reason is not that such methods are more efficient in these domains, but that people are less efficient. There has been no time for domain-specific, and hence non-uniform, proof procedures to develop. Indeed, some of these branches of mathematics may never give rise to such procedures and they may never warrant further development. Human mathematicians working in these branches of mathematics are often forced to resort to the brute-force methods of uniform proof procedures. They have little or no advantage over computers using these techniques.

Uniform proof procedures have been comparative failures both as artificial intelligences and as models of human mathematical ability. These facts, together with a more careful consideration of how expert mathematicians actually try to prove mathematical theorems, have led to a number of alternative proposals about theorem proving. Many of these are highly technical (see Bundy, 1983, part III). However, there is one method that is comparatively easy to understand – the use of domain-specific knowledge to guide proofs. An early AI program, Gelernter's (1963) Geometry Machine, provides an example of a theorem prover that uses such a technique.

*Gelernter's Geometry Machine*
Euclidean Geometry was the first branch of mathematics to be successfully formalised. Its proofs were originally developed, and they continue to be taught, with the aid of *diagrams*. The diagrams depict the figures – squares, triangles, parallelograms and so on – that geometry problems are about. They provide a *semantic interpretation* of the premises – they show what those premises mean. A person working on a geometry proof does not have to rely solely on the structural properties of the premises, in the way that a resolution theorem prover would have to. The diagrams are domain-specific. They are used only in geometry, and not in, say, arithmetic or calculus. The use of diagrams is, therefore, a non-uniform proof procedure, that is only employed to prove theorems of geometry.

Gelernter's (1963) Geometry Machine is a program that proves theorems of Euclidian Geometry. It uses (an internal representation of) a diagram to guide its proofs. The Geometry Machine works by chaining backwards from the theorem, attempting to reach statements that follow immediately from the axioms of Euclidean Geometry. It effectively constructs part of an AND/OR tree for the problem. The axioms used by the Geometry Machine are not those favoured by advanced mathematicians, but are supposed to reflect a high school student's understanding of Euclidean Geometry. The set of axioms is not complete, neither are all the axioms independent of one another.

Each backward chaining step generates a number of additional statements to be proved. These statements are checked against the diagram, and those that are not true in it are set aside. However, they are not totally forgotten. If the Geometry Machine gets stuck, it can revise its diagram, and make a second attempt to prove the theorem. By remembering apparently useless results, it may save itself work on this second pass. Discarding statements that are not true in the diagram only works efficiently if care is taken to ensure that the diagram does not have 'accidental' properties. Similarly, in school geometry proofs, it is important not to be misled by, for example, angles that appear to be equal, but are not really so. As well as discarding statements that are false in the diagram, the Geometry Machine also rejects statements that it is already trying to prove, to avoid getting into infinite loops.

Gelernter introduced two further ways of improving the search for a proof. First, the Geometry Machine knows that certain types of statement can be proved in a single step, if at all. It tries to prove those statements before any others. Second, as in best-first search, the Geometry Machine makes estimates of how close it is to a solution of each of the subproblems it is working on. It chains backwards from those statements that are closer to the premises first.

Gilmore (1970) showed that the success of the Geometry Machine depends partly on the fact that the axioms and statements it works with do not require the full expressive power of predicate calculus. They can all be expressed as horn clauses, which are a proper subset of predicate calculus statements. Bundy (1983) shows that the principle of *semantic checking* used by the Geometry Machine can be extended to other domains, providing that axioms and statements in those domains can be formalised using horn clauses. The general idea behind semantic checking is the building of a *model* of the premises, and using that to eliminate developments of the proof that are incompatible with the model. In Euclidean Geometry a diagram provides such a model.

### Mathematical induction

*Mathematical induction*, not to be confused with the induction of general statements from particular facts, described in chapter 6, is a common method of proof in mathematics. It is one that poses problems for resolution theorem provers. A typical proof by mathematical induction runs as follows:

(1) Prove that the number 1 has some property, P.
(2) Prove that if any number n has property P, then the number n + 1 has the property P.

(3) Conclude that every number (every positive integer) has property P.

The reason why induction is hard to formalise in the resolution framework is that the rule of induction cannot be captured by a single axiom, but only by an axiom *schema* that stands for an infinite number of separate but related axioms. Resolution systems work with a finite set of axioms. They cannot cope with infinite sets of axioms (there is not enough room in a computer's memory!). A resolution system might be able to use an axiom schema directly and generate only a few instances of it at a time. However, it is difficult to see how it could produce the instance relevant to the problem it was working on, except by a time-consuming trial-and-error procedure. Some systematic method of guiding the induction process is needed. Such a method is provided by the Boyer-Moore theorem prover (Boyer and Moore, 1979). The principal theorem-proving method used in the Boyer-Moore system is called *symbolic evaluation*. It comprises a set of heuristics for rewriting mathematical formulae, a technique that is very common among human mathematicians. When symbolic evaluation fails, the way it fails is used to guide the subsidiary theorem-proving methods of induction and generalisation.

*Meta-level reasoning*
Bundy's own preferred alternative to uniform proof procedures is *meta-level reasoning*, which he defines as reasoning about the representation of a (mathematical) theory. Since different branches of mathematics use different notational devices, meta-level reasoning is domain-specific. Bundy argues that meta-level reasoning captures an essential aspect of the way that human mathematicians reason.

Bundy and Welham (1981) describe a program, PRESS, that uses meta-level reasoning to solve algebraic equations. Solving such equations requires the isolation of a single variable, usually x, on the left-hand side, leaving an expression on the right-hand side, with no xs in it, that gives the value of x. Finding a solution almost always requires several steps. Bundy and Welham propose three techniques for rewriting equations. The first is *isolation* (of the variable x) itself. This technique will usually be applied when an equation is almost solved. The second is *collection* in which several occurrences of x are brought together. Collection would, for example, transform $2x + y + x = 0$ into $3x + y = 0$. Finally, *attraction* brings two occurrences of x closer together without actually collecting them. The precise definition of 'closer together' makes reference to the structure of the algebraic expression.

## Planning

When people try to solve problems they often make plans. In some cases the plan is simply to carry out a sequence of actions that is known or thought to lead to the solution. In other cases, the attempt to find a solution must be planned. However, planning and problem solving are different from each other, since 'even the best-laid plans can fail'. Plans fall either because they are faulty or because the world changes in an unexpected way. To formulate a plan is not, therefore, to solve a problem. When a plan is executed, progress towards the achievement of a solution must be monitored.

The focus of AI research on planning has been on the choice of a sequence of actions that allow a robot to achieve a predetermined goal. The goal usually involves unstacking and restacking blocks in the BLOCKSWORLD. In the simplest systems, the distinction between planning and problem solving is blurred, because unforeseen changes in the world are not considered. The robot has a set of basic actions, which have known effects on the state of the world. A plan specifies a sequence of actions that changes the world from the initial, or problem, state to the goal state. The problem solvers described above can be considered as planning systems, in this sense. They generate solutions to problems by working on internal representations of them. They could go on to use that solution to drive a robot that brought about the goal state in the real world. Indeed some problem-solving systems, in particular GPS, have been applied to robot-planning problems. However, turning problem solvers into general purpose planning systems reveals several difficulties that are not apparent in the simpler systems.

The first of these problems arises because performing even a simple action can have a variety of effects on the world. Problem-solving systems need to represent states of the world, and to have operators that change the states of the world. Each operator is specified in terms of the changes that it produces. In the systems discussed so far, those changes have been simple. For example, in a chess-playing program, the operators correspond to legal moves, and each operator changes the position of a single piece (and, perhaps, removes one other piece from the board). The rest of the pieces remain where they were, and the operator has no other relevant effects. This feature of the operators in chess-playing programs reflects the nature of chess moves.

In general it is not safe to assume that the effects of an action carried out by a planning system will be as *local* as they are in a game of chess. A single action may have multiple effects. It is, therefore, necessary to specify either explicitly or implicitly not only which aspects of the world change when the action is carried out, but also which aspects remain the same. The problem of formulating such a specification is called the *frame problem* (which has no connection with the frame systems of chapter 2). This problem takes its name from an analogy between successive states of the world and frames in an animated cartoon. To describe any frame completely requires a large number of statements. However, most of these statements remain the same from frame to frame. Only a few change. The frame problem is to specify which ones change as the result of an action being performed.

The second major problem in planning arises because plans are frequently based on problem reduction, more appropriately labelled goal reduction in the context of planning. A planning system has to analyse its overall goal into a series of subgoals that can be fulfilled directly by one of the robot's basic actions. Simple robots can only perform one action at a time. So it is also necessary to decide which order to perform the actions in. Reducing a goal does not, of itself, indicate the order in which the resultant subgoals should be achieved. Each basic action has a set of preconditions that specify the circumstances in which it can be performed. For example, a robot with one simple hand can only pick up a block if its hand is empty. However, preconditions are aspects of the world, which may be changed when a robot performs an action. Achieving one subgoal may, therefore, create, destroy, or leave unchanged the preconditions for another. Only in the simplest cases can all the subgoals be achieved independently. In such cases the plan is said to be *linear*.

## Planning systems

Planning is similar to problem solving, and problem-solving techniques have been applied to plan formulation. The use of GPS as a planner has already been mentioned. Green (1969) showed how robot-planning problems could be solved by a resolution theorem prover. His technique relies on the description of states of the world using predicate calculus formulae. To solve the frame problem he included in every statement a variable that indicated the state of the world in which it was true. ON(blockA, blockB, state0) means that blockA is on blockB in state of the world state0. A planning problem includes a description of the initial (or problem) state, a description of the goal state, and a formulation, as a set of implications (*if . . . then* formulae, or their equivalents in clause form) of the effects that robot actions have on the state of the world. These rules must explicitly indicate which elements of a description are and which are not affected by each action. Thus, Green's method solves the frame problem by brute force.

More recently Kowalski (1979) has devised a more efficient FOPC representation for planning problems. In Kowalski's system ON(blockA, blockB, state0) is replaced by HOLDS(ON(blockA, blockB), state0). The advantage of this representation is that it effectively allows quantification over statements, such as 'blockA is on blockB', by treating them as names for 'individuals'. Kowalski's solution to the frame problem does not require an explicit statement, for each element of each description about whether it is affected by each action. It is possible to make a general (quantified) statement that all descriptions other than those that are explicitly changed stay the same. However, ordinary deductions are more complicated in Kowalski's system than they would be with a more standard predicate calculus representation.

## PLANNER and related languages

In chapter 2 the distinction between procedural and declarative representations of knowledge was introduced. Encoding knowledge into procedures was originally a reaction to the perceived limitations of some AI programs of the 1960s. These programs encoded all their data in the same way, using declarative representations. Any mechanism for controlling the use of knowledge had to be incorporated into the general data manipulation part of the program. The result was either a uniform procedure which, like the uniform search procedures described above, was inefficient, or a very complex control structure that was difficult both to write and to generalise. In an attempt to solve this problem, languages were created in which control information can be explicitly expressed. In these languages, procedures can be invoked by specifying, for example, the goals that they are intended to achieve. Indeed, a program in such a language is little more than a list of goals. To put this another way, plans can be expressed very straightforwardly in these languages.

The first such language was PLANNER (Hewitt, 1972) – partially implemented as MICRO-PLANNER (Sussman, Winograd and Charniak, 1971). The best-known application of PLANNER is in Winograd's language-understanding system, SHRDLU (see chapter 5). Ironically, PLANNER proved too inflexible for writing realistic planning systems. In searching for solutions to planning problems, PLANNER used strictly depth-first search with automatic backtracking on failure to the last choice point. It made no use of the reasons why a plan failed. PLANNER's successors include CONNIVER (McDermott and Sussman, 1972) and QLISP (Sacerdoti *et al.*, 1976). A CONNIVER program benefits more from its failures than a PLANNER program. The reasons why a plan did not work are used in deciding which alternative to pursue next. However, despite several successful applications, notably Sussman's (1975) HACKER (see chapter 6), CONNIVER programs proved difficult to write and expensive in computer time to run.

*STRIPS and its successors*
Fikes and Nilsson (1971) describe a robot-planning system called STRIPS (STanford Research Institute Problem Solver), which uses a combination of GPS and resolution theorem-proving techniques. The means-end analysis of GPS is used to find a path from the problem state to the goal state through the space of possible states of the world. Resolution is used within single states of the world, which are described by sets of predicate calculus formulae, to discover whether goals are satisfied and what operators can be applied to those states. The main interest of the original version of STRIPS is the way that it solves the frame problem. Each basic STRIPS action is encoded as a three-part rule. The first part is a set of preconditions for the action. The other two are lists called the *add list* and the *delete list*. The add list contains statements that become true when the action is performed, having previously been false. The delete list is a list of true statements that cease to hold when the action is performed. If a robot picks up a block it becomes true that the robot is holding the block and it ceases to be true that the robot's hand is empty. The truth or falsity of any statement not mentioned on either of these lists is assumed to be unaffected by the action. The idea of add lists and delete lists is computationally most useful when those lists are comparatively short – when the basic actions do not cause major changes in the world.

STRIPS was designed for problems that can be solved by linear planning – where achieving one subgoal does not interfere with achieving others. However, even in simple robot planning problems plans often interact. Sometimes a linear system can solve in an inelegant way problems that have simpler interactive solutions. But there are some problems that STRIPS-like systems cannot solve at all, because they irretrievably destroy preconditions for actions that they must perform later.

Nilsson (1980, pp. 321ff.) describes a system, RSTRIPS, that begins to solve this problem. RSTRIPS stores its goals on a (last-on, first-off) stack. It looks down the stack at the goals still to be achieved and determines whether any of their preconditions are (i) already satisfied, and (ii) about to be undone by the present action. If any are, RSTRIPS determines whether they can be recreated later. If they cannot, it decides against the action it was going to perform, backs up one step, and tries to formulate a new plan in which the subgoals are achieved in a different order.

A different solution to the problem of interactions between plans was developed by Sacerdoti (1977) for his NOAH system. Like STRIPS, NOAH divides goals into subgoals, but it develops independent plans for achieving each subgoal. These plans can be represented in an AND/OR graph. Such a graph does not completely specify the order in which the actions should be performed. Subgoals must, of course, be satisfied before the goals of which they are part, but subgoals of the same goal can be achieved in any order. The graph provides a *possible* solution to the overall planning problem, but the solution will only work if all of the subgoals are independent – that is to say, if none of the plans interact. In this case, the actions can be performed in any order. If the robot is capable, they can be carried out simultaneously.

When the plans do interact, NOAH attempts to find a way of performing the actions that allows every precondition to be met at the right time, and which, therefore, solves the problem. There is no guarantee that this attempt will be successful, though it almost always produces a plan that is less flawed. If this second stage of NOAH's operation still fails to produce a satisfactory plan, new subplans are added to re-establish the preconditions that are still not met, and a further attempt is made to generate a satisfactory plan.

Another aspect of NOAH's planning was first developed by Sacerdoti (1974) for his ABSTRIPS system. Sacerdoti noted that when people make plans they work at several levels. First they sketch a high-level plan in which the major steps towards the solution are identified. Lower-level details are then filled in. The high-level plan controls which lower-level details are considered and thus reduces the number of possibilities considered by the planning system. STRIPS works at only a single level – all the basic actions in a plan are treated as equally important. In ABSTRIPS some preconditions for actions are marked as more important than others and a high-level plan is formulated in which only the most important preconditions of actions are taken into consideration. This high-level plan is then filled out by considering the next most important conditions, and so on. If no satisfactory plan can be formulated at one level, control passes back to the level above, and an alternative is sought at that level.

Wilkins (1984) describes a more sophisticated domain-independent hierarchical planner, SIPE (System for Interactive Planning and Execution monitoring). The principal innovations in SIPE are the ability to consider the effects of carrying out more than one action at the same time, as would be possible for a robot with two arms, and the ability to reason about available resources.

## Summary

Thinking and reasoning are central components of human intelligence. However, of the wide variety of skills that fall under these heads, only some of the simpler ones have succumbed to AI analysis.

AI research on problem solving is most successful when both the problem and the operations that can be performed in an attempt to solve it can be clearly specified. Examples of problems that AI programs can solve include some kinds of puzzle-book puzzles, which are intended for a single person, and the adversary problems posed by games such as chess. AI techniques have been much less successful in solving the comparatively ill-formulated problems of everyday life and of academic endeavour.

Some simple problems, such as geometric analogies, have been solved by programs that examine all solutions that are possible given the way that the problem is encoded. However, for most problems there are too many possibilities for such methods to work. For these problems control strategies are required to guide the search among possible solutions. Possible solutions can be mapped out using either state-space or problem-reduction representations. The two can be combined in AND/OR graphs. The simplest control strategies are depth-first and breadth-first search. If a program can estimate how near to a solution it is, these strategies can be modified to hill climbing and best-first search, respectively. A useful method for finding the best solution to a problem is the A* algorithm, which takes account of both distance travelled and distance to go, and which can quickly classify some solutions as inevitably longer than others.

Chess-playing programs do not try to solve the problem of finding a winning strategy for chess. They choose, at each point in the game, the move that they estimate to be best. They look ahead for several moves, make a static evaluation of the positions that can be reached, and use the minimax procedure to compute the best move. They assume that their opponent is rational. Some programs follow up all possible moves. Others select a subset of moves to examine.

Theorem proving is, in many ways, like problem solving, though it has usually been treated separately in AI. Newell, Shaw and Simon's Logic Theory Machine proved theorems in propositional calculus. Its use of heuristic methods made its proofs similar to those produced by people.

Resolution is a theorem-proving method that is guaranteed to prove any predicate calculus theorem that can be proved. It may, however, take an arbitrarily long time. Chaining, or rule-based, methods are similar to resolution and suffer from the same drawbacks. To produce quick proofs of boring theorems or any proofs of interesting theorems it is usually necessary to go beyond the uniform methods of resolution and chaining and use domain-specific methods similar to those employed by, for example, human mathematicians. Examples of such methods include the use of diagrams in proving geometry theorems and of meta-level reasoning about mathematical representation systems.

Forming a plan to achieve a goal is similar to solving the problem of achieving that goal. However, the term *planning* highlights the possibility of things going wrong and the necessity of monitoring the execution of the plan to see if the goal is being achieved. AI research on planning has focused on plans for robots stacking blocks. The actions that a robot can perform tend to have more diverse effects on the world than the operators used in solving puzzles and playing chess.

This fact generates the frame problem – the problem of providing an insightful specification of which aspects of the world stay the same when a robot acts. Another consequence of the diverse effects of robot actions is that actions within a plan must be sequenced so that one action does not destroy the prerequisites for another. Finally, plans are often generated hierarchically. One approach to modelling this fact is to treat some prerequisites for actions as more important than others. Only the more important ones are taken account of in high-level plans.

# 5 Language

Computational techniques have been used to investigate many aspects of language processing, from identifying spoken words to the use of knowledge about the world to produce a full interpretation of a text. This chapter reviews the main aspects of this work. It begins by discussing the computer processing of speech. Techniques for encoding speech on a computer are introduced first. Then research on speech recognition and speech synthesis is described. The second major topic is parsing – the identification of the structural relations between the words in a sentence. To parse a sentence is not to understand it, but it is a step towards understanding. Four parsing methods are discussed: augmented transition networks, chart parsing, Marcus parsing and semantic parsing. Finally the comprehension of discourse and text is examined. Two major projects of the 1970s, Winograd's SHRDLU and Schank's MARGIE, are described in detail. Some issues at the forefront of current research are then taken up: dialogue, non-literal language and the use of knowledge about the world.

A long-term goal of applied AI is to produce computers that converse with people, computers that understand spoken language and that speak themselves in response to it. Such systems remain a distant prospect. Before they become a reality, research on a number of relatively independent topics in language comprehension must progress to the stage where they can be combined to produce a useful system.

## Speech

One of the abilities required by a talking computer is the ability to process speech itself. Speech-processing research investigates the relation between speech waves and words or phonemes – the individual sounds, such as /a/, /e/, /b/, /ch/, out of which words are made. It leaves to one side questions about meaning. There are two broad divisions of research on speech processing: speech recognition and speech synthesis. Speech recognition is working out the identities of words from properties of the speech wave. Speech synthesis is the production of speech from a specification of words and/or phonemes and, possibly, information about syntax and intonation.

A full understanding of the literature on speech processing requires knowledge of both the acoustic and the phonetic properties of speech. However, this section aims to provide a brief, non-technical, introduction to this work.

Although speech-processing research is part of AI in the broad sense, historically it has been separate from mainstream AI. It has been strongly influenced by work on signal processing carried out by electrical engineers. This influence is reflected in the fact that speech-processing programs are often written in FORTRAN, rather than one of the list-processing languages.

Computational research on speech processing requires a way of storing a continuous signal, such as a speech wave, on a digital computer. This requirement poses no real problem, since any continuous (analogue) signal can be approximated digitally (as a series of 1s and 0s) to any degree of accuracy. All that is necessary is to choose a method of approximation that does not lose important information about the signal. The simplest way of digitising a speech wave is to measure its amplitude at regular intervals and to store the amplitude in digital form. Amplitude is typically stored as a 12-bit number, so 4096 (i.e. $2^{12}$) different amplitudes can be distinguished.

Young people can hear sounds up to about 20,000 Hz, and speech waves have components at this frequency. However, almost all the important information is at lower frequencies. A typical *sampling rate* for digitising speech signals is 10,000 Hz (10,000 samples, or amplitude measurements, every second). This sampling rate preserves frequencies up to about 5000 Hz, which compares favourably with a telephone line. It loses all information above 4000 Hz.

Digitisation is the first of many transformations that speech waves undergo in speech processing. However, it is not a psychologically interesting one, simply one that allows speech to be represented inside the computer. Digitised waveforms take up enormous amounts of computer memory, and are unlikely to correspond to any representation in the human brain. Signals leaving the ear already contain much less information than digitised waveforms. In computer speech processing, digitised waveforms are transformed into more compact representations from which important information is more readily accessible.

The earliest transformations produce representations that remain *acoustic*, rather than linguistic. There are three main ways in which this early, acoustic, processing of speech waves can be achieved: vocoder analysis, formant tracking, and LPC analysis (cf. Isard, 1986). For each type of representation a sampling rate of about 100 Hz is sufficient – 100 times less frequent than the rate needed for the initial digitisation of speech. However, the representation of each sample is more complex than the single 12-bit number representing the amplitude of the wave, so the transformed representation is only about ten times smaller than the original.

*Vocoder analysis* is the simplest, but least used, of these methods. A vocoder separates a sound into a series of *frequency bands*. A low frequency band might, for example, run from 100 Hz to 500 Hz, covering sounds with pitches about one octave on each side of middle C. For each frequency band the vocoder measures the amount of energy in the sound and encodes it digitally. Vocoder analysis can be applied to any sound. It does not make use of the special properties of speech sounds. Vocoders are also comparatively slow. For these reasons vocoder analysis has not found favour among the speech community.

The other two types of representation exploit special properties of speech. *Formant tracking*, as its name suggests, depends on the presence of *formants* in speech signals. In much of normal speech the vocal cords are vibrating. The frequency of the vibration varies from speaker to speaker. It also varies over time for a single speaker. However, it is usually in the range 80–200 Hz. This *fundamental frequency* gives rise to *overtones* at integer multiples of itself. So, if the vocal cords are vibrating at 150 Hz there will be overtones at 300, 450, 600, . . . Hz. The shape of the vocal tract, which varies depending on the position of the lips, tongue, jaws and teeth, determines which of these overtones are emphasised and which de-emphasised, by providing *resonances* centred on certain frequencies. A resonance centred on 1300 Hz, for example, will give most emphasis to the 1350 Hz and 1200 Hz overtones of a 150 Hz tone. In the sounds that come out of the mouth, energy is, therefore, concentrated in certain bands of frequency. These bands are the formants. They are more or less independent of the fundamental frequency of the voice. The first three formants are important in determining the identity of sound, especially vowels. Their values for an English vowel might be 500 Hz, 1500 Hz, 2500 Hz. Formant tracking represents a speech wave by the values of the first 3 or 4 formants in each sample. Unfortunately there is no completely reliable algorithm for extracting formants from a digitised waveform.

*Linear predictive coding* (LPC) is a way of coding speech sounds in terms of a simplified model of the vocal tract. The code is a set of numbers, called LPC coefficients, that reflect the shape of the vocal tract. The model represents the vocal tract as a sectioned tube, in which all the sections are of equal length and each can vary in diameter independently of the others. Each section has a resonance that depends on its diameter, but the relation between the resonances of the sections and those of the vocal tract as a whole, which produce the formants, is complex. Twelve LPC coefficients are typically used, two for each of six sections of tube.

The major advantage of LPC analysis is that there are efficient algorithms both for deriving LPC coefficients from speech and for generating speech from them. In the case of speech recognition in particular, LPC analysis can be automated, whereas formant tracking cannot. LPC techniques are also widely used for resynthesising real speech, when digitisation is required.

The availability of efficient algorithms is closely associated with two simplifying assumptions made in LPC analysis. The first is that the vocal tract is a *single* tube. In fact, the nose forms a side branch, which is important in the production of some sounds, the *nasals* (e.g. /n/, /m/). Second, all sounds are assumed to be either *voiced* or *unvoiced*. A voiced sound is one produced when the vocal cords are vibrating. In LPC analysis such a sound is assumed to be the result of a *buzz* at the fundamental frequency of the larynx passing through the vocal tract. An unvoiced sound is produced when the vocal cords are not vibrating. The source of the sound is the rush of air from the lungs. In LPC analysis this source is represented by a particular type of noise, in the technical sense of that term. LPC assumes that every sound has either a buzz source or a noise source, but not both. Many real speech sounds involve both vibration of the vocal cords and a rush of air from the lungs. The effect of these simplifying assumptions is that LPC representations of nasals and of sounds with a mixed buzz and noise source are poorer than those of other sounds.

## Automatic speech recognition

An *automatic speech recognition* program takes a speech wave as input and provides a 'label' for that input. That label can be thought of as a transcription of the input as a string of words or, less ambitiously, phonemes. The goal of automatic speech recognition research is to provide a transcription, in real time, of natural speech by any speaker, in any context in which a person would have no difficulty recognising the words spoken. However, this goal is a distant one. Current programs can only identify a comparatively small number of words (1000–2000) spoken clearly in relatively noise-free conditions by a limited number of speakers, sometimes only one. They usually need to be trained to recognise the voices of those speakers they can deal with.

Some of the more successful automatic speech recognition

systems have used a technique that would be costly, in computational terms, to generalise, and is unlikely to reflect the way that people recognise spoken words. This technique is to match representations of whole words against templates held in memory. Human speech varies in many ways, so it is difficult to match words to templates directly. To overcome temporal variations in the way a word is spoken, the programs have to treat the templates as though they were elastic. They do so using the mathematical technique of dynamic programming to produce the required 'time warping'. Dynamic-programming techniques can be extended so that successive parts of a sentence (or word string) can be matched against different templates.

There are two reasons why it is unlikely that people recognise speech by matching inputs to word templates. First, they have too many words in their vocabularies. Second, words are made up of smaller and much less numerous units – syllables, phonemes, phones, diphones – whose identification could form the basis of more efficient word recognition procedures. Unfortunately these smaller units vary greatly in their acoustic properties from context to context. It is hard to determine what constant features they have and, hence, difficult to write procedures that identify them. Furthermore, it is likely that people use grammatical and semantic constraints to help them recognise words in connected speech. It may not, therefore, be necessary to rely on a complete acoustic analysis. Bridle, Brown and Chamberlin (1982) have shown how grammatical constraints can be incorporated into a dynamic programming algorithm.

The most intensive work on automatic speech recognition was carried out as part of the ARPA speech-understanding project in the USA. In this project, several teams of researchers tried to write speech-understanding systems that met specifications laid down by the ARPA research agency. Among those specifications were that the vocabulary size should be about 1000 words, and that the programs should demonstrate how syntax and semantics can aid word identification. The term *understanding*, rather than recognition, was used because the programs were to be judged by whether they responded correctly to spoken input, rather than by whether they transcribed it properly. However, much of what the programs did was automatic speech recognition.

The most successful of the speech-understanding systems, according to the ARPA criteria, was HARPY (Lowerre and Reddy, 1980). HARPY effectively stored a template for every sentence in the fragment of English it could understand, making it even less plausible than word-template systems as a model of human speech understanding. The program did contain information about how words are made up from acoustic segments and how sentences are made up out of words. However, this information was not used directly to identify words. It was used to produce a large set of sentence representations, in the form of a transition network, when the program was compiled. HARPY was not intended to be a realistic model of human speech understanding. In particular, speakers of natural languages cannot use syntactic constraints to produce representations of sentences, because those languages have indefinitely many sentences. However, some aspects of HARPY, for example its comparatively small demands on working memory, do have psychological plausibility (cf. Norman, 1980).

Two other systems, HWIM (Hear What I Mean, Wolf and Woods, 1980) and HEARSAY (Erman and Lesser, 1980), were not as successful as HARPY in meeting the ARPA criteria, but they were more ambitious. The HEARSAY system comprises a set of *knowledge sources*, which are used during identification itself, not to produce precompiled representations of sentences. A single knowledge source might contain information about phonemes or syllables or syntax or semantics. All knowledge sources have access to a data structure called the *blackboard* on which current hypotheses about the input are written. HEARSAY does not depend very heavily on the acoustic properties of the words it hears, particularly in the case of short common words that tend to be pronounced sloppily in real speech. It focuses on longer infrequent words, which provide *islands of reliability*, because they are acoustically clearer. It works outwards from these, both to the left and to the right, attempting to identify the rest of the words in the sentence. Syntactic, semantic and pragmatic knowledge play a relatively large role in identifying words, so incorrect hypotheses that are syntactically and semantically appropriate are difficult to reject. HEARSAY makes more mistakes of this type than people do, presumably because people make more use of the acoustic properties of the speech signal.

Speech synthesis

In the speech-processing literature the term *synthesis by rule* refers to the production of speech from linguistic, as opposed to acoustic, information (see Linggard, 1985, for an overview). Synthesis from an acoustic representation is usually resynthesis of, for example, speech coded by LPC analysis. There are two main methods for synthesising speech by rule. In the first, and more widely used technique (Holmes, Mattingly and Shearme, 1964), each phone is defined by a pattern of formants (phones are acoustic realisations of phonemes – a phoneme may have several variants, or *allophones*). Words and longer utterances are formed by stringing together the phones of which they are made up, and smoothing out the irregularities.

There are two major difficulties with this first synthesis technique. The first is that it is hard to select formant values that are suitable for every occurrence of a phone. Acoustically, phones vary from context to context. This problem has been 'solved' by making detailed measurements on natural speech. However, it takes a long time to produce values that correspond to the speech of a single speaker. Furthermore, these values do not allow the voices of other speakers to be synthesised. Each voice must be coded separately.

The second problem is finding a suitable way to join one phone to another. In natural speech, formant frequencies usually change smoothly through time. The formant values associated with each phone are *target values*, through which the formants should pass in moving from the preceding phone to the next phone. In natural speech the smoothness, or otherwise, of formant transitions is largely governed by the way the soft parts of the mouth move. Techniques for interpolating between target values have been designed to reflect, approximately, the kinds of movement that occur and are described by Holmes *et al.*

*Diphone synthesis* (Isard and Miller, 1986), the second technique used to produce synthetic speech, avoids the problem of having to interpolate between target values by having a much larger catalogue of elements on which to draw. A *diphone* is the second half of one phone and the first half of the one following it. The maximum number of diphones in a language is the square of the number of phones. In practice not all of these will be legal. For diphone synthesis a library of diphones is created from natural speech. A selected speaker produces a set of utterances that includes all legal diphones. Synthetic speech can be produced by doing little more than 'gluing' diphones together. In practice the formants (or LPC coefficients) at diphone boundaries do not match exactly, because the first and second halves of the phone are taken from different utterances. However, only relatively minor adjustments are needed to avoid an audible glitch.

It is almost possible to produce diphone libraries automatically from a recording of a suitable set of utterances. Only a small amount of hand correction is necessary. This development makes it easy to synthesise different voices using diphone synthesis.

Speech synthesised by simply putting together phones or diphones sounds unnatural, for several reasons. The two primary ones are that it lacks natural timing and that it lacks natural intonation. In normal speech the duration of a single phone varies, though there is still some dispute about the form that this variation takes. It has been claimed, for example, that English is a *stress-timed* language – that stressed syllables in English are approximately equally spaced. Since the number of unstressed syllables between two stressed syllables varies, the length of a phone will not be constant in a stress-timed language. Several algorithms are available for adjusting phone durations for English. Some assign standard lengths to each phone and adjust them according to the context in which the phones occur. Others start from the pattern of stressed and unstressed syllables in the sentence and fit the phones to that.

*Intonation contours* show the changes in the fundamental

frequency produced by the vocal cords across a sentence. For example pitch rises towards the end of a declarative sentence if it is used as a question. Synthetic speech can be much improved by adding appropriate intonation contours.


## Parsing

The words in a sentence are grouped into larger structural units – phrases, clauses and sentences. *Parsing* is the process that identifies such groups of words. It is, or can be, a stage in the interpretation of sentences, though simply grouping words together is not, in itself, deriving the message that they carry. The fact that the words in a sentence form groups can be established intuitively. For example, in the sentence:

I believe that the box fell off the kitchen table.

the words *the kitchen table* form a group, whereas other sequences of three adjacent words, such as *box fell off* do not. Furthermore, *the kitchen table*, which is an example of a noun phrase, is itself part of the larger prepositional phrase *off the kitchen table*. This prepositional phrase is, in turn, part of the verb phrase *fell off the kitchen table*. Because one phrase can be part of another, sentences have a hierarchical structure, as illustrated in Figure 5.1. Linguists refer to such structures as *syntactic structures* or *phrase markers*. Grouping the words in a sentence is a step towards interpreting it, because phrases and clauses have simple meanings. For example, when the sentence above is used in an appropriate context, *the kitchen table* will refer to a specific item of furniture.

Although the existence of groups of words in a sentence can be established intuitively, the exact structure of complex sentences and the theoretical concepts needed to describe them are sources of much debate in the discipline of linguistics. In AI and psychology there have been arguments about whether linguistic descriptions of syntactic structure, which are usually formulated without reference to processing considerations, are relevant to a psychological theory of language processing; about the extent to which syntactic analysis is a necessary stage in sentence comprehension; and

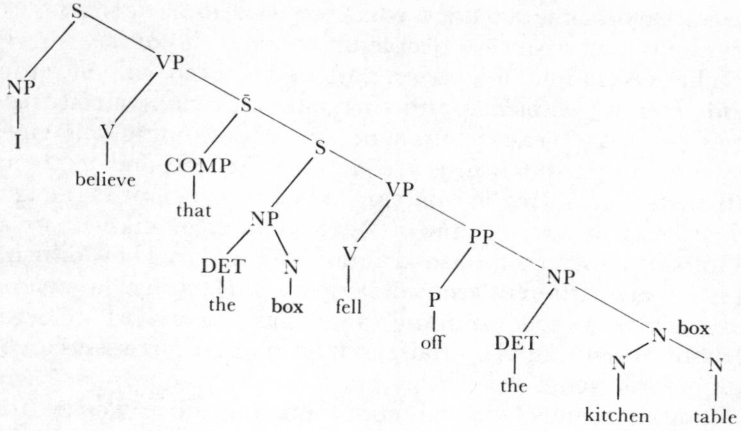

Figure 5.1

about how parsing interacts with other stages in sentence comprehension, such as the derivation of the message an utterance conveys.

There have been two main types of work on parsing in AI. On the one hand people have tried to write programs that understand or produce natural language. These programs inevitably include parsers. On the other hand, AI techniques have been applied to the problem of parsing, studied for its own sake.

The early language understanding programs used a variety of techniques for determining the structure of sentences. Many produced only very superficial analyses, for example by looking for keywords or by matching patterns. The pattern-matching technique proved effective only when the range of inputs to be analysed was very restricted, as it was for example in Green *et al*'s (1961) BASEBALL program, which answered questions about opponents, venues and scores in the baseball games of a single season. Weizenbaum's (1966) ELIZA program, which simulated a non-directive Rogerian psychotherapist, showed that these techniques could be used in a program that engaged in what were apparently realistic conversations. However, as Weizenbaum himself realised,

ELIZA neither understood what was said to it, nor provided many insights into how people understand discourse.

The second line of work on parsing has been influenced by both computer science and linguistics. Computer scientists study parsing because commands in programming languages have to be parsed before a computer can respond to them. Efficient algorithms for parsing different types of languages have been discovered and a large number of mathematical results have been established about, for example, how difficult it is to parse different kinds of languages. If natural languages are similar to programming languages – a matter of fierce debate – then results established by computer scientists can be applied to them.

Linguists have worried about parsing since Peters and Ritchie (1973) published some results about languages with transformational grammars – the kind of grammars proposed for natural languages in the 1960s. Peters and Ritchie showed that there could be no guarantee that a sentence from a transformational language could be parsed in a finite amount of time. This conclusion seemed at odds with our intuitions about natural languages, such as English. Even if a sentence is difficult to understand, the way its words are grouped is usually clear, as long as it contains no unfamiliar words. Some linguists have, therefore, developed new kinds of grammars for natural languages, which allow for easier parsing. In particular they have investigated the possibility that natural languages have *context-free phrase structure grammars*, or something very like them (Kaplan and Bresnan, 1982; Gazdar *et al.*, 1985; Joshi, 1985; Peters and Ritchie, 1982). Most programming languages have grammars of this kind, and a sentence from a language with such a grammar can always be parsed in a time proportional to the cube of its length in words (Earley, 1970; Younger, 1967).


General parsing methods

Parsing can be thought of as the construction of a phrase marker. There are a number of ways in which this construction might occur. First, a parser could start at one end of a sentence, or in the middle, or at all points simultaneously. Since people process sentences from left to right, literally in reading and figuratively in listening, human parsing is probably basically 'left-to-right'. This mode of operation is more necessary for spoken language, with its transient signal, though the analysis of an ambiguous stretch of speech may have to be postponed until it has been disambiguated by subsequent information.

A second decision is whether the phrase marker should be constructed from the top S(entence) node downwards (*top-down* parsing) or from the words upwards (*bottom-up* parsing). The same set of grammatical rules can be used to build the tree either way. For example the rule S → NP VP could be used top-down to expand an S node, as the first step in trying to make contact with the words of the sentence. Alternatively, it could be used bottom-up, to combine an already constructed noun phrase and verb phrase to form a sentence. However, some structures lend themselves more readily to bottom-up analysis, and others to top-down. A single parsing algorithm may combine top-down and bottom-up procedures. For example, a left-corner parser (see Johnson-Laird, 1983, pp. 345–54) analyses the beginnings of phrases bottom-up and the ends of them, which are fairly predictable, top-down.

A third decision concerns not how to build a single tree, but how to proceed when there is more than one possible tree. Parsing can be regarded as a search problem – it is a search for an analysis of the current sentence in the space of possible sentence analyses. Parsing algorithms guide the search of this space. In chapter 4 the ideas of *breadth-first* and *depth-first* search were introduced. In parsing, breadth-first search corresponds to developing all possible analyses of a string in parallel. Depth-first search corresponds to pursuing one analysis until it is completed or until it can be developed no further. If a parsing algorithm uses depth-first search it will almost certainly need a *backtracking* facility to allow it to recover from errors.

## Augmented transition networks

Towards the end of the 1960s a general parsing technique was developed that could be used with any language, including ones with transformational grammars. However, Peters and Ritchie's result meant that it could not guarantee to parse a sentence in finite time. The technique is known as *augmented transition network* (ATN) parsing. The definitive presentation is Woods (1970), which is based on earlier work by Thorne, Bratley and Dewar (1968).

A transition network is a network of nodes and links (or arcs) through which transitions can be made when certain conditions are fulfilled. The conditions correspond roughly to finding correct analyses for parts of the sentence. The ATN is a top-down parser. It starts building a parse tree from the top, by looking for a sentence, and then goes on to look for smaller constituents.

The fact that English sentences usually comprise a noun phrase followed by a verb phrase is represented by the network shown in Figure 5.2. This network is interpreted as

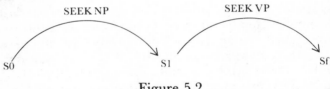

Figure 5.2

follows. S0 is the starting state. When in S0, the parser is ready to look for a sentence. SEEK NP, the condition for a transition from S0 to S1, means that a noun phrase must be found before the transition can be made. Similarly, SEEK VP means that a VP must be found for a transition to the final state Sf. If in the course of processing a string of words the state Sf is reached from the state S0, and there are no words left over, then the string of words is a sentence. There are separate networks for finding NPs and VPs, and control passes to these networks during parsing. They are said to be *called* by the sentence network.

Part of a VP network for English sentences is shown in Figure 5.3. It illustrates the fact that phrases in English may have alternative structures. CAT V means that a word of the lexical category V (erb) must be found for the transition VP0

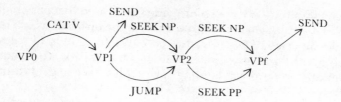

Figure 5.3

to VP1 to be made. JUMP means that the transition from VP1 to VP2 can be made without any part of the sentence being analysed. SEND means that control passes back to the calling network. So if the VP network was called by SEEK VP in the sentence network, SEND passes control back to the sentence network, together with the information that a VP has been found. The transition labelled SEEK VP (S1 to Sf in the sentence network) can then be made. SEEK, CAT, JUMP, and SEND are the four main types of arc in ATNs, though occasionally WORD arcs, which look for specified lexical items (e.g. WORD *to*), have been used. The VP network can analyse the following types of VP: V (slept), V NP (saw the dog), V NP NP (gave Susan a book), V PP (climbed over the fence), V NP PP (hit the ball over the roof).

CAT and SEND arcs are sometimes referred to as PUSH and POP arcs respectively. These terms derive from the fact that information about which networks have called others is held in a last-in-first-out memory called *the stack*. PUSH indicates that a new item is pushed on to the top of the stack, POP that one is to be taken off. The item on top of the stack is, therefore, the current network, and the next item down the calling network. When a POP occurs at the end of a phrase, the top of the stack indicates where control should be passed back to. The last-in-first-out property of the stack means that control can only return to the immediate caller.

In the VP network above there are a number of places at which the parser is faced with a choice. For example, when a verb is found should control return to the sentence network (SEND), should an NP be sought (CAT NP), or should a move be made to the next state (JUMP)? An ATN parser makes such decisions using *scheduling principles*, which specify which possibilities to explore first. It would be possible to label the arcs at each choice point with the order in which they should be tried. However, for both ATN models of human parsing and intelligent machines that use ATNs it is usual to formulate general scheduling principles (see e.g. Wanner, 1980).

The networks described so far are recursive transition networks. Their *augmentation* to produce ATNs has not yet been described. Transition networks can be augmented by labelling arcs with (parsing) actions that are to be performed when those arcs are traversed. Examples of such actions are the (provisional) labelling of the first noun phrase in a sentence as its subject, and the relabelling of it, if subsequent parts of the sentence show that it is not the subject. For example, if a passive verb is encountered, as in the sentence:

The mouse was caught by the cat

then the noun phrase *the mouse* must be relabelled as the (logical) object of *caught*. The noun phrase *the cat* is then labelled as subject.

Another example of augmentation is found in Wanner and Maratsos's (1978) proposal for analysing relative clauses using ATNs. When a relative pronoun is encountered, for example *who* in the sentence:

The young man who travelled to Paris enjoyed himself there.

Information about the preceding noun phrase, which contains the so-called *head noun* of the relative clause, is placed in a special HOLD register. The CAT RELPRO arc is augmented by the action STORE NP in HOLD. At some point in the following clause – between *who* and *travelled* in the example above – the parser must 'find' a noun phrase in a place where there is no lexical material. This procedure assumes that the ordinary S network is used to analyse relative clauses and that relative clauses are sentences with noun phrases missing from them (*travelled to Paris* is *the young man travelled to Paris* with *the young man* missing). One option in the NP network must, therefore, be a JUMP from NP0 to NPf with the augmentation RETRIEVE HOLD. The result of retrieving information from the HOLD register in the above case is that *the young man* is identified as the subject of the verb in the relative clause, *travelled.* Exactly the same mechanism handles object relative clauses, in which the head noun is the object of the verb in the relative clauses, for example:

The young man who(m) the editor admired was successful.

In object relatives the information in the HOLD register is retrieved during the analysis of the VP in the relative clause.

Wanner (1980) further developed ATN models of human parsing. He showed how parsing principles identified by Kimball (1973) and Frazier and Fodor (1978) could be captured by simple ATN scheduling principles, such as try CAT and SEEK before SEND and JUMP.

### Applications of ATNs

ATNs have been used in real-life applications as well as in models of human parsing. The most important was in the BBN LUNAR system (Woods, 1977). LUNAR comprised a database of information about samples of rock brought back from the moon during the Apollo missions and a natural language interface for interpreting questions about those rocks. The questions were parsed using an ATN and converted into database queries.

### Chart parsers

*Chart parsing* (Kaplan, 1973; Kay, 1973; and see Winograd, 1983, for a good introduction) is a more recent, more versatile and more popular alternative to ATNs. Unlike ATNs, chart parsers make a clear distinction between linguistic information and parsing principles. The linguistic information, or grammar, that a chart parser uses is stored as a set of rules in whatever format is most convenient. The parser itself has two parts, a *chart* and an *agenda*. A chart is a data structure in which possible syntactic analyses of the various parts of a sentence are stored. An agenda is a list of tasks to perform. The parsing principles of a chart parser govern the way in which tasks are added to the agenda and carried out once they are on it.

In mathematical terms a chart is a labelled acyclic graph. In some ways it is similar to a phrase marker that displays the syntactic structure of a sentence. It comprises a set of nodes joined to one another by edges. There is one more node than there are words in the sentence – one between each pair of words, and one at each end. Each edge provides an analysis for a subpart of the sentence. At the lowest level there is one edge corresponding to each word. These edges are labelled with the syntactic categories of the words, taken from a dictionary. Examples of higher-level edges that might be found in a chart are an edge labelled NP spanning the words *the kitchen table* and one labelled VP spanning *fell off the kitchen table*.

There are two crucial differences between a chart and a phrase marker. First, alternative analyses of a sentence or part of a sentence may be represented in the same chart. Second, a chart may contain partial analyses. Partial analyses are represented by *active edges*. For example, if a chart contains the word *the*, it can be hypothesised that a noun might follow it to complete an NP, since there is a grammar rule saying that an NP can be a DET(erminer) followed by an N. This hypothesis is represented in the chart by an edge spanning *the* labelled as an NP for which the noun has yet to be found (NP/N). If that active edge has to its right an ordinary (or inactive edge) spanning a noun, then a new edge, in this case an inactive one, representing an NP can be entered in the chart. It will span *the* and the noun following it. It is also possible to insert active edges into a chart when no material has been identified. For example, an edge labelled S/(NP VP) might be added at the beginning of a string of words, indicating a sentence of which both the NP and the VP are still to be found.

Although chart parsing is a versatile technique, it is particularly suited to languages with context-free phrase structure grammars. The reason is that, for such languages, once a *substring* of a sentence has been correctly analysed it need never be renalysed (barring lexical ambiguities). The chart is an ideal way of keeping track of such *well-formed substrings* of a sentence. Indeed it is closely related to the well-formed substring table in Earley's (1970) highly efficient algorithm for parsing context-free languages. If an ATN parser makes a mistake and has to backtrack, it may have to reproduce the analysis of a well-formed substring of the part of the sentence it has misanalysed. ATNs are, therefore, less efficient than chart parsers.

One way in which chart parsers are more versatile than ATNs is that they can operate top-down, bottom-up or in a mixed mode. To make a chart parser operate top-down, like an ATN, the first task on the agenda must be to add to the chart, at the left-hand end of the sentence, one active edge corresponding to each type of sentence. All of these edges have everything to find. One of them is the S/(NP VP) mentioned above. A further condition for top-down parsing is that whenever an active edge is added to the chart, further active edges are added, corresponding to the first missing constituent, if any such edges are licensed by the grammar rules. Once S/(NP VP) has been added, for example, NP/(DET N) and NP/(DET ADJ N) will be added. However, no active edges of the form DET/(. . . . .) are licensed. There are no grammar rules with DET on the left-hand side. The parser must look to see if the firstword in the sentence is a DET.

Bottom-up parsing can be implemented by adding active edges only when new *inactive* ones are found. The active edges start at the same node as the inactive edge. They are those which, according to the grammar rules, have the inactive edge as their first missing constituent. In bottom-up parsing, the first active edges are, therefore, added to the chart by looking at the lexical categories of the words. So, if the first word is a DET, NP/(DET N) and NP/(DET ADJ N) will be added.

Marcus parsing

When parsing sentences from natural languages, both ATNs and chart parsers can be faced with a choice of actions to perform next, and they may make the 'wrong' choice. If an ATN makes an incorrect choice it eventually reaches a dead end and has to backtrack. A chart parser may expend unnecessary effort by building active edges that never find all their constituents.

Marcus (1980) argued that the human sentence-parsing mechanism does not usually do unnecessary work or make mistakes, except when analysing garden-path sentences, such as:

> The horse raced past the barn fell.

(which means: the horse that was raced past the barn fell). Recovering from the errors induced by these sentences is notoriously difficult. No comparable problems are caused by other sentences that are initially misanalysed by ATNs and chart parsers. Marcus, therefore, tried to design a parser that never revised its parsing decisions and that only made mistakes on garden-path sentences. He called such a parser *deterministic*. Marcus based his parser on the then current version of transformational grammar (e.g. Chomsky, 1977; Chomsky and Lasnik, 1977). Its output is, therefore, the type of annotated surface syntactic structure (S-structure) proposed in that theory. Marcus also attempted to explain, in terms of parsing operations, supposedly universal properties of natural languages, such as the constraints on transformations proposed by Chomsky and others.

Marcus's goal of producing a deterministic parser appears to be inconsistent with the existence of sentence pairs such as:

> I believe that man.
> I believe that man is a fool.

When a parser encounters the word *that* in these sentences it has to decide whether it is an adjective or a complementiser. However, that decision cannot be made until either the full stop or the word *is* is encountered. The parser cannot make a deterministic choice about the lexical category of *that* without risking a mistake. Marcus overcame this problem by giving his parser a limited ability to look ahead. The limiting of the lookahead facility is crucial, since there is, in principle, no difference between unrestricted lookahead and unrestricted backtracking after an incorrect choice. Marcus proposed that lookahead should be limited to three *constituents*, each of which might contain several words. However, for some constructions – complex NPs – he was forced to allow five-constituent lookahead. He provided no general principle to rule out further extensions to the amount of lookahead permitted.

A Marcus parser has two principal data structures, an *active node stack* and a *buffer*. Like the ATN's stack, the active node stack is a last-in-first-out memory. It contains bits of syntactic analysis trees that cannot be revised, but which are in some way incomplete. The item on top of the active node stack is the one currently being analysed. The buffer, which mediates lookahead, contains items waiting to be attached into trees. By default it works on a first-in-first-out basis. Items in the buffer may be single words or complete phrases, though they cannot be incomplete phrases like those on the active node stack. Words enter the buffer from the right. Nodes from the stack, which have been completed, but which cannot yet be fitted into any higher-level structure, may enter from the left. Once an item is in the buffer it cannot be dislodged. If a node is to enter the buffer from the stack, at most two of the three buffer slots can be full. Otherwise the buffer overflows, and the sentence cannot be parsed.

The linguistic rules used by a Marcus parser are encoded as productions (see chapter 2). These rules are organised into groups, called *packets*, only one of which is active at any time. The rules in a packet are those likely to be needed in a single context. The node currently being analysed – the one at the top of the active node stack – determines which packet is active. A rule may refer to both the currently active node and, when lookahead is required, to the contents of the buffer.

### 'Semantic' parsers

The parsers discussed so far analyse a sentence regardless of what it means. Interpretation is assumed to be the work of a distinct semantic processor. However, many AI practitioners have argued that, in models of human language understanding, it may be both unnecessary and unrealistic to postulate an independent syntactic parser.

There are several related questions about the relation between syntax and meaning in sentence comprehension that have not always been clearly distinguished. In particular two very different uses of the term *autonomy* require comment.

*Formal autonomy*

One influential view, which has often been misunderstood, is that the study of syntax should be *autonomous* of the study of meaning (Chomsky, 1957). More precisely, Chomsky's claim, which is referred to as the *formal autonomy thesis*, is that syntactic primitives, such as *noun, verb, noun phrase, verb phrase, phrase-structure rule*, and *transformation*, should be defined without using any semantic notions. It is useful for syntacticians to assume that this thesis is true, because if it is, they can proceed with their studies without worrying about semantic theory.

Two points about the formal autonomy thesis should be noted. First, formal autonomy must be distinguished from *processing autonomy*. Second, the formal autonomy thesis is explicitly rejected in some AI language-understanding projects.

A grammar that does not obey the formal autonomy principle is sometimes referred to as a *semantic* or a *pragmatic* grammar, depending on the meaning-related notions that are used in the definition of its syntactic primitives. One type of semantic grammar that has enjoyed wide popularity in AI research (see Bruce, 1975, for a review) is *case grammar*, originally proposed by Fillmore (1968, 1971). Syntactic categories in case grammar have names such as AGENT, PATIENT, and BENEFACTIVE. An example of a pragmatic grammar is one designed by Bruce (1982) for the HWIM system. This grammar has among its syntactic categories CITY, STATE, and COUNTRY. Semantic and pragmatic grammars typically allow a simpler description of the structures of sentences from a limited domain of discourse than do grammars with autonomous syntax. However, a separate grammar is needed for each such domain.

An important set of language-understanding programs that use semantic grammars, though they have not always been described as doing so, are those written by Schank and his colleagues. Marcus (1984) refers to the kind of syntactic analysis that Schankian parsers perform as *positional template matching*. Template-matching parsers use two kinds of information. The first is information about word meanings stored in the lexicon. In particular, template-matching parsers need to know, for each verb, how many arguments it takes, and which of those arguments are obligatory. They also need to know of any restrictions on the values of those arguments. Those restrictions specify the semantic types of the noun phrases and prepositional phrases that fill the argument slots. Those phrases inherit their semantic types from the nouns in them. Semantic types of nouns are recorded in the dictionary – a semantic type is a semantically defined syntactic category. The second type of information used by Schankian parsers is a set of templates that specify the preferred order (or orders) of the arguments for each verb.

Marcus points out that the ability of Schankian parsers to analyse a large number of sentences does not show that they provide an adequate description of how people understand sentences. He shows that a syntactic processor making use of only the first type of information can correctly parse many sentences, though it fails on many others. Such a processor is equivalent to the case-frame analyser discussed by Garnham (1985, pp. 69–70). Marcus further shows that there are sentence structures in English that people have little difficulty in parsing, but which are misinterpreted by template-matching parsers using semantic grammars of the kind proposed by Schank.

*Processing autonomy*

A processor, such as the parser, is said to be *autonomous* if its operation is not influenced by that of other processors, such as those that compute meaning. Processing autonomy is distinct from formal autonomy. It refers to the way in which bits of machinery operate together, and not to the way that concepts are defined. The simplest example of an autonomous parser would be one that computed the syntactic structure of an entire sentence and only then passed that structure on to be interpreted by message-level processors. Our intuitions suggest that people do not understand sentences in this way, and so does experimental evidence (Marslen-Wilson, 1973, 1975). When repeating a passage played over headphones – a task called *shadowing* – people can correct speech errors, such as the mispronounciation of *company* as *compsiny* – but only if the word *company* is semantically predictable. Shadowers do not wait until the end of a sentence to respond. Indeed, some of them lag only about one syllable behind the tape recorder. They are using semantic information to correct errors well before the end of the sentence.

There are autonomous parsers whose operation is compatible with our intuitions about comprehension. Such parsers do not wait until the end of a sentence before producing an output. They produce an output after each word. Because sentences of natural languages contain local ambiguities, this output comprises a *set* of partial analyses – all those compatible with the sentence so far. The parser remains independent of semantic and pragmatic processors if all (non-syntactic) decisions about which of those analyses is worth interpreting are made without the parser being 'informed'. Some partial analyses will be syntactically incompatible with later parts of the sentence. These analyses will be abandoned later on syntactic grounds, without violating the principle of processing autonomy.

Non-autonomous parsers can interact either weakly or strongly with semantic processors. *Weak interaction* occurs when the parser is 'told' to discontinue analyses that are leading to implausible or impossible interpretations even though those analyses are syntactically acceptable. A *strong interaction* is one in which parsing choices are guided by semantic considerations, so that phrase markers with implausible interpretations are never constructed.

In both AI (e.g. Winograd, 1973) and psychology (e.g. Marslen-Wilson, 1973, 1975) it has been argued that language understanding is an interactive process. In many ways this conclusion is an unfortunate one, because autonomous systems are easier to model than interactive ones. However, more recently it has become apparent that interactive and non-interactive systems are not so easy to distinguish as was previously believed (e.g. Norris, 1982).

## Comprehension of text and dialogue

The 1960s and 1970s saw the writing of a number of programs, or suites of programs, that were intended to understand text and dialogue, and often to produce it as well.

The early programs – chiefly those of the 1960s – are often described as *semantic information-processing* systems. Some of the most important of them are described in a book of that name (Minksy, 1968). These programs exemplify an approach to natural language processing that was intended to rectify the faults of earlier machine translation programs, which had focused on syntax, and which had been a comparative failure.

Semantic information-processing systems differed from their predecessors in two main ways. First, they were usually restricted to a limited semantic domain. One program, BASEBALL, only understood statements and questions about baseball games (Green *et al.* 1961). Another, STUDENT, confined itself to high-school algebra problems (Bobrow, 1968). The reason for such restrictions was the growing conviction that language understanding required the mobilisation of a large amount of knowledge about the world. It was impossible to encode anything but a minute fraction of this knowledge into a computer program that would run in a reasonable amount of time.

The second novel feature of semantic information-processing programs was that they translated sentences of English into a formal language that was supposed to represent the meaning of those sentences in a perspicuous way. Bobrow's STUDENT program, for example, translated algebra problems stated in words into sets of linear equations.

The following sections describe two of the most elaborate language-understanding systems, Winograd's SHRDLU and Schank's MARGIE. Some current research issues are then discussed.

## Winograd's SHRDLU

The apotheosis of semantic information-processing came in the late 1960s and early 1970s when faster, more powerful computers became available for AI research (usually DEC PDP10s). The best-known program from this period, and the one whose performance is most impressive to those familiar with the problems of language understanding, is Winograd's

(1972) SHRDLU. SHRDLU engages in dialogues about the BLOCKSWORLD – a table top on which blocks of various shapes, sizes and colours can be placed and moved about. The BLOCKSWORLD was inhabited by many MIT AI programs of this era, particularly vision programs that attempted to recognise objects on the table top (see chapter 3). SHRDLU moves blocks around in this world, at the user's command, and answers questions about what it has done. More precisely, it interacts with a simulation of the BLOCKS-WORLD, stored in the computer's memory. It was never attached to a robot arm nor did it move real blocks.

SHRDLU takes to an extreme the idea of a limited knowledge domain. Not only is the BLOCKSWORLD physically small, there is very little to know about the objects in it. The amount of knowledge required to understand even the simplest texts about people, for example, is very much greater. By severely restricting SHRDLU's domain of competence Winograd was able to make it linguistically sophisticated. However, because the BLOCKSWORLD is so different from the real world, it cannot be assumed that language works the same way in both.

Although SHRDLU engages in dialogues (of a kind) about BLOCKSWORLD, it is primarily an understanding system. The complexity of its own contributions to the conversation is limited – they are produced from a small set of syntactic templates, though this fact may not be apparent to the casual observer.

SHRDLU's comprehension system is remarkable in a number of ways. First, it can handle a variety of so-called *anaphoric* expressions, such as definite pronouns, indefinite pronouns (*one*), and elliptical verb phrases. These expressions must be assigned a meaning from another part of the dialogue. Second, it uses a model of the world, including information about the discourse so far, to determine the referents of definite noun phrases, such as *the red pyramid*. Third, it knows when it has not understood something, and can ask for clarification.

SHRDLU's comprehension system comprises three main subprocessors – a syntactic analyser, a semantic processor and an inference mechanism that uses both general knowledge about the BLOCKSWORLD and specific knowledge about the current state of the table top. The processors operate interactively. Information passes freely between them during the analysis of a single sentence. However, despite Winograd's own claims (e.g. 1973), it is doubtful that such interaction is essential to SHRDLU's success.

SHRDLU's syntactic analyser uses Halliday's (e.g. 1970) *systemic grammar*, though again this choice is not as crucial as Winograd implies. The grammar rules are encoded as procedures in a specially developed language called PROGRAMMAR. A more important application of the idea that knowledge can be represented in procedures (see chapter 2) is found in SHRDLU's semantic processor. The meanings of words, phrases and sentences are all procedures. The procedural representations of the meaning of more complex expressions are constructed from those of the simpler expressions that are their parts. SHRDLU, therefore, embodies a version of *procedural semantics* (see also Johnson-Laird, 1977; Woods, 1981). For example, the meaning of *block* is a procedure that tests whether an object has the properties that blocks have, and the meaning of *the* determines whether there is only one thing of a certain type in the current model. The meaning of *the block* is, therefore, a procedure to test whether there is one thing with the properties of a block in the current model. If there is, the procedure returns that object as its value, and the phrase *the block* refers to that object. The meaning of a declarative sentence is a procedure that adds the fact expressed by the sentence to the database. That of a question is a procedure that searches the database for a fact.

Although SHRDLU's semantics is adequate in the BLOCKSWORLD in which the program operates, it is difficult to extend to language used in other domains. For example, it fails to account for the vagaries of the meaning of definite descriptions in other contexts (see e.g. Woods, 1975; Ritchie, 1980; Marcus, 1980; Crain and Steedman, 1985). However, the arguments that these authors make are against Winograd's specific proposals, not against procedural semantics in general.

## Schank's MARGIE

Another influential set of programs, MARGIE (Memory, Analysis, Response Generation, and Inference on English), was written by Schank and his coworkers. An overview of the original version of this system can be found in Schank (1975). Unlike Winograd, Schank did not restrict his program's expertise to a narrow domain. He addressed himself to the problems of how texts about human behaviour are understood. Some aspects of MARGIE's operation have already been discussed. High-level knowledge structures used by MARGIE and its successors were discussed in chapter 2, and its semantic parser was described above.

MARGIE displays its understanding by paraphrasing the texts it reads and by answering questions about them. It has three main modules: a semantic parser, an inference mechanism, and a response generator. The parser converts English sentences into meaning representations called conceptual dependency diagrams; the inference mechanism elaborates those diagrams using knowledge about the world; the response generator uses the elaborated diagrams to produce paraphrases and to answer questions.

*Conceptual dependency* is a universal 'semantic' notation in which, Schank claims, the content of any sentence in any natural language can be expressed. Conceptual dependency gets it name from the fact that it makes relations or dependencies between concepts explicit. A conceptual dependency diagram is a special type of semantic network (see chapter 2). As in other semantic network representations of sentence meaning, the verb plays a central role in a conceptual dependency diagram, and the things denoted by noun phrases and prepositional phrases stand in certain relations to the verb. The novel part of Schank's theory is the idea that the meaning of any verb can be expressed in terms of a dozen or so primitive acts, such as PTRANS (physical transfer), MTRANS (mental transfer, i.e. of information), PROPEL, CONC(eptualise), and INGEST.

Since the completion of the MARGIE project Schank and his coworkers have continued to develop their ideas on how texts about human behaviour are understood. The most important aspect of this work has been the investigation of higher-level knowledge structures. These developments have already been outlined in chapter 2. Scripts and plans, the first of these knowledge structures to be studied, are used in text comprehension by their respective Applier Mechanisms SAM (Cullingford, 1978) and PAM (Wilensky, 1983). Other ideas include sketchy scripts (de Jong, 1982), MOPs (Memory Organisation Packets) and TOPS (Thematic Organisation Points) (Schank, 1982), story points (Wilensky, 1982), plot units (Lehnert, 1982), and AFFECTs (Dyer, 1983). There is no room here to explicate these proposals – the interested reader is referred to the original literature – but the list serves to emphasise two points. First, understanding texts about people, even highly stereotyped texts such as the stories that MARGIE deals with, is a highly complex process. Second, AI researchers have yet to impose order on their theories of memory organisation and its relation to text comprehension.

SHRDLU and MARGIE are two very different responses to the challenge of producing a computer program that can 'understand natural language'. Their effects on the AI/cognitive science community have also been very different. In SHRDLU Winograd seemed to have provided a complete demonstration of what could be done in a restricted domain. To some extent the existence of SHRDLU inhibited other work of a similar nature. There seemed little point in producing a SHRDLU for another domain. But attempts to relax the limited domain assumption made it difficult to retain both linguistic sophistication and realistic inference in a system that would run in a respectable time.

MARGIE and subsequent Schankian programs, on the other hand, because of their more ambitious nature, continually suggested problems that apparently required new types of knowledge structure. Little order thas yet been imposed on the ideas that have emerged and it seems reasonable to seek a rationalisation of these proposals rather than to investigate more and more complex types of structure whose nature and generality is worked out in less and less detail.

Current research issues

*Dialogue*

MARGIE does not attempt to take part in conversations and although SHRDLU enters into linguistic exchanges of a sort, careful examination shows that they lack many of the features of ordinary human dialogue. However, dialogue is the most basic and the most common use of natural language. One of the central tasks for a theory of language processing is, therefore, to explain how people formulate appropriate contributions to dialogue and how they understand them.

Conversation is a usually a co-operative enterprise, as Grice (1975) has pointed out, and participants in conversations have goals that they hope to achieve through dialogue. SHRDLU's contributions to conversations are limited because it has no goals of its own. Some goals, such as obtaining information, may be satisfied as a direct result of a linguistic exchange. In other cases conversation is required to achieve a subgoal in a larger plan – getting someone to agree to help carry out a complex task, for example.

Another feature of ordinary conversations emphasised by Grice is that what people (literally) say may be far removed from the message they intend to convey. Yet other people have little difficulty in understanding what is meant. A program like SHRDLU, however might get stuck in the following kind of exchange.

> *Operator*: Are there any pyramids on top of blocks?
> *Program*: Yes.
> *Operator*: Would you mind finding out their colours?
> *Program*: No.
> *Operator*: Could you let me know their colours?
> *Program*: Yes.
> *Operator*: I haven't been told their colours yet.
> *Program*: I know that.
> *Operator*: You might tell me what their colours are.
> *Program*: Yes, I might.
> *Operator*: (swears, picks up an axe, etc.)

SHRDLU assumes that everything the operator says is either a statement, question or command. It uses linguistic form to decide which is which. It does not know that, in normal conversations, the form of a sentence – whether it is declarative, interrogative or imperative – is only a rough guide to its intended import – statement, question or command. Neither does it know that there are things other than making statements, asking questions and issuing commands, that can be done with words – making promises and getting married, for example. These acts that we can perform by saying certain things have been dubbed *speech acts* by Searle (1969). The use of an interrogative sentence, which would usually be a question, as, for example, a request is referred to as an *indirect* speech act.

The comprehension of ordinary dialogue has been one of the major research topics in post-SHRDLU work on natural language processing. This research has attempted to show how recognising the plans of other participants in a conversation helps to determine the import of what they say. A program written by Power (1979) uses plans to direct conversations. Two copies of the program, each of which represents a robot, converse with each other. The two robots inhabit a very simple world with two regions, IN and OUT, linked by a door with a catch that can only be opened from inside. If one robot plans to move from OUT to IN it may need help from the other one, for example if the catch is closed and the other is already IN. Power's program generates conversational contributions from plans, but its conversation is unnatural. For example, it always establishes that it is about to ask a question by saying, 'May I ask you a question?' The program is unable, and not intended to be able, to work out the import of what is said without an explicit context.

Two recent research projects have shown how more natural conversation can be produced from plans. Houghton and Isard (in press) describe a program that inhabits a similar world to Power's, but which is linguistically more sophisticated. Perrault and his colleagues (Allen and Perrault, 1980; Cohen and Perrault, 1979; Cohen, Perrault and Allen, 1982; Perrault and Allen, 1980) have investigated the role of beliefs and wants in the interpretation of speech acts. Allen's program answers questions about arrivals and departures at a train station. It assumes that people making enquiries have one of a limited number of top-level goals, the chief of which are catching a train and meeting a train. By making this assumption it is able to interpret a wide range of indirect speech acts.

Further aspects of the planning of conversational contributions have been studied by McKeown (1985) and Appelt (1985). McKeown tackles the problem of how longer contributions are internally structured. Her TEXT program produces paragraph-length responses to database queries. It uses discourse strategies that fulfil three types of communicative goal – definition, comparison and description – to structure those responses. Appelt's program KAMP (Knowledge And Modalities Planner) is addressed to the more local problem of selecting appropriate referential NPs. Such NPs need to be co-ordinated with speakers' actions and they have to fulfil communicative intentions, such as focusing the audience's attention on a particular object and informing them what sort of object it is. Given a set of high-level goals, KAMP can plan referring expressions that fulfil multiple goals.

## Non-literal language

A further problem with systems like SHRDLU is that they cannot interpret non-literal language. There has been only a small amount of work within AI on the comprehension of figures of speech. Most of it has focused on similes and metaphors. In both one thing is compared with another, either explicitly in a simile, or implicitly in a metaphor. Understanding metaphors is more difficult to explain. In a metaphor one thing is referred to as if it were another, but only some aspects of the second thing are relevant to the comparison being made. The problem in metaphor interpretation is to decide which properties are relevant, and to use those properties to reconstruct the intended message. There is no simple formula for deciding which those properties are.

Although metaphor is usually thought of as a literary device, found chiefly in 'serious' writing, the metaphors created by poets and novelists are atypical in that they are hard to understand. People often have to give them some thought before they appreciate their meaning. There have been no attempts to get computers to understand them.

However, literary metaphors are just extreme examples of non-literal language. In more mundane language less creative examples of metaphor are surprisingly frequent. One common type of metaphor, identified by Carbonell (1982), depends on the equation *more-is-up, less-is-down*. Carbonell argues that if *types* of metaphor can be identified, general mechanisms for interpreting non-literal language can be postulated. These mechanisms will be activated if the literal meaning of a sentence is, in context, impossible or highly implausible. Carbonell makes a further observation that is likely to be useful in theories of language understanding: a single type of metaphor tends to recur throughout a conversation or text. Once that type has been identified, it can be used as a default for subsequent interpretation.

One important question about the interpretation of metaphors – a question that can also be asked about indirect speech acts – is whether they are understood by first computing and then rejecting their literal meanings. The issue is complicated by the fact that metaphors can become dead – what was once a metaphorical meaning can become a new literal meaning. From a processing point of view, it may be difficult (and perhaps unnecessary) to distinguish between the literal interpretation of a dead metaphor and its direct interpretation while it remains metaphorical. If computation of the literal meaning is not always necessary, then some alternative mechanism for understanding metaphors will have to be proposed.

### Discourse models and focusing

Information from the beginning of a text creates the context for interpreting what comes later. This aspect of text comprehension has been studied recently by both psychologists and AI researchers. They have proposed that the information in a discourse is encoded into a *model* of the part of the world, real or imaginary, described by the discourse. Such a model is updated as each new sentence or clause is processed and the new model provides the context for the interpretation of the next sentence. Recent research on discourse models provides a good example of how cognitive science should be done. On the other hand, the level of detail of the analyses owes much to AI, and to the notion that theories ought to be translatable into computer programs. On the other hand, the concern with general principles as opposed to working programs is reminiscent of experimental psycholinguistics.

SHRDLU uses a discourse model of sorts, but it leaves unanswered many questions about such models, in particular questions about the information they encode. First, do they contain a record of the linguistic form of a text or do they simply represent its content? Although discourse models are usually described as representations of content, it is sometimes necessary to remember linguistic form in order to interpret a sentence. For example, the second sentences in the following passages have different interpretations, though the content of the first sentences is the same:

> Bill had seen John.
> Jeff had, too.

> John had been seen by Bill.
> Jeff had, too.

What the second sentence means is determined by the form of the first.

Second, discourse models contain (representations of) things that may be referred to in subsequent text. These items are introduced by linguistic expressions. A theory of language understanding must specify what items are introduced by which expressions. In some cases the answer is straightforward. For example, the first occurrence of the name *John* introduces a person of that name into the model. However, as Webber (see e.g. 1983) has shown, a wide variety of back references may be possible after a definite description. For example, a plural definite description introduces several objects, which can subsequently be regarded as either distinct things or as a set:

> John gave Mary five dollars.
> It was more than he gave Sue.

> John gave Mary five dollars.
> One of them was counterfeit.

(Webber 1983, p. 331). Further complications arise in the

presence of quantifiers, such as *some*, *all* and *many*, and numbers. For example,

> Three boys bought five roses.

could mean that the boys bought five roses each, that they formed a collective and bought five, or that they bought five among them (two bought two each, and the other bought one, say). These different possibilities have different consequences for the subsequent use of referring expressions.

Third, participants in a conversation must recognise that not only their world knowledge but also their discourse models may differ (Johnson-Laird and Garnham, 1980). Speakers need to take account of differences in world knowledge when choosing referring expressions, and hearers in interpreting them.

Finally, how do speakers use their discourse models to follow what Grimes (1975) calls 'the thread of discourse'? One mechanism that limits the way this 'thread' can develop is *focusing*. At any point in a text of some length only some items are easy to refer back to. The ones that are are said to be focused. Focusing permits the unambiguous use of expressions, such as pronouns, which have relatively little semantic content. If only a few items are focused, and only one is male, then *he* can refer unambiguously, on the assumption that it refers to something in focus. However, it is unlikely that focusing has developed specifically so that we can use pronouns. Pronouns presumably exploit a mechanism with other origins. In fact, the exact role of focusing in language understanding remains to be clarified, though it is probably related to the relatively small capacity of the short-term memory stores used in discourse comprehension. In AI, focusing is studied primarily with the intention of understanding human language understanding and of building machines that can interact with people, using natural language. Computers do not suffer from the memory limitations that create the need for focusing!

Sidner (1983) proposes a theory of *focus tracking* that incorporates three insights into human language understanding. First, she distinguishes between the discourse focus and the focused agent. The person performing the current action (focused agent) may be doing it to the thing that the discourse is about (discourse focus). Nevertheless, agents can always be subsequently pronominalised, whether or not they are discourse foci. Agents are always focused, unlike other case fillers, such as benefactors or instruments, which can only be pronominalised if they are discourse foci. Second, a focus can often only be computed after a *subsequent* pronominal reference, not from the sentence in which it is first mentioned. There are default foci for many sentence structures, but they are overridden if they are incompatible with subsequent pronominalisations. Third, previous foci are maintained on a stack (a last-in first-out memory). An otherwise uninterpretable pronoun may refer to a previous focus, but to retrieve that focus all intervening foci must be taken off the stack. They are then unavailable for subsequent pronominal reference. However, as Sidner demonstrates, still earlier foci, lower on the stack, remain available.

Although previous foci are always structured, Sidner recognises that the linear ordering of a stack memory is a special case that applies to only one kind of dialogue – narrative. Berwick (1983) suggests that it reflects the expected linear temporal structure of such texts. An alternative type of structure was investigated by Grosz (e.g. 1981), who studied dialogues between experts and apprentices engaged in goal-directed tasks – the assembly and disassembly of mechanical components. She showed that the retrievability of preceding foci depended on the goal structure of the task. Once a subgoal, such as finding a tool, was completed, the domain for focusing switched back to that of the higher-level goal of which finding the tool was a subgoal.

## Summary

Language understanding is mediated by a complex set of processes that operate at three main levels: lexical, syntactic and semantic/pragmatic (message level). Research findings about all these levels must be integrated, if the talking computer is to become a reality.

At the lexical level such a computer will have to convert

speech into words – automatic speech recognition – and words into speech – speech synthesis. If a computer is to be given these abilities, speech waves must be digitally encoded, usually by recording their amplitude about 10,000 times a second. These digitised waveforms are then further transformed to produce more useful representations. Three techniques – vocoder analysis, formant tracking, and LPC coding – have been used to create more compact acoustic representations. The mapping between acoustic representations and phonemes and words is more complex. In automatic speech recognition it can, at present, only be performed for a thousand or so words spoken clearly in a quiet environment by a small number of speakers. The popular technique of using word templates and dynamic programming is not likely to provide a good model of how people understand speech.

In speech synthesis two techniques have been used. In the first, single speech sounds – phones – are represented by target formant values. Speech is produced by stringing these values together and interpolating between them to produce smooth formant tracks. This technique has proved successful, but a single voice takes a long time to encode and the detailed measurements that must be made cannot be generalised to produce other voices. The second technique, diphone synthesis, uses a larger number of primitive elements. A diphone is the second half of one phone and the first half of the next. The advantages of diphone synthesis are, first, that joining diphones is easier than interpolating between formant values for phones and, second, that it is comparatively simple to make a diphone library from the speech of a single speaker. Whichever technique is used to synthesise speech, further processing is necessary to make the output sound natural. In particular, timing must be adjusted and intonation contours added.

Syntactic analysis, or parsing, determines the ways the words in sentences are grouped. The human parser operates in a more-or-less 'left-to-right' manner, but it is less clear whether it builds parse trees top-down or bottom-up, and less clear whether it produces all possible parses in parallel (breadth-first parsing) or constructs them one at a time (depth-first). Parsers developed in AI include augmented transition networks, chart parsers, Marcus parsers and 'semantic parsers'. ATNs and chart parsers can be used to parse any language. Of the two, chart parsers are now favoured, especially for parsing languages with context-free grammars. The Marcus parser is a deterministic parser – one that never changes its mind – that is supposed to provide a model of human parsing. It should only fail to parse sentences that people have difficulty with, so-called 'garden-path' sentences. Many 'semantic parsers' were also intended to model human sentence processing, blurring the distinction between syntax and meaning, which many people have considered unrealistic. They violate Chomsky's formal autonomy principle – that syntactic concepts should be defined without reference to semantics. Formal autonomy should not be confused with processing autonomy. A parser is autonomous from its semantic processor if its operation cannot be influenced by what the semantic processor is doing.

Understanding discourse and text requires the mobilisation of a vast amount of knowledge about the world – more than a computer's memory can hold. One way to circumvent this problem is to write a program that understands and produces language about only a small part of the world. The most elaborate program of this sort is Winograd's SHRDLU, which achieved linguistic sophistication by confining its discourse to the table-top BLOCKSWORLD. Schank's MARGIE attempted to deal with the more difficult problem of under-standing texts about people. MARGIE uses conceptual dependency diagrams to represent sentence meanings. In these diagrams verb meanings are analysed using a small set of primitive acts each requiring a small number of case fillers. To handle less explicit aspects of complex interactions among people Schank proposed more elaborate knowledge structures that could be imposed upon texts. However, he failed to provide any systematic account of the kinds of structures allowed within his theory.

Three current interrelated research issues in discourse comprehension are: dialogue, non-literal language and use of discourse-specific knowledge. One important class of dialogues derives from the plans of their participants. To understand those dialogues is, in part, to determine the plans on which they are based. To compute those plans it may be necessary to interpret some utterances non-literally. Among the common types of non-literal language are metaphor and indirect speech acts. In both cases there is an unsolved question of whether they are interpreted via the computation and rejection of their literal meaning. Many aspects of discourse interpretation are internal to a particular discourse. One recent idea is that participants in discourse form models of the situation in the real or imaginary world that those discourses are about. Those models are updated as the discourse progresses and are used to interpret subsequent parts of it. Certain parts of those models become focused, perhaps because it is difficult to hold a large model in short-term memory. Keeping track of which parts of the model are focused is an essential part of comprehension.

# 6 Learning

When the task of writing a complex program seems particularly daunting, AI researchers sometimes claim that real progress will only be made when machines can learn for themselves. If the right learning algorithms could be devised, then the encoding and programming of the knowledge needed for intelligent behaviour could be avoided. Machines could acquire that knowledge for themselves. On this view, the ability to learn is one of the central aspects of intelligence.

If this argument is accepted, the comparative neglect of learning in AI seems strange. However, there are historical reasons for it. AI researchers initially wanted to establish similarities between human and machine intelligence. They assumed that the nature of intelligence did not depend on its genesis – the fact that people learned most of their skills was irrelevant to how those skills should be described. The neglect of learning was compounded by the fact that most AI researchers rejected behaviourism, the paradigm within which learning was studied in psychology. However, at least initially, they had no suggestions for an alternative framework within which learning could be investigated.

The term *learning* has a multitude of related meanings. The simplest type of learning is getting to know new facts. For many computer systems learning a new fact is simply adding an entry to a database. In more interesting types of learning, new skills are acquired – cognitive skills or motor skills. In AI it has, as yet, only been possible to study the acquisition of cognitive skills. In this chapter a number of different types of learning are discussed: learning by rote, learning from examples, learning from mistakes, learning by exploration, learning language. The programs described provide a glimpse of the capabilities that a truly intelligent learning system would have. However, one important aspect of learning has been ignored in this research – learning is always learning for a purpose. The real problem may be giving a machine a reason to learn.

## Learning by being told

Even the simplest type of learning, in which what is to be learned is directly stated, is not always as simple as it seems. If a machine is told that Ulan Bator is the capital of Outer Mongolia then it can store that fact in its memory and use an indexing scheme (see chapter 2) to ensure that it is readily available for answering queries. However, not all things that people (or machines) are told are facts to be stored away. They can also be given advice and, if they intend to follow it, they need to turn it into a practical plan of action. Mostow's (1983) program, FOO (First Operational Operationaliser), takes advice about how to play the card game, Hearts. FOO translates statements such as 'avoid taking points' into specific plans about which cards to play in which tricks. This process is called *operationalising* the advice. In general, operationalisation is a complex process. For example, to convert the advice 'avoid taking points' into a plan for playing cards, extensive reference must be made to the rules of Hearts.

## Samuel's checkers program

One of the earliest successful game-playing programs was Samuel's (e.g. 1963) draughts (US checkers) program. The rules of draughts are simpler than those of chess, but not simple enough to allow the program to compute a strategy that is certain to win. Samuel was, therefore, able to write a fairly simple program whose standard of play was not hopelessly poor and to make it play better by learning from its experience. The program uses the standard game-playing techniques of lookahead, static evaluation and minimaxing described in chapter 4. It always looks ahead at least three moves (for each player) and, for some positions, continues its exploration further. Its maximum lookahead down any branch of the search tree is twenty moves. The static evaluation is based on a weighted sum of various aspects of the board position. The program favours quick routes to winning positions if it is ahead, and slow routes – to give its opponent more chance of making a mistake – if it is losing.

The program can learn in two ways, which Samuel calls *rote learning* and *learning by generalisation*. When learning by rote the program stores board positions and their valuations, using a very compact code. This rote memory effectively allows the program to extend its lookahead. When it has looked three moves ahead, the program may find it has a stored evaluation of the position that has been reached. It can use that evaluation instead of computing a static evaluation for the new position. The stored evaluation will be based on looking (at least) three moves further ahead, so the effective lookahead is (at least) six moves. The program must be able retrieve board positions efficiently from its rote memory when they are required. As well as using an indexing scheme (see chapter 2). Samuel developed methods for eliminating redundancies and positions judged unlikely to be useful. Thus he was able to reduce the amount of information that had to be stored. On rote-learning tests the program accumulated a catalogue of over 50,000 positions, and improved its openings and endgames considerably. Its midgame did not change much.

When learning by generalisation – a rather odd term to use in this context – Samuel's program uses information about its evaluation of specific board positions to improve its static evaluation function. In this mode, one version of the program, referred to as Alpha, plays against another, called Beta. During play Alpha adjusts the weights in its evaluation function, while Beta keeps its weights constant. For each move, Alpha compares its original evaluation with one based on the way play subsequently develops. It is, therefore, able to assess whether it has over- or undervalued a position, and to adjust its weights accordingly. An evaluation function may include only sixteen out of a possible thirty-eight aspects of the board position. If Alpha finds that the weighting of one of them is always near zero it is replaced. When Alpha is consistently winning, Beta is given Alpha's current evaluation function, and a new learning cycle begins. Alpha uses a hill-climbing procedure (see chapter 4) to find the set of weights that gives the best performance. Samuel takes precautions against the principal problem of hill climbing – getting trapped in a local maximum. If Alpha's performance levels off, it is probably trapped at the top of a hill. To get it out of this trap the largest weight in its evaluation function is set of 0, moving it to a new position in the space of possible evaluation functions.

Generalisation, in contrast to rote learning, improved the program's performance most in the midgame. Rote learning was effective in the opening and endgame because standard positions were quickly added to the rote memory with appropriate evaluations. Generalisation was helpful in the more varied midgame, where the number of options is greater, but the consequences of a move quickly become apparent – usually within the program's lookahead.

In later work Samuel (1970) developed his program so that it performed at the level of a master draughts player. The major change was to the evaluation measure. In the original program Samuel used a *linear polynomial* measure – he assumed that each aspect of the board position contributed independently to its evaluation. With the advent of more powerful computers Samuel was able to relax this assumption, and allow for interactions between the components of the evaluation measure. Interactive evaluation measures are more realistic but there are many more of them than linear ones. Even with increased computing power. Samuel was forced to restrict the values that the weights could take to cut down the number of evaluation measures the program had to consider. The evaluation measure for the master-level draughts player was computed by letting the program analyse 250,000 moves from documented games of draughts. Samuel aimed to find a measure that would predict the actual moves. He assumed that a master-level program should duplicate moves made by draughts masters in published games.

## Sussman's HACKER – learning from mistakes

Sussman's (1975) program, HACKER, takes to heart the adage that one should learn from one's mistakes. Its task is to solve robot planning problems in the BLOCKSWORLD. In computer science, hackers used to be people who spent all their time programming, though recently the term has come to refer to certain types of 'electronic vandal'. Sussman chose the name HACKER because he thought that making a plan was similar to writing a program. He emphasised this similarity by writing HACKER in the CONNIVER language (see chapter 4), which allows goal-based procedure calls. A line in one of HACKERs plans is a line of CONNIVER code.

HACKER learns by 'debugging almost-right plans' (Sussman, 1975, p. xiii). Its design embodies the assumption that learning is easy when the expected deviates only slightly from the actual. A similar idea is embodied in Winston's program described below that learns from examples. Initially HACKER knows only the primitive BLOCKSWORLD actions for moving one block at a time. By solving a series of problems it learns to form plans for stacking and unstacking blocks in complex sequences, producing new configurations and preserving aspects of existing ones. Its preference is for linear plans, but such plans are sometimes inefficient, and sometimes they cannot solve a problem at all (see chapter 4). HACKER can modify linear plans to solve problems for which they are inappropriate.

HACKER assumes that its plans are almost correct – that it has got the right basic idea about how to solve a problem. Indeed, it assumes that, if a plan fails to solve a problem, there is a single error, or 'bug', in the plan that is responsible for the failure. HACKER attempts to correct a plan that does not work by adding some extra steps – a 'patch' – to it. The term 'bug' and 'patch' are taken from computer programming, and again underline the parallel between programming and planning. HACKER has methods for classifying bugs and for patching types of bug. The principal types of bug are failure of a precondition for an action and conflict between goals. Bugs are usually corrected by reordering the goals in a plan and adding extra steps, if necessary, to re-establish preconditions. HACKER uses knowledge of what the various parts of a plan are intended to achieve to help it to debug that plan. This information is provided by its *plan proposer*. Sussman argues that people, like HACKER, are only good at discovering why their plans have gone wrong when there is a simple reason for failure.

In the course of a learning session HACKER discovers new types of bug. It also keeps a record of how common the different types are. It may decide that some types are so common that every plan should be checked to see if it contains them. Under these circumstances HACKER writes procedures called *critics*, which examine plans as they are generated. Other bugs are identified only when the plan is tried out on a simulation of the BLOCKSWORLD.

HACKER keeps a list of plans for solving particular problems, called *the answer library*. When creating new plans, it accesses material from this library using patterns that describe the kind of problem it is working on. The use of CONNIVER, with its extensive pattern-matching facilities, makes this process straightforward. HACKER can use quite broad specifications to access the answer library, because it expects to modify old plans, extending and debugging them, to solve new problems. Once a plan has been debugged, HACKER assumes the amended ('patched') plan is more general than the one from which it was derived. The new plan replaces the old one in the answer library.

What HACKER learns depends partly on its teacher. It is most successful when it is set a correctly graded sequence of problems, one in which each problem can be solved by a relatively small modification to a plan that solved a previous one. If it is given a difficult problem too early in the sequence, it will fail for reasons that it cannot understand – the most appropriate plan it can find contains more than one bug.

Hacker's principal failure, apart from its specificity to the BLOCKSWORLD, is that it *always* tries to solve problems by patching existing plans. It can never step back, as people do, and decide to reconsider its whole approach.

## Induction – learning from examples

Induction is a method of deriving scientific laws from specific facts, first described by Francis Bacon, whose work marks the beginning of modern philosophy of science. There are two sides to induction, generalisation and specialisation. Bacon discussed both, though later philosophers have focused on generalisation. Induction proceeds as follows: a set of facts – positive or confirmatory instances of a putative law – suggests a generalisation. That generalisation is then refined (or specialised) in the light of further facts that are inconsistent with it – negative or falsifying instances. The term induction can be used more widely to describe any method of deriving general knowledge from specific instances. In this sense, concept formation is an inductive process. Some empiricist philosophers have claimed that people learn generalities only by induction. In AI other methods are countenanced.

As Mitchell (1982) points out, learning by induction can be thought of as a search problem (see chapter 4). The search space is the set of possible generalisations. The problem is to find the correct one among them. The positive and negative instances, and the way they are presented, help to determine how the space is searched.

Mitchell also points out that the language in which generalisations are stated may differ from the one in which the instances are described. If the two are different, it may be relatively difficult to decide whether an instance is consistent with a generalisation. However, in most AI research on induction the difference between the two languages has been either small or non-existent. Indeed, induction is often thought of as a search for what Dietterich and Michalski (1981) call the *maximally specific conjunctive description* (MSC) that characterises the positive instances. An MSC is couched in the same vocabulary as descriptions of individual objects – usually predicate calculus (see chapter 2). It attempts to capture what the positive instances have in common, as the following very simple example, in English rather than predicate calculus, shows. If two animals are described as:

(1) small and furry and grey

(2) small and furry and brown

the MSC for these two animals is:

small and furry.

It is important that only conjunctive descriptions should be allowed (those in which the simple predicates are linked by *and*) and not disjunctive ones (those with *or*). Otherwise, the most specific description that applied to both animals would be:

(small and furry and grey) or (small and furry and brown).

This description does not capture what the two have in common.

If induction is a search for the correct generalisation and there are a large number of possible generalisations to consider, a control strategy is needed to guide the search (see chapter 4). Winston's program, described below, searches depth-first, focusing on one hypothesis at a time. If necessary, it generalises its current hypothesis in the light of new positive instances, and specialises it after new negative instances. Breadth-first search for inductive generalisations, in which all possible hypotheses are tested against each new instance, is also possible. An extension of breadth-first induction is the *version space strategy* described by Mitchell (1982). Version space is the set of generalisations that have not been ruled out by the data considered so far. The hypotheses in version space are (partially) ordered by the relation 'is more specific than'. More specific generalisations are ones that cover fewer instances. The version space strategy uses positive and negative instances to eliminate generalisations at the specific and general ends of version space, respectively. The version space strategy, therefore, involves bi-directional breadth-first search. As more instances are considered, version space contracts. Eventually only one generalisation – the correct one – remains. A program that uses the version space strategy is Mitchell, Utgoff and Banerji's (1983) LEX, which learns how to perform symbolic integration.

The strategies described above are *data-driven*. The language that the program uses determines what generalisations are possible, but the possibilities are only narrowed down when data – in the form of positive or negative instances – become available. The philosopher of science Popper (e.g. 1957) claimed that the initial choice of a generalisation to investigate need not be based on observation. All that is essential is that generalisations are *tested* against observations after they have been formulated. This idea can be incorporated into induction procedures in the form of *model-driven* strategies, of which the best known is *generate-and-test*. Model-driven strategies select a hypothesis on the basis of a (data-independent) model of what the world ought to be like. They accept it if it accounts for the data well enough. Unlike data-driven strategies, model-driven strategies can cope with noisy data. Their expectations about the world can override aberrant observations. However, they are poor for incremental learning, since they assume that all instances, or at least a representative sample of instances, are available at the test stage. Subsequent additions to the database may require a radical reappraisal of generalisations produced by model-driven methods, as they may in science. Two systems that use the generate-and-test strategy are RULEGEN, the rule generator in the meta-DENDRAL system (see chapter 7) and Michalski's INDUCE 1.2.

## Winston's program

Winston (1975b) describes a program that can learn simple structural concepts for classifying composite objects in the BLOCKSWORLD. These concepts include ARCH and ARCADE, though their definitions, as learned by the program, make reference only to configurations of BLOCKSWORLD objects, not to the functions of arches and arcades in the real world. Winston intended the input to his program to be a description of a BLOCKSWORLD scene as produced by a scene-analysis program, a description in which the blocks, their shapes and their relative positions have been identified.

The program learns concepts from positive and negative instances, using procedures called *induction heuristics*. Induction heuristics include both methods of generalising concepts and methods of specialising them. As well as stating how concepts can be generalised and specialised, induction heuristics also specify the conditions under which generalisation and specialisation should occur.

Winston's program does not learn by itself but, like HACKER, depends on a teacher. The teacher first presents the program with a positive example of the concept to be learned. The program then constructs, from the output of the scene analysis program, a semantic network representation (see chapter 2) of the example. The nodes in the network correspond to the simple BLOCKSWORLD objects identified by the scene analyser and to concepts in the program's semantic memory – its general knowledge about the BLOCKSWORLD. The links between the nodes correspond to the relations between those objects and concepts. The relations are chosen from a fixed set that includes ISA (see chapter 2) SUPPORTS and HAS-POSTURE (the orientation of a block is described by HAS-POSTURE links to standard orientations such as STANDING and LYING).

The program's initial semantic network represents a particular ARCH, say. Its goal is to produce a *model* representing ARCHES in general. The model is produced by modifying the initial network using information about other BLOCKSWORLD configurations. These configurations are classified by the teacher either as further exemplars of the concept or as *near misses*. Near misses differ from exemplars by only a few features, perhaps only one. The program cannot learn anything from negative examples of a concept that are not near misses. When the program is shown more ARCHES, it deduces what features are *not* essential to being an ARCH, *generalising* its current concept. If the first ARCH that the program sees is built of yellow blocks, it may think that all ARCHES are yellow. It will be disabused of this error if the next ARCH is multicoloured. However, only by using information about near misses can the program determine what the defining features of an ARCH are and, hence, *specialise* its concept. When a feature is discovered to be defining, it is labelled as such in the model. Models can also specify properties that an object must not have – for example, the two sides of an ARCH must not touch.

Winston's program relies on its teacher presenting either examples or near misses. It may never learn a concept if it is not given an appropriate training sequence. However, a near miss need not differ from the current model in only one way. When there is more than one difference, the program assumes that one of them is responsible for the near miss not being an example of the concept. The only exception is when there are two parallel differences. For example, if the LINTEL is removed from an ARCH then both the LEFT SIDE and the RIGHT SIDE fail to SUPPORT it. From this near miss the program can deduce that both SIDES of an ARCH must SUPPORT the LINTEL. In other cases the program makes a(n educated) guess about which of several differences is important. However, the program can only test this guess against subsequent information provided by the teacher. It cannot generate block structures and ask its teacher to classify them.

Many of the heuristics that Winston's program uses are specific to the BLOCKSWORLD and are unlikely to generalise to other domains. In particular, they will probably not be useful when objects must be classified according to their function rather than their structure. One assumption that may be of more general use is that differences between an object and a model are independent of one another – if a difference is important in one context, it is always important. This assumption parallels the assumption that a problem can be solved by a linear plan – that the effects of actions are essentially independent of one another. Neither assumption is true in the real world, though in many domains one or both is nearly true. In the BLOCKSWORLD, the assumption made by Winston's program is almost always true.

Winston's program illustrates two important general points about learning. First, to learn one thing you often need to know a lot of other things already. The program starts with a fund of knowledge about the basic objects of the BLOCKS-WORLD – bricks and wedges – and about possible relations between them. Second, it is easiest to learn something when you almost know it already. Winston's program knows all the atomic concepts out of which its new concepts can be constructed, and it relies on its teacher presenting it with configurations that are almost examples of the concept it is trying to learn.

## Michalski's AQ11 and INDUCE 1.2

The idea of learning from examples and near misses is extended in the work of Michalski (e.g. 1983). The induction heuristics in Michalski's AQ11 program and its successor, INDUCE 1.2, are more powerful than Winston's but they operate in ways that are less like ordinary human learning. In particular, these programs do not need a teacher to present positive and negative examples in a special order. They consider all training instances together. The programs can work from positive examples only, or from both positive and negative examples. Since negative examples help induction procedures to specialise, these programs must avoid over-generalising when presented with positive examples only. They are able to do so by using generate-and-test procedures. Constraints on the way generalisations are generated ensure that less general ones are always considered first.

The induction heuristics of AQ11 and INDUCE 1.2 can be used in a different, but related, task – discrimination learning. Michalski and Chilausky (1980) taught a program based on AQ11 to discriminate betwen soya bean plants with fifteen different diseases. The program was trained on descriptions of 290 previously diagnosed plants. It was then tested on a further 360 such examples. Its performance was better than that of a set of rules formulated by a human expert. The program chose the actual disease as the most likely diagnosis over 95 per cent of the time, while the expert's rules did so in just over 70 per cent of cases.

## Lenat's AM and EURISKO – learning by exploring

Lenat's (1977, 1982) program AM discovers new mathematical concepts, and makes conjectures about them, by reasoning about concepts it already knows. EURISKO (Lenat, 1983) is an improved version of AM that can work in several knowledge domains, including the design of three-dimensional VLSI (very large-scale integration) circuits.

In one representative run, AM was given 115 set-theoretic concepts, such as set, order and relation, represented in a *slot-and-filler* notation reminiscent of frame-system theory (see chapter 2). Its task was to discover concepts of number theory and to make conjectures about them. AM's search for concepts and conjectures is guided by over 200 *heuristic rules*. These rules specify, for example, how to modify the structural definition of one concept to give a new definition, and how to compare two definitions to produce a conjecture about how they are related. AM tries to find examples of the concepts it generates, but it does not attempt to prove its conjectures. One of the concepts that AM was intended to discover, and did, was that of a natural number.

Strictly speaking, AM does not undertake the kind of search described in chapter 2, because it has no clearly defined goal state. It does, however, have an indefinitely large space of possibilities to explore, and it has to make decisions about which parts of the space are the most promising.

In a typical run, AM is allowed about an hour (!) to itself on a large computer. In this time it generates about 200 new concepts. About half of these are of some interest. Among AM's more noteworthy discoveries were the concepts of number and prime number. Its more interesting conjectures included: that every number has a unique set of prime factors, and that every even number is the sum of two prime numbers. The first of these conjectures is called the *fundamental theorem of arithmetic*. The second is Goldbach's conjecture – one that mathematicians have not yet proved either true or false.

AM produces new concepts by modifying existing ones, but it cannot create new heuristics. Part of the reason is that its heuristics are larger and more complex structures than the concepts they are designed to operate on. In EURISKO concepts and heuristics are structures of the same type, so one heuristic can modify another. EURISKO is, therefore, able not only to learn new concepts, but also to develop new ways of learning.

Ritchie and Hanna (1984) criticise Lenat for, among other things, his lack of clarity about AM's contribution to a theory of the nature of mathematical discovery. In reply, Lenat and Brown (1984) claim that the *ad hoc* nature of AM's heuristics – a major contributing factor to the difficulty of assessing the program – is an advantage if AM is considered as a model of human mathematicians.

## Learning language

Almost all children learn a language apparently without effort, and certainly with little formal tuition. These facts might suggest that language learning is a simple task, simpler than learning to play chess or draughts, for example, which requires conscious effort. However, appearances here, as elsewhere, are deceptive. A task that seems straightforward is mediated by a complex underlying mechanism.

There are two major problems in describing how language is learned. First, it is difficult to spell out exactly what adults know about their native languages and to decide how much of that they have to learn. Second, it is not immediately obvious what data children learn language from.

Solutions to these problems were suggested by Chomsky (e.g. 1965), who had rejected an account of language learning based on Skinnerian (neobehaviouristic) learning theory (Chomsky, 1959). First, Chomsky identified the grammar of a language, as formulated by linguistics, with the 'knowledge' about that language that an adult native speaker has. However, grammars are complex, and it is difficult to see how they could be learned. Chomsky, therefore, suggested that much of our knowledge about language is innate and does not have to be acquired. This innate knowledge can be formulated as a set of principles, called *universal grammar*, which describes what all possible natural languages have in common. These principles severely limit the form that grammars for natural languages can take and, hence, make the problem of language learning easier, because many possibilities need not be considered.

Chomsky's answer to the second problem was to suggest that children learn about language, and about syntax in particular, from *positive examples* only. They usually hear grammatical sentences, not ungrammatical ones, and when they do either hear or utter ungrammatical sentences they are not told that those sentences are ungrammatical. Parents may correct their children when they say something false, but they do not correct incorrect sentence forms. Learning from positive examples is more difficult than learning from both positive and negative ones, because there is less information to go on and because there is a danger of overgeneralising. This impoverishment of the data from which language is learned makes Chomsky's innateness hypothesis all the more important, given the complexity of natural language syntax. However, learning transformational grammars – the kind proposed by Chomsky for natural languages – from positive examples only is more difficult than even Chomsky realised (Gold, 1967; Angluin, 1978). There must be further constraints on either the grammars or the learning process, if transformational grammars are to be acquired.

Chomsky's ideas have only recently been incorporated into an AI program for language learning. Berwick (1985) describes a system based on Marcus's PARSIFAL parser (see chapter 5) that learns syntactic rules from grammatical sentences. The system incorporates a set of constraints on the form that these rules can take. The constraints are based on the most recent version of Chomsky's syntactic theory – the theory of government and binding (GB, Chomsky, 1981). There are two sets of constraints, which correspond to the two principal types of syntactic rule in Chomsky's theory – phrase-structure rules and transformations. Phrase-structure rules describe the way phrases are made up out of smaller constituents. The form of these rules is constrained by a theory called *X-bar syntax*. X-bar syntax restricts phrase-structure rules in two ways. First, it ensures that every phrase has, as its principal component, or *head*, a word of the right type. A noun phrase must be built around a noun, for example, and a verb phrase around a verb. Second, X-bar syntax divides the remainder of a phrase into two parts, *specifiers* and *complements*. Head, specifiers and complements must appear in the same order in all types of phrase in a language. In English, for example, the order is: specifiers, head, complements.

In GB, transformations produce structures such as WH-questions and relative clauses from underlying forms that reflect semantic relations more straightforwardly. Trans-formations are, in principle, very powerful tools, but GB severely restricts the form that they can take. These constraints on transformations are incorporated into Berwick's model of language learning.

In order to learn grammar rules Berwick's system must be given sentences that it can almost analyse, using its parsing techniques and the rules of grammar it already knows. Like Winston's program, it learns from 'near misses'. Providing that the first sentences it encounters are simple enough, it can start with the single rule S → NP VP. It has been suggested that this rule, or rather a generalisation of it, is part of universal grammar. When the system encounters a word that it cannot incorporate into a parse tree, it attempts to construct a new phrase-structure rule that accounts for that word and for other constituents that are not yet attached into the syntactic analysis tree. This rule must be consistent with X-bar theory. If no such rule can be constructed, the system performs a transformation and tries again. Only two types of transformation are allowed, the reordering of two constituents and the insertion of a 'dummy' NP. The first type of transformation could be used to change:

> Have you been to the shops?

into

> You have been to the shops.

This transformation allows the question to be analysed by the same phrase structure rules as the statement. The second type of transformation allows, for example, a relative clause to be analysed by the same phrase structure rules as a main clause. As the following examples show, a relative clause has a noun phrase missing when compared to the corresponding main clause.

The man who I met            yesterday offered to buy my car.
        I met the man yesterday

Berwick's system initially proposes the most specific phrase-structure rule that will allow it to parse the current sentence. This rule may refer to specific words rather than phrase types. However, once it has parsed the sentence, it attempts to collapse the new rule with other similar rules to form a more general rule. Providing it encounters the right sentences, overly specific rules soon disappear. Furthermore, because it always constructs the most specific rule compatible with what it knows, the system does not overgeneralise, even though it learns from positive examples only.

A more ambitious computational model of language learning, formulated within the Schankian framework, has recently been presented by Selfridge (1986). As well as learning 'semantic' syntax, Selfridge's CHILD also learns word meanings, and mimics some well-documented facts in language acquisition, such as the regularisation of irregular verbs and the systematic misunderstanding of certain syntactic constructions.

## Learning by connection machines

One worry about many of the programs described in this chapter is that they leave many aspects of learning unexplained. Winston's program, for example, shows how the concept of an ARCH can be constructed from those of a SUPPORT (or PILLAR) and a LINTEL, but it does not explain how those more primitive concepts might be learned. Indeed, traditional AI seems to provide no clue as to how concepts could be learned other than by construction out of more primitive concepts.

Connection machines (see chapter 2), however, can do something very like learning concepts without having to rely on concepts that they already know. They can learn to classify objects as belonging or not belonging to a class by being presented with members and non-members of the class and being told which is which. The connection machine's ability to classify is encoded into excitatory and inhibitory links between its simple processors. The strengths of those links change in response to information provided by the training instances. A connection machine might be described as building concepts out of non-conceptual primitives.

In the most popular learning scheme the connection machine has a fixed number of layers of simple processors between those that encode its inputs and those that produce its output. The strength of the connections between the processors is adjusted after each learning instance by a computation known as *backward error* propagation, embodied in the *generalised Delta rule*. McClelland and Rumelhart (1985) present a distributed memory system that can learn both specific and general concepts using the Delta rule.

A different learning method for connection machines, *competitive learning*, is described by Rumelhart and Zipser (1985). Competitive learning can also result in the ability to classify, but a machine learning competitively does not require a teacher.

A selection of connectionist models of psychological processes can be found in McClelland and Rumelhart (1986). The next few years will show just how successful models of this type will be in explaining those aspects of learning that traditional AI models leave unexplained.

## Summary

Learning has, until recently, been a comparatively neglected aspect of AI research. However, a machine that can learn has a much greater potential for intelligence than one that cannot.

There are many different types of learning, the simplest of which is learning by being told. If a machine is told a fact, it can simply store that fact in its database. Advice, on the other hand, has to be operationalised.

The next simplest type of learning is rote learning. Samuel's draughts player extends its lookahead by storing evaluations of specific positions. Its opening and endgame are greatly improved by this rote memory. However, its midgame only improves when it can change its evaluation function, by generalising from board positions it actually evaluates to produce a new function for evaluating all positions.

People often learn from their mistakes. Sussman's HACKER produces plans that almost solve block-stacking problems in the BLOCKSWORLD, discovers why they do not work and amends them. The new plans are added to a library that can be used to solve subsequent problems. HACKER is only successful if there is a single error in its initial plan.

Induction is the formulation and modification of generalisations, including both laws and concepts, on the basis of specific instances. It can be thought of as a kind of search. New positive and negative instances lead to generalisation or specialisation, respectively.

Winston's program learns BLOCKSWORLD concepts by induction. It relies on a teacher to present positive and negative examples in a helpful order and it assumes that all the negative examples are 'near misses'. Michalski's programs AQ11 and INDUCE 1.2 are more powerful, but their performance is less like that of a person. They do not require a teacher and they can consider many positive and negative instances at a time. These programs can also learn from positive examples only, by using built-in constraints on the form of generalisations, and they can learn to discriminate between concepts as in Michalski and Chilausky's soya bean disease diagnoser.

People often learn by exploring and extending what they already know. This type of learning is simulated in Lenat's AM, which generates mathematical concepts and conjectures from a limited stock of set-theoretical concepts. It does so using a set of heuristic rules that compare and modify concepts. His more advanced EURISKO represents heuristics in the same ways as concepts. It can, therefore, discover new heuristics – new ways of learning – as well as new concepts.

Language learning is deceptively simple – almost all children learn a language without effort. Chomsky argues that they do so partly because much of their knowledge of language is innate and does not have to be learned. He also argues that children learn grammar rules from positive examples only – the sentences that they can interpret and that they assume are grammatical. Berwick's language-learning system is based on a Marcus parser and the most recent version of Chomsky's linguistic theory. It can learn new phrase-structure rules from sentences that it can almost parse. Its knowledge about transformations is built in.

Traditional AI models leave many aspects of learning unexplained. They make it difficult to see how a machine could learn any concepts unless it already had some. Connection machines can build concepts out of non-conceptual primitives. They are likely to make an increasingly important contribution to the study of machine learning in the future.

# 7 Applications

Computers are widely used in business, industry, and research. Many things that we take for granted, such as making telephone calls and withdrawing money from cash dispensing machines, would be difficult or impossible without them. By AI standards most of these computers are not intelligent, neither is there any need for them to be. Although it is annoying to receive bills for £0.00 – and indicative of a 'stupid machine!' – a trivial change to a program could prevent such bills from being mailed. More efficient bill preparation and dispatch depends primarily on the advent of faster, cheaper printers, and better ways of monitoring which bills have been paid. The performance of computers that perform such tasks will only be improved, and their range of applications increased, by technological developments. There are, however, many tasks that computers would perform better than they do now, and some which could only be performed by computers, if those machines could be made more intelligent.

The widespread application of AI findings will depend on their providing economically viable solutions to real-world problems. Economic viability is difficult to define in this context because of such factors as the prestige, or otherwise, of using new techniques. However, a number of considerations will inevitably be important, in particular the availability of comparatively cheap machines with reliable and reasonably rapid performance. Most of the techniques described in this book have been developed in laboratories where these constraints were less important. AI researchers typically have access to large machines, though they have to share them with many other people. Many have developed the habit of programming at night! Little except pride, and perhaps a PhD, depends on the success of a project, and there is no need for a program to run in what, in an application, would be regarded as a reasonable amount of time. A researcher may not care if a program takes two minutes to analyse a single sentence, but a machine answering a query in a busy information bureau would not normally be expected to take so long.

This chapter discusses a number of applications and potential applications of AI research. In some cases, such as image processing, computer-aided instruction and CAD/CAM, computers are already widely used, though AI techniques have yet to make a significant contribution. In these areas there is reason to believe that such techniques, when they can be applied, will produce better results. The case of expert systems is different. Expert systems have always been firmly based within AI but, until recently, they have been enormously expensive in manpower to develop. The aim in expert systems research is to make systems that are cheap enough and reliable enough to augment (or, in some cases, replace) human expertise.

## Image processing

The human visual system has remarkable image-processing powers, but it works best when extracting the kind of information that people need in the kind of visual environment they usually inhabit. Many artificial images contain important information that the human visual system is poor at extracting or that it cannot extract at all. Two such types of image are those used in medical diagnosis and those used for military intelligence gathering. The most common 'low-grade' images in medical diagnosis are X-rays. X-rays can only be interpreted by experts, and often only with difficulty. More recently, doctors have had to interpret computer-aided tomography (CAT) scans and to infer three-dimensional structures from sequences of them. Military intelligence gathering relies on satellite photos in which important details are small, blurred, and invisible to the untrained eye.

A variety of computer-based techniques have been devised for extracting 'hidden' information from images. Most of them lie outside AI, and play no part in attempts to model the human visual system. However, AI techniques are increasingly used in machine vision and image-interpretation systems. This trend is likely to continue as it becomes possible to implement AI vision algorithms cheaply and efficiently. In particular, many of the low-level vision algorithms described in chapter 3 are suitable for implementation on massively parallel hardware when it becomes available at a reasonable price.

A longer-term goal is to make AI vision systems and models of higher-level cognitive processes work together. This combination will produce machines that can make knowledge-based inferences both before and after visual processing. For example, a system that reasons about illnesses could make a diagnosis based on superficial symptoms. This diagnosis could, in turn, suggest features that should be present in a an X-ray or a CAT scan and could guide the interpretation of that image.

## Expert systems

The synonymous terms *expert system* and *intelligent knowledge-based system*, which are part the jargon of *information technology*, have rapidly become among the most common in AI, particularly when its applications are being discussed. Expert systems themselves have been in existence, under other names, for about twenty years. *Knowledge engineering* is the new term for writing expert systems.

An expert system is a program that embodies (some of) the knowledge of a human expert in a domain in which expertise comes with experience. In such fields it is difficult to formulate the knowledge that an expert has – if that knowledge could be explicitly formulated, human experts would be easier to train. Human expertise is expensive, both to produce and to hire, so expert systems promise to be a money-earning application of

AI. Because of these positive connotations the term 'expert system' is used more widely than it perhaps should be. There have been two main types of overgeneralisation. First, programs that embody any kind of knowledge that is hard to formulate are sometimes called expert systems. For example, the speech understanding programs HARPY and HEARSAY-II (see chapter 3) have been so described. (In the case of HEARSAY, the reason is partly that its architecture has been used as a model for that of expert systems.) Second, many small programs that embody specialist knowledge, rather than expertise, are called 'expert systems' in an attempt to make them commercially attractive. The result of this overgeneralisation has been that, in many people's minds, the term *expert system* has been devalued. In particular, it has become associated with the attempt to make a fast (and fraudulent) buck out of AI.

The following sections discuss some general questions about expert systems. Some important expert systems are then described in detail.

What kind of problems do expert systems solve?

As the name implies, expert systems are intended to do (some of) the work of human experts. The first condition that a problem must satisfy, if it is to be tackled by an expert system, is that there should be recognised experts at solving that problem, and that their performance should be demonstrably better than that of non-experts. There are, of course, many fields of human endeavour in which so-called experts do not do better than anybody else. A medical consultant is a typical expert of the first type. A consultant not only performs better than the layman in diagnosing and treating diseases but, in his or her own speciality, better than a general practitioner.

Medical diagnosis illustrates a number of other features that a problem should have, if it is to be solved by an expert system. First, medical experts take a long time to train and there are not enough of them. Expert systems are intended to make human expertise, which is expensive, more widely available. Second, the difference between consulting a medical expert and not consulting one can substantially alter the subsequent course of events. It can literally be a matter of life or death. However, this aspect of medical diagnosis raises questions about the delegation to computers of decisions on how people should be treated. Third, there is no simple set of rules that a medical consultant can follow in diagnosing illnesses. If there were, diagnosis could be done by non-intelligent programs (and there would probably be no experts). Rather, a consultant draws on a wide range of experience about the connection between *manifestations* of illnesses and their underlying causes. Fourth, a single manifestation – a symptom, a sign, or a test result – may indicate a number of different diseases, but it is unlikely to be associated with any one of them in every case. Furthermore, some of the data on which a diagnosis is based may be misleading or incorrect. In other words, reasoning about diagnoses is, in some sense, probabilistic. Finally, diagnosis does not depend on general knowledge about the world. It requires a large, but relatively tractable, amount of domain-specific knowledge.

### What should expert systems do?

The primary goal of an expert system is to solve problems from the domain – medical diagnosis, for example – that it works in. However, most expert systems interact with people to solve problems, and their users often need to know how a decision has been reached. An expert system should, therefore, be able to explain how it came to a particular conclusion. In addition expert systems could improve their performance if, like human experts, they could learn. Some expert systems can develop new rules, similar to the ones they already use. However, more complex kinds of learning, such as developing new ways of thinking about problems, are not yet possible.

### The design of expert systems

Davis (1984) identifies four principles for the design of expert systems. The first is that the domain-specific knowledge used by an expert system should be kept separate from the rules that manipulate that knowledge – sometimes called the *inference engine*. The second principle is that domain-specific knowledge should be represented uniformly (see chapter 2). The first two principles allow additional pieces of knowledge – new discoveries about medical diagnosis, for example – to be added to an expert system without changing the system itself. The third principle is to keep the inference engine simple. The fourth is to exploit redundancy by using multiple sources of information about a single topic. The first three principles all contribute to the goal of having a system that can explain its conclusions in a comprehensible way. These principles are most readily satisfied by writing an expert system in the form of a rule-based (production) system (see chapter 2). A recent trend is to write such systems, particularly small ones, in the logic programming language PROLOG. Productions can be expressed straightforwardly in PROLOG.

### The source of the knowledge in an expert system

The inference engine of an expert system should be kept simple. Writers of expert systems are, therefore, primarily concerned with what knowledge should be encoded into an expert system and how it should be used to make decisions. That knowledge comes largely from human experts. Encoding it into the system is called the *transfer of expertise*. Transfer of expertise is hard, because experts cannot always formulate explicitly the knowledge that they use in, for example, medical diagnosis. Nor can they say how they combine different items of information to make a judgment about a particular medical case. The expertise to be transferred must usually be extracted from lengthy interviews with experts in which they are asked to give their opinion on sample cases. Furthermore, what the experts themselves say may have to be supplemented by survey data, in which, for example, patterns of medical symptoms and test results are correlated with eventual diagnoses. These facts make the writing of expert systems difficult and time-consuming. The early systems each took several tens of man-years to encode.

## The treatment of uncertainty in expert systems

In a domain such as medical diagnosis, simple productions of the form:

If [symptom] then [diagnosis]
or If [test result] then [diagnosis]

are rarely appropriate. Symptoms and results of tests give varying degrees of support to diagnoses, rather than confirming them absolutely. A medical diagnosis system will often, therefore, provide a set of possible diagnoses for a given case. Each diagnosis in the set should have a probability associated with it. Since a diagnosis may be based on many pieces of information, an expert system needs a way of combining probabilities as it works towards its final assessment.

One statistical theorem that appears relevant to this problem is Bayes' theorem. Bayes' theorem allows one to calculate the probability of a hypothesis – in the medical case, a diagnosis – from two other sets of probabilities:

(1) the probabilities of a set of alternative hypotheses before any evidence has been collected (e.g. how common certain diseases are).
(2) for each of those hypotheses, the probabilities of the actual symptoms and test results being found if that hypothesis is correct. This second set of probabilities can be estimated from statistical surveys (e.g. of previously diagnosed cases).

Bayesian methods have been used in several expert systems (e.g. PROSPECTOR, Duda *et al.*, 1978). However, they are not always appropriate. Ironically, medical diagnosis is one area in which the assumptions underlying Bayes' theorem do not hold. There are two reasons why Bayesian methods cannot always be applied to medical diagnosis. First, a patient may have more than one disease. Bayes' theorem assumes that the hypotheses (possible diagnoses) are mutually exclusive.

Second, micro-organisms evolve rapidly. They develop new strains more quickly than statistical data about their association with symptoms and reactions to drugs can be collected. A different method of handling uncertainty, based on assigning probability values to *rules*, has been developed by Shortliffe and Buchanan (1975) for the MYCIN system described below.

Example expert systems

Programs that would now be called expert systems were first developed in the mid-1960s. Two large systems, now in regular use, were conceived in that period. MACSYMA helps mathematicians perform tasks such as simplifying algebraic formulae and symbolic integration. Although MACSYMA grew out of earlier AI research, and was partly written in LISP, it is of more interest from a mathematical than an AI point of view. However, it is the most widely used program that could reasonably be called an expert system. The other early expert system was DENDRAL, a program for determining the structural formulae of organic molecules from their molecular formulae and data from mass spectrography.

*DENDRAL*
DENDRAL (Lindsay *et al.*, 1980) is an expert system, with several components, that works out the structure of large organic molecules. These molecules are made up chiefly of carbon, hydrogen and oxygen atoms. The number of each type of atom in one molecule of a compound – its molecular formula – is easy to determine, but there are many ways in which those atoms could be linked in a three-dimensional structure. Organic chemists are interested in the relation between the structure of a compound and its properties. More specifically, the structure of a compound can suggest ways of synthesising it, for example. One way of determining the structure of a molecule is to break it up in a mass spectrograph and 'weigh' the pieces. If the spectrogram shows that there are pieces with weight 17 units, the compound probably has an oxygen atom (weight 16 units) attached directly to a hydrogen atom (weight 1 unit). Working out a structural formula from a

mass spectrogram is complicated by the fact that after a molecule has been broken up, the atoms in the fragments may be subject to rearrangement.

DENDRAL works in three stages – plan, generate and test. In the planning stage simple measurements from the compound's mass spectrogram are used to produce two lists of substructures. The first list comprises those substructures that the molecule definitely contains; the second those that it definitely does not. Planning is rule-based. The output of the planning stage is used by the second, generation, stage, in which possible structures for the compound are computed. The lists of substructures eliminate many structures that are otherwise consistent with the molecular formula. The generator depends on an algorithm for enumerating possible structures. The original version of this algorithm, formulated by Lederberg, was restricted in scope. Nevertheless, for the classes of compound it could deal with, it produced all possible structures. It was, therefore, unlike human experts who sometimes fail to identify the correct structure for a compound, because they do not work systematically through the possibilities. In the mid-1970s a new algorithm, CONGEN (the CONstrained GENerator), was developed. CONGEN can be used either on its own or as part of DENDRAL. It works from a compound's molecular formula and from basic chemical knowledge about the number of bonds that each type of atom forms – carbon atoms form four, oxygen atoms two and hydrogen atoms one. It can also accept further constraints on a compound's structure, which might come from the DENDRAL planner or from a chemist using CONGEN in its stand-alone mode. CONGEN has two major advantages over Lederberg's original algorithm. First, it can generate cyclic structures, such as those of benzene and its derivatives. These compounds are both common and important in organic chemistry. Second, it can distinguish between stereoisomers – mirror-image versions of a compound. Differences between stereoisomers are biologically important.

The third part of DENDRAL is the tester. It takes the structures that remain as possibilities after the second stage, and synthesises mass spectrograms for them using yet another set of rules. These spectra are then compared with the spectrum of the compound under analysis. After a fairly gross comparison, structures corresponding to spectra very different from that of the compound are rejected. The remainder are then compared against the actual spectrum in more detail. The matching procedure uses information about the aspects of a spectrogram that are particularly important in determining the structure it corresponds to.

Although DENDRAL uses domain-specific knowledge about the structure of organic molecules, it does not model in detail the steps by which an organic chemist works out a structural formula. For this reason its operation may be comparatively opaque to someone using it. Unlike other expert systems, DENDRAL was never intended to explain its reasoning. Its users can trust it because of mathematical results, mainly relating to the completeness of its generators, that have been established about it. These results give DENDRAL one of its principal advantages over a human scientist – it does not overlook unlikely, but nevertheless possible, solutions to a problem. Its success is shown by the fact that several papers published in chemistry journals describe results obtained with the program's help.

A further part of the DENDRAL project is the program meta-DENDRAL, which attempts to show how an expert system can learn for itself and hence overcome the transfer-of-expertise problem. Meta-DENDRAL learns rules of the type used in the test phase of DENDRAL. It takes as its input pairings of structural formulae with mass spectograms. The rules it proposes are constrained by general knowledge about mass spectrometry. It knows which types of bond are likely to break, and which unlikely, and it knows how fragments rearrange themselves after cleavage. This information is known as a *half-order* theory, because it lies between the zero-order theory of mass spectrometry, which simply says that any bond can break, and the first-order theory, the set of specific rules for interpreting spectrograms that the program is trying to discover. Some of the rules for interpreting mass spectrograms discovered by meta-DENDRAL have been considered important enough to be published. The program has also been used to generate rules for interpreting the output of another analysis technique, nuclear magnetic resonance (NMR).

DENDRAL is not the only expert system designed to help chemists. There are also programs, such as SYNCHEM (Gelernter *et al.*, 1977), that suggest methods of synthesising organic chemicals.

## Medical diagnosis

DENDRAL does not pose any serious ethical problems. An organic chemist deciding whether to use it need only worry about whether it really helps in working out the structure of complex molecules. Other expert systems, such as those that perform medical diagnosis, do raise moral questions. Doctors have a responsibility for the well-being of their patients. They cannot afford to use diagnostic techniques that put those patients at unnecessary risk. For this reason, medical diagnosis systems, although among the first expert systems to be developed, have not come into general use. Only PUFF, a system for diagnosing pulmonary diseases, has been routinely consulted, at the Pacific Medical Center near San Francisco. However, as diagnosis systems improve, there will be increasing pressure to bring them into use. If doctors do anything that could be construed as negligent – if they do not use the best techniques available – they risk being taken to court.

The two most important diagnosis systems are MYCIN and CADUCEUS. MYCIN (Shortliffe, 1976), has been under development since the early 1970s. It diagnoses bacterial infections whose treatment requires the prescription of anti-biotics. It is intended for situations in which drugs must be prescribed before the micro-organism responsible for infection has been positively identified in laboratory tests. Such identification can only be made after a culture has been grown, which can take up to two days. A chronically sick patient cannot always wait that long before drugs are administered. Drugs must therefore be prescribed on the basis of symptoms and the results of tests that can be performed quickly. These indications eliminate some diagnoses, but the choice of an antibiotic or antibiotics is still not an easy one. A doctor cannot simply prescribe one drug for each possibility, since some are highly toxic, especially in combination with other antibiotics.

MYCIN interacts with a medical expert, requesting

information and suggesting treatments. It makes inferences mainly by backward chaining (see chapter 2), using its currently favoured diagnosis to predict symptoms and test results. This method of operation helps keep MYCIN's language processor simple. MYCIN asks only specific questions related to the hypothesis it is currently considering ('Does the patient have such-and-such a symptom?' 'What is the result of such-and such a test?') and it knows what sorts of answers it should receive. If it chained forward – from indications to diagnoses – it would have to understand a much wider range of inputs, because it could not use hypothesised diagnoses to help it interpret what it was told.

MYCIN knows of about 100 micro-organisms that produce infections amenable to antibiotic treatment. It uses about 500 *if . . . then* rules to reason about them. Each rule has an associated *certainty factor*. This factor reflects how certain the conclusion would be if the premises were known to be true. A certainty factor of 1 means that the conclusion is certain; $-1$ means it is certainly false. In addition there are rules for determining the certainty of a conclusion drawn from premises that are themselves uncertain.

Davis (1982) describes a program, TEIRESIAS, that helps human experts to formulate rules for MYCIN. TEIRESIAS enables its user to monitor MYCIN's performance and to find out which rules were responsible for a particular decision. TEIRESIAS also allows the MYCIN's rules to be changed, if they have led to what the human expert believes to be an incorrect conclusion. This process is aided by TEIRESIAS's meta-level knowledge about MYCIN's rule formats and methods of reasoning. The ideas underlying TEIRESIAS can be generalised to help solve the problem of transfer of expertise in other domains.

Another spin-off from the MYCIN project is E-MYCIN (E for empty). E-MYCIN is MYCIN stripped of its domain-specific knowledge. If a different database is put into E-MYCIN, a new expert system results. Facilities such as E-MYCIN are known as *expert system shells*. They allow users to create their own expert systems quickly. However, expert system shells are most useful for domains similar to the one the shell was originally written for. The most successful applications of E-MYCIN have been in medical diagnosis systems, such as the PUFF system for diagnosing pulmonary diseases.

The second major medical diagnosis system embodies the knowledge of one particular expert, Jack D. Myers, MD, a specialist in internal medicine at the University of Pittsburgh. The first version of the program was called INTERNIST. INTERNIST-II is also known as CADUCEUS (Pople, 1982). CADUCEUS differs from MYCIN in several ways. First, and most obviously, it diagnoses a different type of illness. Second, CADUCEUS knows about many more diseases than MYCIN. Third, CADUCEUS tries to mimic the way a human expert (Myers) reasons, not just the conclusions he comes to. Although MYCIN can explain how it came to a conclusion, it does not reason in the same way that doctors do. Fourth, CADUCEUS only diagnoses illnesses, it does not recommend treatments. Fifth, CADUCEUS stores its knowledge about illnesses in a semantic network, rather than as a set of productions.

CADUCEUS knows about more than 500 diseases and over 3500 manifestations, which include symptoms, signs and test results. The diseases are arranged in a tree, whose organisation corresponds roughly to that of the organ systems of the body. Manifestations may be associated either with particular diseases or with types of disease – jaundice is associated with all liver diseases. CADUCEUS also knows the strength of the associations between diseases and manifestations, in both directions – the likelihood of the disease given the manifestation and the likelihood of the manifestation given the disease. Furthermore, CADUCEUS knows how expensive each manifestation is to test for.

In a diagnostic session CADUCEUS starts from the readily determined manifestations of disease in the patient. It uses these manifestations to focus its attention on an area (or areas) of its semantic network. It then works out what manifestations would best allow it to discriminate between diseases in the area(s) it has focused on. The consultant using it must then find out whether the patient shows those manifestations. By focusing on smaller and smaller areas of the network, until a specific disease (or diseases) is diagnosed,

CADUCEUS is said to follow the *differential diagnostic model*. It asks questions that best allow it to decide among those diagnoses that have not yet been ruled out. The diagnostic session ends when all the manifestations are accounted for and one or more specific diseases have been diagnosed.

The differential diagnostic method, which amounts to considering related hypotheses in parallel, was introduced to overcome a weakness in the original INTERNIST program. Medical experts like to formulate at least a partial diagnosis fairly quickly, and use that to give focus to their further investigations. Pople tried to incorporate this aspect of the human behaviour into his program. However, INTERNIST always worked with specific diagnoses, looking for manifestations that would distinguish them from the most likely alternatives. It tended to begin with entirely inappropriate hypotheses, although it usually reached the right conclusion in the end. Consultants working with INTERNIST found this aspect of its behaviour both unfamiliar and disconcerting. The problem was solved by the introduction of associations between manifestations and *types* of disease. INTERNIST did not use information of this sort.

Another weakness in the original INTERNIST program was that, unlike consultants, it knew only about associations between diseases and manifestations. It did not know about the causes of illness or about the way manifestations change through time. An attempt has been made to remedy this problem in CADUCEUS, enabling the later program to give better explanations of its diagnoses.

A diagnosis system that, from the start, gave a central place to causal explanations is CASNET · (Causal ASsociative NETwork, Weiss *et al.*, 1978). CASNET was developed at Rutgers University for diagnosing and suggesting treatments for the various types of glaucoma. Unlike MYCIN and CADUCEUS, CASNET has a dynamic, rather than a static, model of diseases. This type of model is possible because the way glaucomas develop is fairly well understood. It is necessary because the recommended treatment depends on how advanced the disease is.

## XCON

One of the most successful expert systems in regular use is XCON, (eXpert CONfigurer), formerly known as R1 (McDermott, 1982). XCON was developed by Digital Equipment Corporation (DEC) in conjunction with Carnegie-Mellon University. It is a rule-based system with about 2500 rules. XCON is used by DEC to configure the VAX mainframe computer systems that they manufacture. To configure a system is, roughly speaking, to find a sensible layout for the major components inside the cabinets and to connect them up correctly. XCON can configure fairly complicated systems with a few hundred components. Configuration is necessary because, unlike home computer buyers, purchasers of mainframe computers generally want their systems tailor-made. Each order must be treated separately. By 1984 XCON had configured over 20,000 orders. Its successful rate, measured in terms of satisfied customers, was over 95 per cent (Kraft, 1984). It is reputed to have saved DEC a great deal of money.

### Geological prospecting

Two expert systems have met with some success in the field of geological prospecting. Both are consultation systems. Like MYCIN and CADUCEUS, they are intended to assist relatively knowledgeable people. PROSPECTOR (Duda *et al.*, 1978) was developed at the Stanford Research Institute (SRI International). It is the successor to an earlier computer-based consultant, which gave advice to novice mechanics working with electromechanical equipment. PROSPECTOR reasons about possible mineral deposits using information gathered mainly from the surface of a new site, or *prospect*. It uses a partitioned semantic net (see chapter 2), rather than a set of productions, to model its domain-specific knowledge. In field tests, PROSPECTOR predicted the existence of a previously unknown molybdenum deposit in Washington State.

The DIPMETER ADVISOR (Davis *et al.*, 1981), developed at the Schlumberger-Doll Research Center, gives advice about where to sink new oil wells – an expensive, but potentially lucrative enterprise. A *dipmeter* is a device that can be lowered into a bore-hole. It emits electrical, sonar, and nuclear energy, and measures the reflection of that energy from the surrounding rock. As the dipmeter progresses down the hole, a series of readings is taken from four sensors at the same level on the dipmeter. Since different types of rock reflect the emitted energy in different ways, these readings provide information about the tilt of the rock formations that the dipmeter is passing through. From these local measurements, it is possible to infer more global patterns of tilt, called *structural dip*. These global patterns in turn provide evidence for *structural features*, such as faults. Finally a *stratigraphic analysis* indicates what rocks and minerals have been deposited and how. On the basis of this analysis a decision is made about whether to drill a full-scale oil well. If the decision is 'no', the DIPMETER ADVISOR can advise where the next bore-hole should be sunk.

## AI in education

Computer-aided instruction and learning

Computer-aided instruction (CAI) is not a recent development, nor is it one that originated within AI. Early CAI systems did not use AI techniques. Indeed, one of their chief architects and proponents was the behaviourist B. F. Skinner. These systems presented students with material to learn, asked them questions about it, and told them if they were right or wrong. When the answer to a question was incorrect, remedial material was presented, and sometimes the subsequent path through the syllabus was altered.

Carbonell (1970) pioneered the application of AI to CAI. Since 1970, many intelligent computer-aided instruction (ICAI) systems have appeared. Such systems have three main components: a representation of the subject matter that they teach, a model of the student, and a set of teaching strategies.

*The knowledge base*
Older CAI systems often simply taught lists of facts. However,

such lists are not an appropriate representation of the more complex subject matter than ICAI systems teach. In these systems the knowledge base is more likely to be an expert system that can explain how it makes decisions. This knowledge base is used to formulate problems for the student and to evaluate the student's solutions. The ICAI system tries to teach the expertise embodied in the expert system.

## The model of the student

ICAI systems not only tell students that they are wrong, they also explain to them why they are wrong. An ICAI system must, therefore, have a model of the person it is teaching so that it can identify misconceptions that are leading to mistakes. The simplest technique is for the system to keep a record of those ideas it has evidence the student has mastered and to assume that misconceptions arise elsewhere. However, this approach ignores the fact that a student may have an incorrect hypothesis that does not correspond in any simple way to what the system knows. A more sophisticated model of the student can be developed if the program conceptualises its own knowledge as a set of procedures for solving different types of problem. A student error can then be thought of as a bug in one of those procedures.

## Teaching procedures

Several approaches to teaching have been explored in ICAI systems. The most straightforward is to set problems and evaluate proposed solutions to them. If information about why solutions are wrong can be provided, students should be able to learn from their errors. An alternative is to pose further, usually simpler, problems that make any misconceptions more obvious. Students will then discover the bugs in their procedures for themselves. This teaching method is harder to implement. It depends on the tutoring system having a sophisticated model of the student that allows misconceptions to be accurately located.

Two other teaching procedures that have been used are the *socratic method*, in which students are repeatedly asked questions, in an attempt to make them think about what they know, and *coaching*. Coaching, as its name suggests, is used primarily for teaching computer games. Coaches let their pupils learn mainly by practice. However, at comparatively infrequent intervals they interrupt and suggest better methods of playing the game.

*Some example ICAI systems*

Carbonell's (1970) own contribution to ICAI was the SCHOLAR system, which teaches facts about South American geography. SCHOLAR engages in English dialogue with students. It is a *mixed initiative* system – SCHOLAR can both answer questions and generate tutorial questions of its own. When it takes the initiative, SCHOLAR uses the socratic method of probing with questions in an attempt to make students realise their mistakes. SCHOLAR has some ability to answer 'unexpected' questions. It knows that its knowledge base, which takes the form of a semantic network (see chapter 2), is incomplete and is able to make plausible inferences from material that is explicit in the knowledge base. It is also able to vary the level of detail in its questions according to its assessment of the student's level of knowledge.

WHY (Collins, 1976) is a development of SCHOLAR, which is more sophisticated in three ways. First, it uses the ideas underlying the socratic teaching method to produce structured tutorial dialogues. SCHOLAR's teaching sessions often appear undirected, because it does not plan sequences of questions to make a point. Its next question is based on the student's reply to the previous one. Second, WHY has a more comprehensive classification of the kinds of misconception that students can have. It is therefore better able to frame questions that allow students to see what is wrong with the way they are thinking. Third, WHY teaches more complex geographical material, for example about the causes and effects of rainfall. It therefore needs to know how a complex physical system can be explained to a student with a partial understanding of it.

SOPHIE (SOPHisticated Instructional Environment, Brown, Burton and de Kleer, 1982) teaches students to find faults in electronic equipment that is not functioning properly. SOPHIE puts the initiative for learning on the student. It provides detailed feedback about the correctness or otherwise of proposed solutions to problems. This feedback includes counterexamples to incorrect hypotheses that students put forward. Because it lets the student take the lead, SOPHIE, unlike WHY, does not spontaneously identify misunderstandings that the student may have. Neither does it suggest ideas that have not occurred to the student. The sophistication of SOPHIE lies in its natural language interface and its inferential abilities. Its language processor, which is based on a semantic grammar (see chapter 5), allows SOPHIE to engage in more complex dialogues than SCHOLAR and WHY. Its inference mechanism underlies its ability to explain to students why their ideas are incorrect.

GUIDON (Clancey, 1984) teaches the kind of medical diagnosis performed by the expert system MYCIN (see pages 205–7). Indeed, GUIDON has the same knowledge about infectious diseases as MYCIN. However, MYCIN's rules have been reformulated for GUIDON. The new rules make up a system called NEOMYCIN, in which the diagnostic information is in a form more suitable for teaching purposes. In particular, NEOMYCIN makes explicit, information, for example about diagnostic strategies, that is only implicit in MYCIN. NEOMYCIN also contains additional information about the justification for NEOMYCIN's rules. This information is useful in deciding when a rule has been inappropriately applied. GUIDON, like other ICAI systems, engages in dialogues with students. However, it has more elaborate rules for structuring dialogues than many other systems. Its *discourse procedures* take account of the complexity of the material it is trying to teach, the student's understanding and the system's current teaching goal.

## LOGO

ICAI systems take a traditional approach to instruction – they attempt to *teach* subjects to students. Some AI researchers, particularly Papert (1980), have proposed more radical uses for computers in education. Papert suggests that children should be allowed free access to computers running the programming language LOGO. LOGO is a derivative of

LISP, but it is much simpler to use and to understand. Papert claims that if children use machines that solve problems in sensible ways, they will learn how to solve problems themselves as a by-product of using those machines. They will learn by doing rather than by being taught. His ideas are based partly on those of the child psychologist Piaget, who claimed that people learn primarily by interacting with their environment.

The best-known application of LOGO is *turtle geometry*. In turtle geometry, geometric concepts are learned through writing programs that control a 'turtle'. A turtle is basically a pencil holder that can move about on a sheet of paper leaving a track. It is made to look like a robot to hold the child's attention. Commands in TURTLE TALK, the subset of LOGO that controls the turtle, include FORWARD n and BACK n, which move the turtle n units in a straight line, and RIGHT n and LEFT n, which turn the turtle through n degrees. A program, which comprises a sequence of such commands, makes the turtle draw a picture. Papert claims that children who would otherwise have problems learning geometry find turtle geometry easy. However, he does not provide systematic empirical support for this claim. The educational worth of LOGO should become easier to evaluate now that versions of the language itself, together with turtles, are available for home microcomputers.

## CAD/CAM

CAD/CAM stands for *Computer-Aided Design and Computer-Aided Manufacture*. The long-term goal of CAD/CAM research is to develop environments in which the industrial processes of design and manufacture are integrated and automated through the use of computers. Much CAD/CAM research has its origins in branches of computer science other than artificial intelligence, but AI techniques are becoming more important in this field.

Design

The principal design tool in CAD/CAM is the computer

graphics package. Such packages produce displays that supplement or replace traditional technical drawings and blueprints. The major advantages of computer graphics are the ability to simulate the third dimension and the ability to scale and rotate displays on the screen. Such facilities create a much better impression of what a product will look like than 2-D drawings. The graphics display techniques used in CAD are not taken from AI. However, AI can suggest ways of organising information about the kinds of objects to be depicted.

## Robotics

Robotics is the CAM side of CAD/CAM. For many people the term *robot* suggests a metallic humanoid of the sort portrayed in science fiction stories and films. These fictional robots bear little resemblance to the devices called robots that are increasingly used in manufacturing industries. These robots perform such tasks as moving large parts on assembly lines, spray painting and spot welding. They are not intelligent.

The first generation of industrial robots carried out only *pick-and-place* tasks. Their movements were controlled by fixed stops. Second-generation robots – the painters and welders – go through fixed sequences of movements 'learned' from a human operator. These movements are stored in the robot's memory as the operator moves the robot through the series of positions that it occupies in performing its task. Third-generation robots will perform complex tasks without human intervention. These robots will be controlled on-line by one or more computers. Because they will be programmable, they will be more intelligent than second-generation robots. They will also have their own sensors – vision systems and touch receptors. Such robots are at present under development (see Brady, 1984, for a summary of current research).

### Motion

A typical industrial robot has much in common with a single human arm and hand. However, unlike human arms, most industrial robots are fixed in a permanent position – work is taken to the robot rather than vice versa. Mobile robots are only just becoming the subject of serious research. The problem of robot motion is how to get the *manipulator* at the end of the robot arm to the right position to carry out the various tasks that the robot has to perform. This problem can be solved using techniques from three branches of mathematics: *kinematics, statics* and *dynamics*.

Kinematics describes the movements of the parts of a robot in terms of positions, speeds and accelerations. The kinematics of robot motion is complicated by the fact that robots cannot only move in three dimensions, but can also twist at their joints. It is easy to determine the position of the robot's manipulator in its *workpace* from the positions of its joints. However, the much more useful computation of appropriate joint positions to get the manipulator to a particular point in space is harder. Indeed, for some types of robot arm this problem has no simple solution. Interestingly, one way to make the problem tractable is to give the robot an arm that can move like a human arm.

Statics gives an account of the forces and torques (turning forces) in the robot arm and their relation to forces and torques that the robot exerts on its environment. Dynamics deals with the forces needed to move the robot itself, and hence its manipulator, to a desired position. In robot dynamics, as in robot kinematics, the so-called *inverse* problem – given a desired position, determine the forces needed to move the manipulator to that position – is both the more important one and the more difficult one to solve.

The kinematics, statics and dynamics of any robot, intelligent or unintelligent, must be understood, if it is to be used successfully. However, those of first and second-generation robots can be treated in a simplified way, because of assumptions those robots make about their workspace. These assumptions, which require that assembly lines are arranged so that the robot's workspace is always the same, will not be made by intelligent robots. Such robots will, therefore, require different *control* techniques from earlier robots. In particular, they will have to perform kinematic and dynamic calculations on-line.

The simplest form of control is *open-loop control*. A robot under open-loop control does not monitor its environment. It simply executes a fixed sequence of actions. The kinematic specification of these actions can, therefore, be held in memory – on-line computations are not needed. However, if robots are to work in complex, changing environments they will have to plan different trajectories through a workspace to reach the same final position. They will also have to modify movements that are in progress to avoid obstacles that change from moment to moment. Such robots need to perform kinematic calculations quickly enough to enable them to make the required changes to their movements. They need to use *feedback control*.

AI techniques will play an important role in programming the movements of intelligent robots. The complex reasoning about 3-D space that such robots engage in will require methods of knowledge representation of the kind discussed in chapter 2. Planning techniques (see chapter 4) will also be needed, both for working out trajectories and for making higher-level decisions about the order in which tasks should be performed.

One final point about robot motion. If intelligent robots are to be programmed and reprogrammed in factories, relatively straightforward, high-level programming languages will be required. A number of such languages, such as PUMA, VAL, RAIL and AML, are being developed. They are intended for 'non-programmers'.

### Sensors

If they are to make rapid use of information from their environments, programmable robots will need more sophisticated sensory systems than those of first- and second-generation robots, many of which had no real sensors. In particular, intelligent robots will have tactile and visual sensors.

Robot hands that can pick up fragile objects have been in existence for some time. They use feedback about an object's reaction to the force they are applying to control the pressure of their grip. However, they have proved unsuitable for industrial applications, because their operation is slow and unreliable. Robots could also make use of other sorts of tactile information. If they could sense the precise shape and orientation of objects, for example, they could assemble delicate components, making the final small locatory movements under tactile control.

A major goal of robotics research is to provide robots with good visual inputs. Simple robot vision systems are already available. They provide two-dimensional information, which is sufficient for many tasks. For example, a robot may view from above items, such as machine parts or doughnuts, travelling along a conveyor belt. Any whose 2-D shape indicates a fault can be pushed or blown off the belt. In principle the visual-processing algorithms discussed in chapter 3 could be incorporated into robot vision systems. Robots could, for example, use 3-D information computed from two views of an object using a stereopsis algorithm. However, such algorithms are, at present, too slow. A stereopsis algorithm takes several minutes of processor time on a mainframe computer to analyse a single pair of images.

New technology will allow many current problems to be solved, and enable the production of robots with much better sensory systems. The most important development will be the use of *distributed processing*. Instead of a single computer controlling a robot, different aspects of its operation will be the responsibility of different processors. The kind of distributed processing that is needed will be made possible by VLSI (Very Large-Scale Integration) technology, which allows powerful computers to reside on small pieces of silicon ('chips'). Such processors can be mounted, for example, in robot hands. There they can carry out tactile processing locally (and extremely rapidly), only occasionally communicating with the processor with overall control of the robot.

VLSI will also make possible vision systems that process images quickly. The steropsis algorithms discussed in chapter 3, for example, perform the same computation over and over again at different points on the visual image. In the human visual system these computations are performed simultaneously by different neurons. VLSI will make parallel processors, and hence fast 3-D vision systems, a reality (see also chapter 2).

## Automatic programming

The study of *automatic programming* sounds like an attempt by AI researchers to make themselves redundant! In practice, the goal of this research is to make writing and debugging programs less tedious. There are two main approaches to this problem. The first is to provide tools that help to manage large programs. These tools are typically part of programming environments, such as those described in chapter 1. One of the most important kinds of tool is the *debugging* aid, which finds errors in programs. The simplest of these are the spelling checkers and syntax checkers that are built into many compilers and interpreters. More sophisticated debugging techniques require detailed knowledge about programming and what programs are intended to achieve. They use ideas from AI.

Sussman's (1975) HACKER, discussed in chapter 6, debugs faulty plans that it writes in the language CONNIVER. It uses information about the intentions underlying plans to help it find its mistakes. Goldstein's (1975) MYCROFT, also developed at MIT in the early 1970s, has similar debugging capabilities. MYCROFT helps children learn to write programs in TURTLE TALK that draw turtle geometry pictures. Among other things, it finds errors in the programs children write, so it can help them understand their mistakes. In order to identify and explain mistakes, MYCROFT uses detailed descriptions of the programs it assesses. MYCROFT takes two inputs. The first is a faulty program written by a child. The second is a *model* of the picture that the program is intended to draw. MYCROFT can construct plans for drawing pictures. It is therefore able to determine how the child's program differs from one based on a correct plan for drawing the picture.

The second approach to making programming easier is to get one program to write others. A program that writes programs takes as its input a description of the program it is trying to write. This description cannot be in the target programming language. It may be a statement in English, for example, or a specification of the input-output function to be computed. Systems that construct programs from specifications in English include PSI (Green, 1977), which writes LISP programs, and NLPQ (Natural Language Programming for Queuing Simulations, Heidhorn, 1975), which writes programs to solve queuing problems in a language called GPSS. However, programs that accept input in English are not very efficient, and they have produced only comparatively simple programs. They devote too much effort to natural language processing and not enough to automatic programming. CHI (Green and Westfold, 1982), a more powerful extension of PSI, requires its input descriptions to be in a more restricted format. They must be written in the 'very high-level language' V.

CHI combines the two approaches to automatic programming. It provides debugging and program-management facilities together with automatic code generation from high-level descriptions. The *programmer's apprentice* is a similar system, produced at MIT by Waters, Rich and Shrobe (See Rich, 1984, for a summary). There are versions for LISP and for FORTRAN. Like human apprentices, the programmer's apprentice carries out the routine parts of the task that it assists with. However, unlike them, it is not, at present, expected to learn the more difficult aspects of its trade. If apprentices are to be useful, they need some understanding of the task that they are learning. The programmer's apprentice understands programs in terms of plans that it constructs and stores in a plan library. Rich (1984) gives an example of the programmer's apprentice writing a simple procedure. Its plan results from a dialogue with its user, in which it may be given a specification of how a procedure is to be implemented – the apprentice knows about different types of program and can implement a procedure in a specified way. Initially, some parts of the implementation are schematic. Further dialogue determines the details of their implementation, again, perhaps as examples of certain types of procedure.

**Summary**

There are many possible applications for AI, since intelligent machines can, at least in principle, work more quickly, more accurately and in more adverse conditions than people. However, there are many obstacles, apart from inherent conservatism, to be overcome, before AI techniques are widely used in the real world. The most important of these can be summed up as follows: applied AI depends on fast, cheap, reliable computers (and programs).

Image processing is an example of a field in which computational techniques are already widely used, but in which AI has not yet had much influence. The main problem is that potentially relevant AI procedures are, at present, too slow. The AI vision algorithms that could be used to process images – and perhaps the AI knowledge-retrieval and reasoning systems that could predict and interpret visual features – will only work sufficiently quickly when they are implemented on parallel hardware.

The most important application of AI is expert systems. Expert systems were originally developed within AI and have been in existence for many years. They embody the knowledge of human experts, which even those experts find difficult to formulate and teach. That knowledge is typically, but not always, encoded as a set of productions. Most expert systems interact with people rather than working on their own. A reasonably knowledgeable person working with an expert system should perform like an expert. A good expert system can take many man-years to develop, though techniques for the automatic transfer of expertise from people to computers may reduce this period considerably. Problems for which expert systems have been developed include manipulating mathematical formulae (MACSYMA), determining the structure of organic molecules (DENDRAL), medical diagnosis (MYCIN, CADUCEUS, PUFF, CASNET), configuring computer systems (XCON) and geological prospecting (PROSPECTOR, DIPMETER ADVISOR). Some of these expert systems, in particular MACSYMA, DENDRAL and XCON, are in regular use.

Another area in which AI has many potential applications is education. AI techniques can greatly enhance computer-aided instruction systems, allowing them to teach a wider range of skills more successfully. The principal components of an intelligent CAI system are its knowledge base, which may take the form of an expert system, its model of the student and its teaching procedures. ICAI systems explain mistakes to students rather than just telling them when they are wrong. To do so they must combine their own knowledge with information about the kinds of errors that students can make.

A different approach to the use of AI in education has been suggested by Papert. He proposes that children should be allowed to use computers for themselves. To this end he has developed a simple programming language, LOGO. Papert hopes that children will learn problem-solving techniques by using machines to solve problems – a case of learning by doing. TURTLE TALK is a subset of LOGO that can be used to control the movements of a robot and, hence, to teach simple geometric concepts. The educational implications of Papert's ideas have not yet been fully evaluated.

CAD/CAM, computer-aided design and manufacture, is another area in which the influence of AI techniques is just beginning to be felt. These techniques will be more important in CAM than in CAD. They will be used to program third-generation industrial robots. These robots, unlike their predecessors, will be able to cope with changing environments. AI planning techniques will allow them to work out an appropriate way to perform a task, given the current environment. AI vision systems will help them sense the changes in the environment that they must respond to.

There are two approaches to 'automatic programming'. The first is to provide a set of tools for debugging and managing programs. This approach produces programming environments in which book-keeping and proof-reading chores are carried out automatically. The second is to get one program to write another, for example from a description in English of what the program is supposed to do. At present only very simple programs can be written in this way. The two approaches are combined in systems such as CHI and the programmer's apprentice.

# 8  Conceptual issues

This chapter addresses some general questions raised by AI research and the possibility of machines that think. The first is: in what sense can a computer or a computer program be a model of the mind? The mathematical theory of computability – a well-specified account of what computations, in the abstract sense of that term, are possible – provides a partial answer to this question. One view is that computers do not actually think, they merely simulate thought processes. Another is that, particularly when a computer interacts with the world in the way that people do, it can be correctly described as thinking. Searle argues against this view, which he calls *strong AI*. He suggests that we do not attribute mental predicates to people just because of the way they behave. We also take their biological make-up into account. His view has been described as 'protoplasm chauvinism'.

The widespread use of computers in society has already raised a number of moral issues. More intelligent machines will present more pressing problems, particularly if their decision making becomes difficult to understand. Perhaps their use should be discouraged. Weizenbaum (1976) argues that computers already encroach on areas of life that they should be excluded from. He claims that a mechanistic view of people, which is encouraged by the use of computers, can be dehumanising. However, he does not identify problems that are specific to computers, only those associated with technological progress in general. Nevertheless, computers pose these problems in a more acute form than they have been posed before.

## The computer as a model of the mind – Turing's thesis

The mathematical theory of computability was first developed in the 1930s. The theory specifies what computers can and cannot do and how much time and memory they need for the computations that they can perform. It therefore indicates the limitations of computational theories of the mind. The theory had its origins in several branches of mathematics. A number of mathematicians were independently searching for the smallest set of primitive operations needed to carry out any possible computation. When their proposals were worked out in detail, it was shown that they were equivalent.

One approach to the problem of computability was Turing's (1936). Turing formulated his ideas in terms of an abstract computing device called a Turing machine. A Turing machine performs its calculations with the help of a tape divided into squares, each of which can have one symbol on it. The Turing machine's primitive operations are reading and writing symbols on the tape and shifting and tape one square to the left or right. It uses a finite vocabulary of symbols, but its tape can be infinitely long. A Turing machine has only a finite number of internal states. When it reads the symbol on a square its state may change, depending on what state it is currently in and what the symbol is.

The structure of a Turing machine is very simple and so are the operations it performs. However, additional bits of 'machinery' – more tapes for example – do not increase the range of computations that a Turing machine can perform. They only increase its speed. Furthermore, these gains in efficiency are of no theoretical interest, since they speed up the machine's operation by only a constant factor.

It is possible to describe a *Universal Turing Machine*, constructed on the same principles as other Turing machines. The Universal Turing Machine can mimic the operation of any other Turing machine. To simulate another machine it must be given a description of how that machine works. This description can be written on to its tape in standard Turing machine format. Every general purpose digital computer is an approximation to a Universal Turing Machine. When it runs a program it behaves as if it were a machine for performing just the task that the program performs. It is a 'universal' machine simulating a more specific one. Digital computers can only be approximations to the Universal Turing Machine because no real machine has an infinitely large memory. It has nothing corresponding to a Turing machine's tape.

For technical reasons Turing called his theory the theory of *computable numbers*. It, and equivalent formulations of what became the theory of computability, such as Church's theory of *recursive functions*, can be seen as attempts to capture the informal notion of an *effective procedure*. An effective procedure is one that could be carried out automatically by a machine, with no human intervention – one whose result, when computed by a person, does not depend on 'intuition' or any other process not open to objective inspection. Turing conjectured that any effective procedure could be computed by a Turing machine – that his theory of computable numbers was a theory about effective procedures. He found support for this idea in the fact that all attempts to formalise the notion of an effective procedure led to the same result.

As Turing himself recognised, this conjecture – known as *Turing's thesis* – has far-reaching consequences for the study of human behaviour. If psychological processes are not inherently mysterious, but are a legitimate object of scientific study, then the truth of Turing's thesis would guarantee that those processes could be described in computational terms. In one sense, therefore, the computer metaphor for the mind is, despite Searle's (1984) claims, fundamentally different from earlier ones that compared minds with windmills, hydraulic systems and telephone exchanges. Anything the mind can do can be described as a computation. In Marr's terminology (see chapter 3) there is a computational theory for any psychological process. However, the existence of that theory leaves open the questions of what representation and algorithm the mind uses and how they are implemented. In particular, the mind is, in many respects, different from any digital computer.

## Can computers think?

The question that AI raises in most people's minds is: can a machine (really) think? This question can be asked in more and less sophisticated forms. One common reaction to the concept of artificial intelligence is: surely a collection of circuit boards and wires cannot think in the same way that a person can! But once the question is given serious consideration, it becomes clear that a satisfactory answer depends on an analysis of what is meant by *thinking* and also of what counts as a *machine*.

Turing (1950) was one of the first people to consider these questions in detail. He devised a test for whether a machine could think; or, rather, he suggested that the vaguely formulated question 'can a machine think?' should be replaced by an objective test. His test is based on a game in which one person, the interrogator, has to find out which of two other people, X and Y, is a man and which a woman. The interrogator asks X and Y questions by some means that allows them to conceal their identities. A modern version of the test might use an electronic mail system. One of X and Y gives helpful answers and the other tries to fool the interrogator, but the interrogator does not know which person takes which role. Turing asked the question: what would happen if a machine took the role of the person trying to fool the interrogator? If the machine is sophisticated enough to fool the interrogator as often as a person can, Turing suggests that we should admit it is intelligent.

There are no reports of machines playing Turing's 'imitation game'. There are, however, anecdotes about computers being mistaken for people. Weizenbaum's program ELIZA, which simulates a non-directive psychotherapist (see chapter 5), figures in most of them. People interacting with ELIZA often behave as if they were communicating with another person. Occasionally someone has apparently thought that ELIZA's responses were being typed at another terminal (see McCorduck, 1979, pp. 225–6 fn. for one such anecdote). These stories are embarrassing for adherents of Turing's thesis because ELIZA is not a very intelligent program. It does not really understand what is 'said' to it (see chapter 5), so it would be unfortunate if Turing's test suggested that ELIZA can think. However, it is harder to pass Turing's test than to generate output that could have been produced by a person. There are many circumstances in which a person, faced with the output of a program, might justifiably think that they were communicating with another person. In such circumstances context contributes to their being fooled. Nevertheless, these anecdotes about ELIZA raise the question of whether Turing's test provides an adequate criterion for whether a machine can think.

Turing formulated his ideas as the first computers were being constructed. There was no question of ascribing mental predicates to such machines, partly because there were no working AI programs – though Turing himself had suggested how write one that played chess. In general, AI researchers have not worried too much about whether machines can think. Most of them have accepted, at least implicitly, a functionalist account of mental predicates. This account holds that such predicates are ascribed on the basis of behaviour, not on the details of the mechanisms – neurons vs. integrated circuits – that produce that behaviour. If a program's behaviour is sufficiently like that of a person, then it can be called intelligent, even if no program yet written meets this criterion.

The deeper implications of AI research for our ideas about what constitutes thinking have been left for philosophers to consider. One question that philosophers have raised is whether computer programs (or machines running those programs) actually think, or whether they only simulate thinking. This question can also be asked of more specific cognitive predicates that might be ascribed to machines. Do they really see or do they just simulate seeing? Do they understand language or do they just simulate understanding? And so on.

The idea that computers only simulate thought processes is suggested by an analogy between AI programs and certain other types of program. Computer programs can simulate a country's economy or a weather system. However, such programs do not take out billion-dollar loans from the IMF or blow from the south-west. They simulate economic or meteorological phenomena without instantiating them. Perhaps AI programs are better described as simulations of, say, language understanding rather than as 'machines' that understand language.

One difference between AI programs and simulations suggests a reply to this argument. The input to a program that simulates a country's economy is a *representation* of various aspects of that economy. Language-understanding programs process, or at least they might eventually be expected to process, real sentences. A different analogy may, therefore, be more illuminating. An economic simulation does not enter into financial transactions, but a bank's computer does, particularly if the bank has cash dispensers. Its computations result in decisions about what to do with real cash. Perhaps the question of whether a machine thinks depends on what it is used for. A program written as part of a research project might only simulate language understanding. Furthermore, it might be described as processing *representations* of sentences, though the distinction between a sentence and a representation of one is difficult to draw, because a sentence is itself symbolic. A computer program answering questions about train times in a railway station, and thus guiding people's actions, might truly be said to understand (certain aspects of) language.

## Can symbols have meanings for computers?

The questions of whether machines can think is closely related to another: do the symbols that a computer uses have any meaning for it, or do they only mean something to its operator? The answer to this question depends on what it means to say that a symbol has a meaning for a person. Those people – again mainly philosophers – who have tried to answer this question have always found it perplexing. It cannot be resolved in an introductory text on AI. However, it is worth devoting some space to.

Consider a computer working on a 'difficult' multiplication problem. The operator types in two (large) numbers; the machine multiplies them together and prints the answer. If the program is easy to use, the input and output should be the same as those of a mathematician (say 384757, 79685 and 30659361545). However, it seems wrong to say that these symbols have the same meaning for the computer as they do for the person. The computer does not, for example, use numbers to count in the way that people do. Furthermore, it seems that the operations of the computer are determined solely by the *form* of the symbols it processes, and not by any relation that those symbols have with things outside the computer. To put this another way, the computer apparently treats its input and output as numerals, not as numbers. Only the programmer makes a connection between the two.

The idea that computers manipulate symbols solely on the basis of their *formal* properties has been championed by Fodor (e.g. 1980). Since Fodor accepts the computer metaphor for the mind, he concludes that mental processes are formal processes. However, although this view is true in one sense, it is misleading insofar as it suggests that the relation between symbols and the world is unimportant in explaining psychological processes. A computer program for multiplication, say, or language understanding, contains rules that refer to the formal properties of symbols. However, those rules must be formulated so that they are appropriate for manipulating representations of numbers or natural language. The rules make *direct* reference only to formal properties of symbols, but the choice of rules depends on what the symbols they manipulate stand for.

Searle (1980) argues that because computer programs are only symbol manipulators they cannot actually be intelligent. He refers to the view that a computer (running the right program) has mental states and is, therefore, an artificial intelligence, as *strong AI*. Weak AI, which Searle accepts, rests on the uncontroversial claim that the computer is a useful tool for studying the mind. However, it denies that mental predicates can be ascribed to computers.

Searle tries to make a case against strong AI in his *Chinese room argument*. The Chinese room is a place where, in a certain sense, questions about stories in Chinese are answered. They are answered by people who know no Chinese, but who are able to perform complex manipulations of Chinese symbols using rules stated in (say) English. In particular, Searle considers a person in the Chinese room who is given three sets of symbols, together with rules in English. To someone outside the room – someone who understands Chinese – the three sets of symbols correspond to a script, a script-based story and a set of questions about the story (see chapter 5). The rules can be used to compute new sets of symbols that are to be sent out of the room (answers to the questions). *Ex hypothesi*, the person in the Chinese room does not understand Chinese. Searle argues that, therefore, a computer program that performs the same task as that person cannot be said to understand Chinese either. Cognitive states cannot be attributed to something 'solely in virtue of [its] being a computer with a right sort of program' (1980, p. 422).

This statement reveals that Searle is arguing against a straw man. Few people have claimed that a machine can think *solely* because it runs the right sort of program. We attribute cognitive states to things that interact with the world in certain ways, things that are sufficiently like ourselves to warrant that attribution. The interesting question is: what counts as being sufficiently like ourselves? It is a question that is notoriously hard to answer. For example, there are many cases in which we are undecided about whether a cognitive attribution to an animal is justified. Do monkeys have fears, intentions or beliefs, for example? And what about rats, pigeons and butterflies?

The Chinese room turns out to be irrelevant. The crux of Searle's argument is a claim about the basis on which cognitive states are attributed. Among the possible replies to the Chinese room argument that he discusses is one in which it is not a program that is said to understand Chinese, but a robot whose behaviour is controlled by the program. Most AI researchers would not find it unreasonable to say that such a robot understands Chinese. Searle rejects this idea, along with the suggestion that the robot provides an argument for strong AI, on two grounds. First, he claims that our willingness to say the robot understands Chinese depends on its *behaviour*, not on the fact that it runs a program of a certain type (cf. his definition of strong AI). Second, he holds that, once it is discovered that the robot's behaviour can be explained by a program, the ascription of cognitive states will be withdrawn. Searle regards 'this robot has mental states' and 'a program is running inside this robot' as alternative explanations of its behaviour. He does not allow the possibility that the two explanations operate at different levels and are, therefore, compatible.

Searle's view is that, ultimately, we are only prepared to attribute cognitive states to things that are made from the same sort of stuff as ourselves. The reason, he claims, is that we believe certain causal properties of that stuff give rise to those states. Intentionality – the ability of mental representations to refer to things outside minds – is, according to Searle, a *biological* phenomenon. It cannot be explained in terms of programs, since they only manipulate symbols and do not take account of what those symbols stand for. Searle's view has been referred to (e.g. by Torrance, 1986) as *carbon* (or *protoplasm*) chauvinism. Searle's only basis for denying that robots think is that they are not made of flesh and blood.

## The limits of AI

Are there limits to what the science of artificial intelligence can achieve? One limitation is suggested by Searle's arguments. If he is right, we will never make machines that think unless we learn to construct artificial people out of biological building blocks.

Searle's views were, to some extent, anticipated by Dreyfus (1979) in his book *What Computers Can't Do*. Dreyfus's critique of AI is based largely on his assessment of early AI research – his book was first published in 1972. It is based on a small number of recurring arguments. One is that AI programs rely too much on *ad hoc* solutions to problems. They do not point to the general principles that underlie intelligent behaviour. This point has been answered in part by the recent systematisation of AI findings and in part by Marr's demand for computational theories (see chapter 3). Dreyfus's second argument is that no program – at least no program written before 1972 – behaves in a way that could really be called intelligent. Dreyfus held this view even though he was defeated at chess by Greenblatt's

MACHACK (see chapter 4). He still holds it, despite the greater sophistication of recent programs. However, Dreyfus does not say what a program would have to do for him to accept that it was intelligent, so the empirical content of his claim is unclear.

Dreyfus's remaining arguments suggest that certain aspects of human thought, particularly its creative and affective aspects, have never been, and can never be, modelled using AI techniques. He makes three main points in support of this claim. First, many thought processes are essentially *analogical*, not digital. They cannot be described or explained in terms of rules that manipulate symbols. They cannot, therefore, be embodied in a computer program. However, since any analogical process can be simulated digitally, Dreyfus's claim is about the implementation of mental computations, not their results. It has no direct bearing on what sorts of thing a machine can do. The other two points are more closely related to Searle's claims. They are that computers do not have human-like bodies, and that they do not take part in human *forms of life*. Dreyfus argues that the attribution of intelligence and other cognitive predicates depends crucially on both how people are constituted and how they behave. A computer cannot enjoy a prawn cocktail, or suffer the consequences if the prawns are off. It cannot, therefore, understand what it is for a person to do these things.

As an alternative to AI, Dreyfus offers the philosophical doctrine of phenomenology as a way of understanding human behaviour. Most AI researchers and experimental psychologists find phenomenology too vague. If behaviour can only be explained – or rather described – phenomenologically, there is little hope of a *scientific* psychology.

## Moral issues

Almost inevitably, scientific discoveries have applications – applications that may have good or bad effects or, more commonly, a mixture of the two. Partly as a result of their participation in the development of atomic weapons, scientists have become more aware of their responsibility for the uses to which their findings are put. AI workers are no exception. They have worried about possible misapplications of intelligent machines.

Computers have many uses. Some of them, for example the maintenance of large databases, have already posed ethical problems and prompted legislation. More intelligent programs could lead to more serious moral dilemmas, particularly if some of the wilder speculations of science fiction writers (and AI workers!) become reality. This possibility raises the following question: in what circumstances should our choices be guided by computers that are, in some sense, more intelligent than ourselves? This problem becomes particularly acute when the decision-making processes of those computers are difficult, or even impossible, for people to understand.

The answer cannot be that we should never be guided by computers. We already use machines that are better at arithmetic than we are. However, we understand how they carry out their computations and we know that they (usually) produce results that we call correct. We also know, at least in principle, how to tell when they are malfunctioning. If intelligent machines pose only the same sorts of problem as payroll computers, we will simply have to be cautious about relying on them. The more momentous the consequences of a decision, and the more difficult it is to assess whether a proposed decision is correct, the more cautious we will have to be. In particular, there would be a problem if a computer's justification for a decision was too long to absorb before action had to be taken. There remains, also, the possibility of machines that are both more intelligent than us and more autonomous than present-day computers. They might act in ways that we can neither understand nor control.

Such speculations are, to some extent, idle. However, Weizenbaum (1976) argues that, even now, there are areas of our lives from which computers should be excluded, in particular those in which there is any kind of interpersonal interaction. Weizenbaum argues that a mechanistic view of people can be dehumanising. It is, therefore, one that should be treated with caution. He believes that we have been too eager to embrace such a view, and that it has already had detrimental effects. For example, he argues that it was partly to blame for Nazi atrocities against the Jews. Weizenbaum also claims that computers have been used to preserve aspects of our society that otherwise would, and in his view should, have succumbed to pressure for change. What Weizenbaum fails to show, however, is that computers pose any special threat that other products of technology do not, except in so far as people are prepared to turn decisions made by computers into choices for action. The 'decisions' of previous machines have been to easy to see through. Computers, at least for the present, are only tools that may be used for good or evil, depending on the motives of their users. Furthermore, there is nothing intrinsically wrong with mechanical metaphors. It is the uses to which those metaphors are put that are good or bad. Indeed, it can be argued that AI suggests better mechanical metaphors – one that do more justice to the complexities of human thought and behaviour – without claiming that the mind is essentially mysterious. Showing that the mind can be understood is not necessarily to devalue it.

## Summary

Computer programs that behave intelligently raise two kinds of 'philosophical' question. First, there are questions about the way computers and computer programs help us to understand mental processes. Second, there are those about the use of such machines.

There have been many attempts to compare minds to mechanical devices: windmills, pumps and telephone exchanges, for example. These metaphors were inadequate, but the computer metaphor promises to be different, because of the theory of computability and Turing's thesis. The theory of computability can be seen as an attempt to formalise the notion of an effective procedure – any series of operations that can be carried out by a mechanical device. If it does formalise this notion – if Turing's thesis is true – and if the mind can be understood scientifically, then any mental process can be described in computational terms.

The question of whether a computer can think is one that AI has always prompted. Simulations of weather systems do not rain, so perhaps AI programs only simulate thinking rather than instantiating it. However, an AI program could control a robot whose behaviour was similar to that of a person. It would be hard to deny, on behavioural evidence, that such a robot could think. Searle has suggested that, nevertheless, such machines cannot think, because they are not biologically constituted. Only things like people think and to be like a person is to be built out of organic components. This view has been disparagingly referred to as carbon chauvinism.

A related question is whether symbols have meanings for computers or only for their operators. Again an answer in terms of what the computer does with those symbols suggests itself – if it uses them to interact with the world they have meaning for it. However, Searle would reject this argument.

On Searle's view AI has definite limits. Machines made of silicon and metal can never think. Dreyfus has also argued that there are limits to what AI can achieve. Some of his arguments are similar to Searle's and make reference to our biological constitution. The others rest on his evaluation of early AI programs. However, Dreyfus's failure to respond to recent developments, and his suggested alternative to AI – phenomenology – have not been well accepted in the AI community.

Some uses of computers, for example, the maintenance of large databases, have already posed ethical problems. More intelligent machines will probably give rise to more serious dilemmas. Weizenbaum argues that there are areas of life, particularly those involving human interaction, from which computers should be excluded. He claims that computers encourage a dehumanising, mechanistic view of human behaviour that has already been responsible for much evil. However, he has failed to show that computers are fundamentally different from any other technological development. They are simply more complex.

# 9 Future directions

AI began about thirty years ago, soon after the first electronic computing devices were constructed. Great progress has been made in those thirty years and that progress seems likely to continue. What direction will AI take? Predicting the future is always a dangerous occupation. Nevertheless, I will close this book by indicating developments that are likely in the next few years.

Chapter 1 identified two reasons why psychology students should find out about AI. The first is that psychological theories already incorporate ideas from AI and can be difficult to understand without a grounding in that discipline. In the future cognitive psychology will be even more closely integrated with AI in the discipline of cognitive science, so a knowledge of AI will be even more crucial. The second is that, because of their professional training and interests, psychologists are well placed to investigate the efficient use of computers in everyday life. Both of these reasons for getting acquainted with AI will increase in importance. In the study of cognition, psychologists will no longer simply borrow ideas from AI. The inter-disciplinary approach of cognitive science will put psychologists who do not know about AI at an impossible disadvantage. Cognitive scientists will need skills drawn from both AI and psychology. Nevertheless, cognitive science may not provide the answer to every problem in the study of cognition. It remains to be seen, for example, whether cognitive science, with its broadly functionalist perspective, can explain the 'biological' and 'social' components of cognition – those aspects that depend on our biological constitution and our social institutions. However, at present there is no viable alternative to the computational (functional) approach to cognition and most work in the foreseeable future will be carried out within that framework.

As computers become more common and easier to use, ordinary people will interact with them more often in their daily lives. The task of making these computers easier to use *ought* to fall, in large part, to psychologists. However, there is a danger that psychologists will not be consulted, for two reasons. First, computer scientists may not always realise the importance of psychological questions. Second, some of the early psychological work on Man-Machine Interaction (MMI), or Human-Computer Interaction (HCI) as it is known in non-sexist circles, has been poor. HCI is not strictly part of AI. However, psychologists with a knowledge of computers can expect, if they ensure that their expertise is taken account of, to make increasingly important contributions to HCI and, indeed, to human factors in general research. Furthermore, as the machines with which people interact become more intelligent, human factors researchers will need to take increasing account of AI.

Chapter 1 also discussed the research tools of AI, both hardware and software. AI will, of course, continue to benefit from the increasing sophistication and power of both computers and computer programs. However, the availability of more powerful computers by itself cannot produce insights into the nature of intelligence. Computers and programs are tools that can be used wisely or foolishly. A more powerful computer can perform more computations, but more computations are of little interest in pure AI research unless they help to produce insights into the principles underlying intelligent behaviour. Chess-playing programs such as CRAY BLITZ (see chapter 4), for example, play better chess than earlier programs with heuristic rules, but they provide fewer insights into human chess playing. Computational power can be an advantage in the applications of AI, where it may directly remove obstacles to progress, but in pure AI research human brain power is still of prime importance.

It is more difficult to predict where advances will occur in the substantive areas of AI research discussed in chapters 2 to

6 – representation, vision, thinking, language and learning. In the realm of knowledge representation two things are fairly certain. First, the formalisation of mundane knowledge and common-sense reasoning, including reasoning about other people's mental states (cf. Haas, 1986) and naive physics, will remain an important, and very difficult, area of research. Non-monotonic logics will be further investigated, and formal results of the type reported by Etherington (1987) will become increasingly important. Whether non-monotonic logics will provide the basis of the solution, or set of solutions, to the problems of everyday reasoning is hard to foresee.

Second, there will be continuing development of massively parallel models of cognitive processes. The diversity of the assumptions underlying these models, which has been obscured by broad labels such as connectionism and parallel distributed processing (PDP), will also become more apparent. The controversy surrounding connectionist models is likely to increase. Proponents of PDP claim that it represents a new paradigm for studying cognitive processes, while its detractors say it is just a new way of implementing old ideas. However, even if it is at present primarily the latter, it may yet develop into the former. PDP models are not part of mainstream AI. However, because the brain is a massively parallel, distribute processing system, such models will play an increasingly prominent role in cognitive science.

Work on computer vision continues apace, though there are signs that it is separating off from mainstream AI. There are three related reasons for this development. First, Marr died, prematurely, in 1980 and subsequent research has tended to lack two important qualities that he brought to the study of vision. One is the desire for a maximally general theory of (human) vision. The other is the ability to link computational results to findings from psychology and neurophysiology. Second, Draper's work, discussed in chapter 3, showed that research on the interpretation of line drawings of the BLOCKSWORLD and related domains could not form the basis of a general theory of object recognition. BLOCKS-WORLD object-recognition research has always been the point of closest contact between computer vision and main-stream AI. The only other general approach to object recognition, the generalised cone approach of Marr and Nishihara, has not been developed to any great extent since Marr's death. The general problem of object recognition is very difficult. It is unlikely that a solution will emerge in the near future. Nevertheless, much will be learned from applied research in which specific discriminations between objects have to be made to perform particular tasks.

The third reason why computer vision research is drifting away from the rest of AI is implicit in this last comment. Much of the current work on low-level vision is applied research. It forms part of an attempt to develop robot vision systems. This work is becoming increasingly technical and requires a grounding in mathematics as well as in AI programming. An example of the kind of mathematical development that is becoming increasingly important in computer vision research is the widespread use of Hough transforms (see Mayhew and Frisby, 1984, pp. 345–50 for a review of this work).

In low-level vision there will be continuing refinement of the shape extraction algorithms that write information into the 2½-D sketch. More of the processes that contribute to this sketch will be studied in detail (see Ikeuchi, 1984 for the work on extraction of shape from texture gradient). Connectionist models of low-level vision will be further developed and this approach will be extended to higher levels of visual processing (cf. Ballard, 1984).

At a more abstract level, there continues to be a controversy over Marr's claim that low-level vision in humans is a purely bottom-up process. However, since both top-down and bottom-up vision systems can be made to work, it is difficult to see how this debate can be resolved until it is made more concrete. Perhaps the only way to find out how the human visual system works will be to carry out experimental work, in psychology and neurophysiology, testing the predictions of the different models.

Problem solving and game playing is another area of research that is no longer at the forefront of AI. In this case the reason is that the 'simple' obstacles to progress, such as finding general ways of thinking about clearly defined problems and searching for their solutions, have been resolved. Getting machines to solve ill-defined everyday problems is harder, and it is unlikely that there will be major developments in the next few years. However, there will be further progress on technical issues, such as the refinement and efficient implementation of algorithms such as alpha-beta pruning.

In the domain of problem solving, in which attention has traditionally focused on simpler problems, the challenge is not to write programs that can solve the problems, but to relate the behaviour of programs to that of human problem solvers. Achieving this goal is made difficult by such fundamental problems as deciding whether people use rules of mental logic in problem solving (see e.g. Johnson-Laird, 1983, who argues that they do not). Within cognitive science, if not within AI, more adequate models of human problem solving will be formulated. On the computational side, connectionist models will show how, in this as in other areas, people can appear to be using rules when those rules are nowhere explicitly represented in their minds.

In theorem proving uniform methods based on the resolution algorithm are a thing of the past. Except in a limited range of applications, they have to be replaced by domain-specific methods such as those proposed by Bundy for various branches of mathematics. However, formalising those methods for the relatively constrained domain of mathematics has proved difficult. In less constrained domains it will be more difficult still. Indeed, domain-specific methods are required to model everyday reasoning, which is one of the reasons why this type of reasoning poses such a difficult challenge to AI. There will, nevertheless, be a large amount of work on everyday reasoning, because that kind of reasoning has many potential applications in expert systems and other information services.

Computer game playing, and in particular computer chess, is at present dominated by a number-crunching approach that is alien to AI. Again, it is unclear when, if ever, more intelligent programs will regain their former edge in this field, particularly given that, in recent times, the amount of work on the simulation of human chess play has been comparatively small.

AI research on language production and understanding is, to a large extent, driven by the prospect of applications in the form of computers that can converse with people. A great deal of money is already committed to long-term projects on speech perception and production, so the next few years will see a continuing effort on that front. Intelligent speech processing requires syntactic and semantic processing as well as analysis at lower levels. For example, an ambiguity about a word boundary (e.g. *nitrate* vs. *night rate*) or the identity of a word (e.g. *please* vs. *pleas*) can often be resolved on the basis of syntactic and semantic context. Indeed, a uniform approach for grouping sounds into words and words into phrases and sentences, often a version of chart parsing, is currently finding favour.

At a higher level, the topics in dialogue understanding discussed at the end of chapter 5 will remain important, partly because of their intrinsic interest, and partly because they will have to be solved before intelligent dialogue systems can be used in the real world. However, such systems are long-term prospects. Except in very limited domains, realistic dialogue systems are unlikely to come into use in the near future.

Getting machines to learn remains one of the major challenges in AI. Despite the advances sketched in chapter 6, there are few examples of machines learning things that substantially increase their 'intelligence'. Learning is important for many reasons, not least because part of what we mean by intelligence is the flexibility of behaviour that goes along with the ability to learn. That ability enables us to cope with situations that we cannot foresee. Because a person can learn so much, many AI researchers feel that trying to program all the knowledge and skills of a really intelligent system will prove too difficult. Until machines can learn for themselves they will never display certain types of intelligence. The most important recent development in computer learning is learning by connection machines. Such machines, unlike the induction programs discussed in chapter 6, can learn concepts without having to build them out of others that they already know. They can also appear to learn rules without constructing internal representations of them. At present connection machines learn very slowly. The next few years will see a more extensive exploration of the learning capabilities of these machines and provide a clearer indication of whether and how they might help to explain intelligence.

Several areas of AI research that will be driven by their applications have already been mentioned. Since the possibility of applications generates finance, this trend is bound to continue. There will also be an increase in the number of computer applications that incorporate AI techniques. One example was mentioned in chapter 7. Work in robotics – both in robot vision and in robot motion – will, in future, be much more AI-influenced, as more intelligent robots are called for.

It hardly needs saying that work on expert systems will continue apace, at least in the short term. However, many people are sceptical about the usefulness of small expert systems. Such systems can be readily produced – many of them have been or are being developed. The question is whether their decisions can safely be followed by someone who is not an expert or whether they need expert assessment. If their decisions cannot be followed blindly, they will not replace experts, but only make their jobs a little easier. The next few years should provide some indication of how such systems perform in practice and of whether their users are, or should be, satisfied. To answer this question well-designed and conducted field trials are essential, though whether they will be carried out remains to be seen.

The use of computers and, in particular, AI programming languages in education will continue to increase. Languages such as LOGO, PROLOG and POP-11 will begin to replace BASIC both at home and at school. However, the shortage of people able to teach these languages in schools will inevitably slow down their adoption. In the longer term this problem will be alleviated by an increase in computer literacy among young people. This rise in computer literacy will also increase the number of people able to engage in programming projects of all kinds. In an indirect way, these developments will, therefore, contribute to both the quantity and quality of AI research.

I have already alluded to developments in robotics. These developments will contribute to the move towards what is already being called *computer integrated manufacture* (CIM). In

CIM, interconnected computers control all stages in the manufacture of an item, from the initial design to quality control, packaging and dispatch. Robots will also play an increasingly important role on the production line. The initial problems of CIM, for example getting different machines to communicate with one another, are rather far removed from AI, but as these problems are solved, the potential application of AI techniques in CIM will become apparent.

AI programmers already gain considerable benefits from the 'automatic programming' tools provided in the programming environments described in chapters 1 and 7. There is still a long way to go before complex programs can be produced from natural-language descriptions, a possibility that is sometimes referred to as 'using English as a programming language'. However, pressure from users will ensure that increasingly sophisticated software is available for AI programming. This sophistication will, in the next few years, come largely from developments that take the drudgery out of programming, such as those described in chapter 7.

In what sense could there be progress in resolving the philosophical issues discussed in chapter 8? First, it is possible, though highly unlikely, that developments in the foundations of mathematics will throw new light on Turing's thesis. Second, technological developments will force us towards a resolution of the other questions discussed in that chapter – 'do computers think?' and 'what should we do about the moral dilemmas posed by artificial intelligences?' Advances in AI will result in the construction of machines with capabilities that present-day machines do not have. It will no longer be possible to discuss those questions in such a detached way.

One perspective on the question of whether such machines can think is suggested by the work of the philosopher Wittgenstein. Wittgenstein suggests that there is not necessarily a predetermined answer to any question that our language allows us to pose. 'Can machines think?' might be just such a question. The words *machine* and *think* were developed for use in contexts in which this question does not arise. Faced with machines that we are tempted to describe as thinking, we have to make a *decision* about whether to *extend* the senses of mental predicates so that they apply to such machines. Wittgenstein did not claim that this decision was an arbitrary one. It is guided by many considerations about the current use of those concepts. However, it is an illusion to think that present customs of linguistic usage must contain an answer to every question that can be posed.

Technological developments will also force us to face the moral dilemmas posed by more intelligent computers. When those computers can be built, we will be forced to make decisions about their use. However, in the case of these moral dilemmas, unlike that of the conceptual questions, the fact that more intelligent machines are not yet with us does not absolve us of our responsibility for considering the potential problems before they are.

Much of the increased activity in AI will lead to new insights into the nature of intelligence and will, therefore, be of intellectual interest, especially to cognitive psychologists trying to develop an understanding of the human mind. However, there is one danger that psychologists must avoid. If AI flourishes while psychology languishes, it may happen that all the interesting questions about human behaviour are 'stolen' by computer scientists, who will try to answer them without taking notice of potentially relevant psychological research. That would be a pity, because psychologists, particularly those with knowledge of AI, have much to offer to that study.

# A brief guide to the AI literature

The literature of every academic subject has its idiosyncrasies, and that of AI is no exception. Many aspects of that literature reflect the relative youth and comparatively small extent of AI. This brief guide is intended to alert psychologists to points at which their expectations about the AI literature may not be met.

Perhaps the most important difference between the literatures of AI and psychology is the role of periodicals in the two disciplines. In psychology the most important new findings are published in a wide range of more or less specialised journals. In AI there have been, until recently, very few journals, and the best research has often not appeared in them. Before 1970 there were no journals devoted specifically to AI, and for some time after that there was only one. Indeed the fact that this journal, *Artificial Intelligence*, was the only one is reflected in the name by which it is informally known, '*the* AI journal'. Since 1977, *Artificial Intelligence* has been joined by *Cognitive Science*, which, although interdisciplinary in nature, has carried a preponderance of articles on AI. A few other periodicals, for example the *Communications of the Association for Computing Machinery*, have also published articles related to AI (see the bibliography for further examples).

Although some of the best AI research has appeared in *Artificial Intelligence*, much of it has seen less formal publication, as in other comparatively youthful disciplines. Indeed, from about 1970 onwards, technical reports issued by the major AI laboratories and, more recently, commercial organisations supporting AI research, such as Xerox, Bolt, Berenek and

Newman (BBN) and the Rand Corporation, have been a major source of information about new research in AI. Formal accounts of this work appeared much later, if ever. In some cases I have been unable to avoid references to technical reports in the bibliography. Fortunately these reports are more widely available than 'unpublished' manuscripts in psychology.

In the last few years, with the upturn in interest in AI, a number of new journals have appeared, and there has been an increasing trend towards formal publication. Another indication of this trend is the appearance of many more monographs and edited volumes. However, it will be some time before the technical report entirely disappears from the AI literature.

Conference proceedings form another important section of the less formal AI literature. These proceedings typically comprise short reports of new research. The most important are those of the biennial International Joint Conference on Artificial Intelligence (IJCAI), the annual meetings of the American Association for Artificial Intelligence (AAAI) and the Association for Computational Linguistics (ACL), and the irregular Theoretical Issues in Natural Language Processing (TINLAP) conferences.

With technical reports often taking the place of book chapters, and even monographs, the number of books on AI is smaller than might be expected. In the period up to 1970 the edited volumes by Feigenbaum and Feldman (1963) and Minsky (1968) were particularly important. However, as the bibliography of this book indicates, much of the research of this period was reported in obscure conference procedings. The late 1960s also saw the publication of the first volume (Collins and Michie, 1967) in the *Machine Intelligence* series. In the 1970s more edited collections appeared, of which Schank and Colby (1973), Bobrow and Collins (1975) and Winston (1975a) are important examples. A number of doctoral dissertations were also published as books, for example Winograd (1972), Sussman (1975) and Sacerdoti (1977). In the mid-1970s the first AI texts appeared (e.g. Hunt, 1975; Raphael, 1976).

The publication of these texts reflected the fact that undergraduate and postgraduate classes in AI were beginning to attract substantial numbers of students. With the exception of Bundy (1978) and Bowden (1977), these texts were intended primarily for students in the United States. Their style is similar to that of American texts for advanced psychology undergraduates. However, they were written primarily for students in computer science. More recent texts include Nilsson (1980), Rich (1983), Winston (1984, 2nd edition) and Charniak and McDermott (1985). These books differ somewhat in style and content. The last two are broadly similar. They are organised around major research areas and describe particular research projects in some detail. They 'rewrite' the history of AI, in order to present a more coherent picture. Rich takes a similar approach, but presents knowledge representation and problem solving as the central concerns of AI, treating other topics, such as language processing, as 'advanced' applications of ideas from these basic areas. Nilsson's book is rather different, in two ways. First, it treats AI as applied logic. Second, it focuses on general issues rather than on specific research projects. For the beginning student it is less approachable than the others. For those who want to study AI programming, a number of books are available. However, programming cannot be learned from a book – access to a computer is essential. The books each focus on a particular language. Winston and Horn (1984) and Charniak, Riesbeck and McDermott (1980) introduce LISP. Both books also provide extensive tuition in the writing of AI programs. Barrett, Ramsay and Sioman (1985) and Clocksin and Mellish (1981) describe the languages POP-11 and PROLOG respectively, but they devote comparatively little space to the specifics of AI progamming. Ramsay and Barrett (1987) describe how to write AI programs in POP-11.

For those who want more information than a textbook provides, but who cannot consult the primary literature, perhaps because they do not have access to it or because they find it too daunting, one publication bridges the gap between textbooks and the technical literature, *The Handbook of Artificial Intelligence* (3 vols, Barr and Feigenbaum, 1981, 1982; Cohen and Feigenbaum, 1982). Despite its bland and sometimes uninspiring style, this book is an essential reference for AI research up to the early 1980s.

Finally, some lighter reading. McCorduck (1979) outlines the history of AI research, largely as related to her by its practitioners. Hodges (1983) provides a very readable biography of Turing, one of the pioneers of modern digital computing. Haugeland (1985) makes one of many attempts to come to terms with the philosophical issues surrounding AI.

# Bibliography

Allen, J.F. and Perrault, C.R. (1980), 'Analyzing intentions in dialogues', *Artificial Intelligence*, vol. 15, pp. 143–78.

Angluin, D. (1978), 'Inductive inference of formal languages from positive data', *Information and Control*, vol. 45, pp. 117–35.

Appelt, D.E. (1985), 'Planning English referring expressions', *Artificial Intelligence*, vol. 26, pp. 1–33.

Ballard, D.H. (1984), 'Parameter nets', *Artificial Intelligence*, vol. 22, pp. 235–67.

Barr, A. and Feigenbaum, E.A. (1981), *The Handbook of Artificial Intelligence*, vol. 1, Los Altos, Calif., William Kaufmann.

Barr, A. and Feigenbaum, E.A. (1982), *The Handbook of Artificial Intelligence*, vol. 2, Los Altos, Calif., William Kaufmann.

Barrett, R., Ramsay, A. and Sloman, A. (1985), *POP-11: A Practical Language for Artificial Intelligence*, Chichester, Ellis Horwood.

Barrow, H.G. and Tenenbaum, J.M. (1978), 'Recovering intrinsic scene characteristics from images', in A. R. Hanson and E. M. Reisman (eds), *Computer Vision Systems*, New York, Academic Press.

Bartlett, F.C. (1932), *Remembering: A Study in Experimental and Social Psychology*, Cambridge, Cambridge University Press.

Berliner, H. and Campbell, M. (1984), 'Using chunking to solve chess pawn endgames', *Artificial Intelligence*, vol. 23, pp. 97–120.

Bernstein, A., Arbuckle, T., Roberts, M. de V. and Belsky, M.A. (1958), 'A chess-playing program for the IBM 704 computer', *Proceedings of the Western Joint Computer Conference*, vol. 16, pp. 157–9.

Berwick, R.C. (1983), 'Computational aspects of discourse', in M. Brady and R. C. Berwick (eds), *Computational Models of Discourse*, Cambridge, Mass., MIT Press.

Berwick, R.C. (1985), *The Acquisition of Syntactic Knowledge*, Cambridge, Mass., MIT Press.

Bledsoe, W.W. (1977), 'Non-resolution problem solving', *Artificial Intelligence*, vol. 9, pp. 1–35.

Bobrow, D.G. (1968), 'Natural language input for a computer problem-solving system', in M. Minsky (ed.), *Semantic Information Processing*, Cambridge, Mass., MIT Press.

Bobrow, D.G. and Collins, A.M. (eds) (1975), *Representation and Understanding*, New York, Academic Press.

Bobrow, D.G. and Winograd, T. (1977), 'An overview of KRL: a knowledge representation language', *Cognitive Science*, vol. 1, pp. 3–46.

Bobrow, D.G., Kaplan, R.M., Kay, M., Norman, D.A., Thompson, H. and Winograd, T. (1977), 'GUS, a frame-driven dialog system', *Artificial Intelligence*, vol. 8, pp. 155–73.

Bowden, M. (1977), *Artificial Intelligence and Natural Man*, Hassocks, Harvester.

Bower, G.H., Black, J.B. and Turner, T.J. (1979), 'Scripts in memory for text', *Cognitive Psychology*, vol. 11, pp. 177–220.

Boyer, R.S. and Moore, J.S. (1979), *A Computational Logic*, New York, Academic Press.

Brachman, R.J. (1979), 'On the epistemological status of semantic networks', in N. V. Findler (ed.), *Associative Networks: Representation and Use of Knowledge by Computers*, New York, Academic Press.

Brady, J.M. (1984), 'Intelligent robots: connecting perception to action', in P. H. Winston and K. A. Prendergast (eds), *The AI Business: The Commercial Uses of Artificial Intelligence*, Cambridge, Mass., MIT Press.

Bratko, I., Kopec, D. and Michie, D. (1978), 'Pattern-based representation of chess end-game knowledge', *Computer Journal*, vol. 21, pp. 149–53.

Bridle, J.S., Brown, M.D. and Chamberlin, R.M. (1982), 'A one-pass algorithm for connected word recognition', *Proceedings of the IEEE International Conference on Acoustics, Speech and Signal Processing*, pp. 899–902.

Broadbent, D. (1985), 'A question of levels: comment on McClelland and Rumelhart', *Journal of Experimental Psychology: General*, vol. 114, pp. 189–92.

Brown, J.S., Burton, R.R. and de Kleer, J. (1982), 'Pedagogical, natural language and knowledge engineering techniques in SOPHIE I, II, and III, in S. Derek and J.S. Brown (eds), *Intelligent Tutoring Systems*, New York, Academic Press.

Bruce, B.C. (1982), 'Natural communication between person and computer', in W.G. Lehnert and M.H. Ringle (eds), *Strategies for Natural Language Processing*, Hillsdale, New Jersey, Lawrence Erlbaum Associates.

Bundy, A. (ed.) (1978), *Artificial Intelligence: An Introductory Course*, Edinburgh, Edingburgh University Press.

Bundy, A. (1983), *The Computer Modelling of Mathematical Reasoning*, London, Academic Press.

Bundy, A. and Welham, B. (1981), 'Using meta-level inference for selective application of multiple rewrite rules in algebraic multiplication', *Artificial Intelligence*, vol. 16, pp. 189–211.

Burstall, R.M., Collins, J.S. and Popplestone, R.J. (1971), *Programming in POP-2*, Edinburgh, Edinburgh University Press.

Carbonell, J.G. (1982), 'Metaphor: an inescapable phenomenon in natural-language comprehension', in W. G. Lehnert and M. H. Ringle (eds), *Strategies for Natural Language Processing*, Hillsdale, New Jersey, Lawrence Erlbaum Associates.

Carbonell, J.R. (1970), 'AI in CAI: an artificial intelligence approach to computer-aided instruction', *IEEE Transactions on Man-Machine Systems*, vol. 11, pp. 190–202.

Charniak, E. and McDermott, D.V. (1985), *Introduction to Artificial Intelligence*, Reading, Mass., Addison-Wesley.

Charniak, E., Riesbeck, C.K. and McDermott, D.V. (1980), *Artificial Intelligence Programming*, Hillsdale, New Jersey, Lawrence Erlbaum Associates.

Chomsky, N. (1957), *Syntactic Structures*, The Hague, Mouton.

Chomsky, N. (1959), 'A review of B. F. Skinner's "Verbal Behavior"', *Language*, vol. 35, pp. 26–58.

Chomsky, N. (1965), *Aspects of the Theory of Syntax*, Cambridge, Mass., MIT Press.

Chomsky, N. (1977), 'On wh-movement', in P. W. Culicover, T. Wasow and A. Akmajian (eds), *Formal Syntax*, New York, Academic Press.

Chomsky, N. (1981), *Lectures on Government and Binding*, Dordrecht, Foris.

Chomsky, N. and Lasnik, H. (1977), 'Filters and control', *Linguistic Inquiry*, vol. 8, pp. 425–504.

Clancey, W.J. (1984), 'Methodology for building an intelligent tutoring system', in W. Kintsch, J. R. Miller and P. G. Polson (eds), *Methods and Tactics in Cognitive Science*, Hillsdale, New Jersey, Lawrence Erlbaum Associates.

Clocksin, W. and Mellish, C. (1981), *Programming in Prolog*, Berlin, Springer-Verlag.

Clowes, M.B. (1971), 'On seeing things', *Artificial Intelligence*, vol. 2, pp. 79–116.

Cohen, Paul R. and Feigenbaum, E.A. (1982), *The Handbook of Artificial Intelligence*, vol. 3, Los Altos, Calif., William Kaufmann.

Cohen, Philip R. and Perrault, C.R. (1979), 'Elements of a plan-based theory of speech acts', *Cognitive Science*, vol. 3, pp. 177–212.

Cohen, Philip R., Perrault, C.R. and Allen, J.F. (1982), 'Beyond question answering', in W. G. Lehnert and M. H. Ringle (eds), *Strategies for Natural Language Processing*, Hillsdale, New Jersey, Lawrence Erlbaum Associates.

Collins, A.M. (1976), 'Processes in acquiring knowledge', in R. C.

Anderson, R. J. Spiro and W. E. Montague (eds), *Schooling and the Acquisition of Knowledge*, Hillsdale, New Jersey, Lawrence Erlbaum Associates.

Collins, A.M. and Loftus, E.F. (1975), 'A spreading-activation theory of semantic processing', *Psychological Review*, vol. 82, pp. 407–28.

Collins, A.M. and Quillian, M.R. (1969), 'Retrieval time from semantic memory', *Journal of Verbal Learning and Verbal Behavior*, vol. 8, pp. 240–7.

Collins, A.M. and Quillian, M.R. (1972), 'Experiments on semantic memory and language comprehension', in L. W. Gregg (ed.), *Cognition in Learning and Memory*, New York, Wiley.

Collins, N.L. and Michie, D. (1967), *Machine Intelligence 1*, Edinburgh, Edinburgh University Press.

Crain, S. and Steedman, M.J. (1985), 'On not being led up the garden path: the use of context by the psychological parser', in D. Dowty, L. Karttunen and A. Zwicky (eds), *Natural Language Parsing*, Cambridge, Cambridge University Press.

Cullingford, R.E. (1978), *Script Application: Computer Understanding of Newspaper Stories*, Yale University Department of Computer Science, Report no. 116.

Davis, R. (1982), 'TEIRESIAS: applications of meta-level knowledge', in R. Davis and D.B. Lenat (eds), *Knowledge-Based Systems in Artificial Intelligence*, New York, McGraw-Hill.

Davis, R. (1984), 'Amplifying expertise with expert systems', in P. H. Winston and K. A. Prendergast (eds), *The AI Business: The Commercial Uses of Artificial Intelligence*, Cambridge, Mass., MIT Press.

Davis, R., Austin, H., Carlbom, I., Frawley, B., Pruchnik, P., Sneiderman, R. and Gilreath, A. (1981), 'The DIPMETER ADVISOR: interpretation of geological signals', *Proceedings of the Seventh International Joint Conference on Artificial Intelligence*, pp. 846–9.

Dietterich, T.G. and Michalski, R. (1981), 'Inductive learning of structural descriptions: evaluation criteria and comparative review of selected methods', *Artificial Intelligence*, vol. 16, pp. 257–94.

Doyle, J. (1979), 'A truth-maintenance system', *Artificial Intelligence*, vol. 12, pp. 231–72.

Draper, S.W. (1981), 'The use of gradient and dual space in line-drawing interpretation', *Artificial Intelligence*, vol. 17, pp. 461–508.

Dreyfus, H.L. (1979), *What Computers Can't Do*, 2nd edn, New York, Harper & Row.

Duda, R.O., Hart, P.E., Nilsson, N.J. and Sutherland, G.L. (1978), 'Semantic network representations in rule based inference systems', in D. A. Waterman and F. Hayes-Roth (eds), *Pattern Directed Inference Systems*, New York, Academic Press.

Dyer, M.G. (1983), *In-Depth Understanding: A Computer Model of Integrated Processing for Narrative Comprehension*, Cambridge, Mass., MIT Press.

Earley, J. (1970), 'An efficient context-free parsing algorithm', *Communications of the Association for Computing Machinery*, vol. 13, pp. 94–102.

Erman, L.D. and Lesser, V.R. (1980), 'The HEARSAY-II speech understanding system', in W. A. Lea (ed.), *Trends in Speech Recognition*, Englewood Cliffs, New Jersey, Prentice-Hall.

Ernst, G. and Newell, A. (1969), *GPS: A Case Study in Generality and Problem Solving*, New York, Academic Press.

Etherington, D.W. (1987), 'Formalizing nonmonotonic reasoning systems', *Artificial Intelligence*, vol. 31, pp. 41–85.

Evans, T.G. (1968), 'A program for the solution of geometric-analogy intelligence test questions', in M. Minsky (ed.), *Semantic Information Processing*, Cambridge, Mass., MIT Press.

Fahlman, S.E. (1979), *NETL: A System for Representing and Using Real-World Knowledge*, Cambridge, Mass., MIT Press.

Falk, G. (1972), 'Interpretation of imperfect line data as a three-dimensional scene', *Artificial Intelligence*, vol. 3, pp. 101–44.

Feigenbaum, E.A. (1977), 'The art of artificial intelligence, 1: Theories and case studies in knowledge engineering', *Proceedings of the Fifth International Joint Conference on Artificial Intelligence*, pp. 1014–29.

Feigenbaum, E.A. and Feldman, J. (eds) (1963), *Computers and Thought*, New York, McGraw-Hill.

Feldman, J.A. and Ballard, D.H. (1982), 'Connectionist models and their properties', *Cognitive Science*, vol. 6, pp. 205–54.

Fikes, R.E. and Nilsson, N.J. (1971), 'STRIPS: a new approach to the application of theorem proving to problem solving', *Artificial Intelligence*, vol. 2, pp. 189–208.

Fillmore, C.J. (1968), 'The case for case', in E. Bach and R. T. Harms (eds), *Universals in Linguistic Theory*, New York, Holt, Rinehart & Winston.

Fillmore, C.J. (1971), 'Types of lexical information', in D. D. Steinberg and L. A. Jakobovits (eds), *Semantics: An Interdisciplinary Reader in Philosophy, Linguistics and Psychology*, Cambridge, Cambridge University Press.

Findler, N.V. (ed.) (1979), *Associative Networks: Representation and Use of Knowledge by Computers*, New York, Academic Press.

Fodor, J.A. (1980), 'Methodological solipsism considered as a research strategy in cognitive psychology', *Behavioral and Brain Sciences*, vol. 3, pp. 63–73.

Frazier, L. and Fodor, J.D. (1978), 'The sausage machine: a new two-stage parsing model', *Cognition*, vol. 6, pp. 291–325.

Frege, G. (1879/1972), 'Conceptual notation: a formula language of pure thought modelled upon the formula language of arithmetic', in T.W. Bynum (ed. and trans.), *Conceptual Notation and Related Articles*, Oxford, Oxford University Press. (First published in German in 1879, Halle, L. Nerbert.)

Frisby, J.P. and Mayhew, J.E.W. (1980), 'Spatial frequency and tuned channels: implications for structure and function from psychophysical and computational studies of stereopsis', *Philosophical Transactions of the Royal Society of London, Series B*, vol. 290, pp. 95–116.

Garnham, A. (1985), *Psycholinguistics: Central Topics*, London, Methuen.

Gazdar, G., Klein, E., Pullum, G. and Sag, I. (1985), *Generalized Phrase Structure Grammar*, Oxford, Blackwell.

Gelernter, H.L. (1963), 'Realisation of a geometry-theorem proving machine', in E.A. Feigenbaum and J. Feldman (eds), *Computers and Thought*, New York, McGraw-Hill.

Gelernter, H.L., Sanders, A.F., Larsen, D.L., Agarival, K.K., Boivie, R.H., Spritzer, G.A. and Searleman, J.E. (1977), 'Empirical explorations of SYNCHEM', *Science*, vol. 197, pp. 1041–9.

Gentner, D. and Stevens, A.L. (1983), *Mental Models*, Hillsdale, New Jersey, Lawrence Erlbaum Associates.

Gilmore, P.C. (1980), 'An examination of the geometry theorem machine', *Artificial Intelligence*, vol. 2, pp. 171–87.

Gold, E.M. (1967), 'Language identification in the limit', *Information and Control*, vol. 10, pp. 447–74.

Goldstein, I.P. (1975), 'A summary of MYCROFT; a system for understanding simple picture programs', *Artificial Intelligence*, vol. 6, pp. 249–88.

Graesser, A.C., Gordon, S.E. and Sawyer, J.D. (1979), 'Recognition memory for typical and atypical actions in scripted activities: tests of a script pointer + tag hypothesis', *Journal of Verbal Learning and Verbal Behavior*, vol. 18, pp. 319–32.

Grape, G.R. (1969), *Computer Vision Through Sequential Abstractions*, Stanford, Calif., Stanford University Department of Artificial Intelligence.

Green, B.F., Wolf, A.K., Chomsky, C. and Laughery, K. (1961), 'BASEBALL: an automatic question answerer', *Proceedings of the Western Joint Computer Conference*, vol. 19, pp. 219–24.

Green, C. (1969), 'Application of theorem proving to problem solving', *Proceedings of the First International Joint Conference on Artificial Intelligence*, pp. 219–39.

Green, C. (1977), 'A summary of the PSI program synthesis system', *Proceedings of the Fifth International Joint Conference on Artificial Intelligence*, pp. 380–1.

Green, C. and Westfold, S. (1982), 'Knowledge-based programming self applied', in J. E. Hayes, D. Michie and Pao Y-H. (eds), *Machine Intelligence 10*, Chichester, Ellis Horwood.

Greenblatt, R.D., Eastlake, D.E. and Crocker, S.D. (1967), 'The Greenblatt chess program', *Proceedings of the American Federation of Information Processing Societies Fall Joint Computer Conference*, vol. 31, pp. 801–10.

Gregory, R.L. (1981), *Mind in Science: A History of Explanations in Psychology and Physics*, London, Weidenfeld & Nicolson.

Grice, H.P. (1975), 'Logic and conversation', in P. Cole and J. L. Morgan (eds), *Syntax and Semantics, 3: Speech Acts*, New York, Seminar Press.

Grimes, J. (1975), *The Thread of Discourse*, The Hague, Mouton.

Grosz, B. (1981), 'Focusing and description in natural language dialogues', in A. K. Joshi, B. L. Webber and I. A. Sag (eds), *Elements of Discourse Understanding*, Cambridge, Cambridge University Press.

Guzman, A. (1968), 'Decomposition of a visual scene into three-dimensional bodies', *Proceedings of the American Federation of Information Processing Societies Fall Joint Computer Conference*, vol. 33, pp. 291–304.

Haas, A.R. (1986), 'A syntactic theory of belief and action', *Artificial Intelligence*, vol. 28, pp. 245–92.

Halliday, M.A.K. (1970), 'Language structure and language function', in J. Lyons (ed.), *New Horizons in Linguistics*, Harmondsworth, Penguin.

Hart, P.E., Nilsson, N.J. and Raphael, B. (1968), 'A formal basis for the heuristic determination of minimum cost paths', *IEEE Transactions on Systems Science and Cybernetics*, vol. 4, pp. 100–7.

Haugeland, J. (1985), *Artificial Intelligence: The Very Idea*, Cambridge, Mass., MIT Press.

Heldhorn, G.E. (1975), *Simulation Programming through Natural Language Dialogue*, Amsterdam, North-Holland.

Hendrix, G.G. (1979), 'Encoding knowledge in partitioned networks', in N.V. Findler (ed.), *Associative Networks: Representation and Use of Knowledge by Computers*, New York, Academic Press.

Hewitt, C. (1972), *Description and Theoretical Analysis (Using Schemata) of PLANNER: A Language for Proving Theorems and Manipulating Models in a Robot*, Massachusetts Institute of Technology, Laboratory of Artificial Intelligence, Technical Report AI-TR-258.

Hillis, W.D. (1985), *The Connection Machine*, Cambridge, Mass., MIT Press.

Hinton, G.E. (1981), 'Implementing semantic networks in parallel hardware', in G. E. Hinton and J. A. Anderson (eds), *Parallel Models of Associative Memory*, Hillsdale, New Jersey, Lawrence Erlbaum Associates.

Hodges, A. (1983), *Alan Turing: The Enigma of Intelligence*, London, Burnett.

Holmes, J.N., Mattingly, I.G. and Shearme, J.N. (1964), 'Speech synthesis by rule', *Language and Speech*, vol. 7, pp. 127–43.

Horn, B.K.P. (1973), *The Binford-Horn Edge Finder*, Massachusetts Institute of Technology, Laboratory of Artificial Intelligence, Memo no. 285.

Horn, B.K.P. (1975), 'Obtaining shape from shading information', in P. H. Winston (ed.), *The Psychology of Computer Vision*, New York, McGraw-Hill.

Horn, B.K.P. (1977), 'Understanding image intensities', *Artificial Intelligence*, vol. 8, pp. 201–31.

Houghton, G. and Isard, S.D. (in press), 'Why to speak, what to say, and how to say it', in P. Morris (ed.), *Modelling Cognition*, Chichester, Wiley.

Huffman, D.A. (1971), 'Impossible objects as nonsense sentences', in B. Meltzer and D. Michie (eds), *Machine Intelligence 6*, Edinburgh, Edinburgh University Press.

Hunt, E.B. (1975), *Artificial Intelligence*, New York, Academic Press.

Ikeuchi, K. (1984), 'Shape from regular patterns', *Artificial Intelligence*, vol. 22, pp. 49–75.

Ikeuchi, K. and Horn, B.K.P. (1981), 'Numerical shape from shading and occluding boundaries', *Artificial Intelligence*, vol. 17, pp. 141–84.

Isard, S.D. (1986), 'Levels of representation in computer speech synthesis and recognition', in M. Yazdani (ed.), *Artificial Intelligence: Principles and Applications*, London, Chapman & Hall.

Isard, S.D. and Miller, D.A. (1986), 'Diphone synthesis techniques', *Proceedings of the IEEE International Conference of Speech Input/Output Techniques and Applications*, pp. 77–82.

Johnson-Laird, P.N. (1977), 'Procedural semantics', *Cognition*, vol. 5, pp. 189–214.

Johnson-Laird, P.N. (1983), *Mental Models: Towards a Cognitive Science of Language, Inference and Consciousness*, Cambridge, Cambridge University Press.

Johnson-Laird, P.N. and Garnham, A. (1980), 'Descriptions and discourse models', *Linguistics and Philosophy*, vol. 3, pp. 371–93.

de Jong, G. (1982), 'An overview of the FRUMP system', in W. G. Lehnert and M. H. Ringle (eds), *Strategies for Natural Language Processing*, Hillsdale, New Jersey, Lawrence Erlbaum Associates.

Joshi, A.K. (1985), 'Tree adjoining grammars: how much context-sensitivity is required to provide reasonable structural descriptions?', in D. R. Dowty, L. Karttunen and A. M. Zwicky (eds), *Natural Language Parsing*, Cambridge, Cambridge University Press.

Julesz, B. (1971), *Foundations of Cyclopean Perception*, Chicago, University of Chicago Press.

Kanade, T. (1980), 'A theory of the Origami world', *Artificial Intelligence*, vol. 13, pp. 279–311.

Kaplan, R.M. (1973), 'A general syntactic processor', in R. Rustin (ed.), *Natural Language Processing*, Englewood Cliffs, New Jersey, Prentice-Hall.

Kaplan, R.M. and Bresnan, J. (1982), 'Lexical-functional grammar: a formal system for grammatical representation', in J. Bresnan (ed.), *The Mental Representation of Grammatical Relations*, Cambridge, Mass., MIT Press.

Kay, M. (1973), 'The MIND system', in R. Rustin (ed.), *Natural Language Processing*, Englewood Cliffs, New Jersey, Prentice-Hall.

Kimball, J. (1973), 'Seven principles of surface structure parsing in natural language', *Cognition*, vol. 2, pp. 15–47.

Kister, J., Stein, P., Ulam, S., Walden, W. and Wells, M. (1957), 'Experiments in chess', *Journal of the Association for Computing Machinery*, vol. 4, pp. 174–7.

Korf, R.K. (1985), 'Macro-operators: a weak method for learning', *Artificial*

*Intelligence*, vol. 26, pp. 35–77.

Kowalski, R. (1979), *Logic for Problem Solving*, Amsterdam, North-Holland.

Kraft, A. (1984), 'XCON: an expert configuration system', in P. H. Winston and K. A. Prendergast (eds), *The AI Business: The Commercial Uses of Artificial Intelligence*, Cambridge, Mass., MIT Press.

Land, E.H. and McCann, J.J. (1971), 'Lightness and retinex theory', *Journal of the Optical Society of America*, vol. 61, pp. 1–11.

Lehnert, W. (1982), 'Plot units: a narrative summarization structure', in W. G. Lehnert and M. H. Ringle (eds), *Strategies for Natural Language Processing*, Hillsdale, New Jersey, Lawrence Erlbaum Associates.

Lenat, D.B. (1977), 'The ubiquity of discovery', *Artificial Intelligence*, vol. 9, pp. 257–85.

Lenat, D.B. (1982), 'AM: discovery in mathematics as heuristic search', in R. Davis and D. B. Lenat (eds), *Knowledge-Based Systems in Artificial Intelligence*, New York, McGraw-Hill.

Lenat, D.B. (1983), 'EURISKO: a program that learns new heuristics and domain concepts', *Artificial Intelligence*, vol. 21, pp. 61–98.

Lenat, D.B. and Brown, J.S. (1984), 'Why AM and EURISKO appear to work', *Artificial Intelligence*, vol. 23, pp. 269–94.

Lettvin, J.Y., Maturana, H.R., McCulloch, W.S. and Pitts, W.H. (1959), 'What the frog's eye tells the frog's brain', *Proceedings of the Institute of Radio Engineers*, vol. 47, pp. 1940–51.

Levesque, H. and Mylopoulos, J. (1979), 'A procedural semantics for semantic networks', in N. V. Findler (ed.), *Associative Networks: Representation and Use of Knowledge by Computers*, New York, Academic Press.

Lindsay, R., Buchanan, B.G., Feigenbaum, E.A. and Lederberg, J. (1980), *Applications of Artificial Intelligence for Chemical Inference: The DENDRAL Project*, New York, McGraw-Hill.

Linggard, R. (1985), *Electronic Synthesis of Speech*, Cambridge, Cambridge University Press.

Lowerre, B. and Reddy, D.R. (1980), 'The HARPY speech understanding system', in W. A. Lea (ed.), *Trends in Speech Recognition*, Englewood Cliffs, New Jersey, Prentice-Hall.

McCarthy, J. (1980), 'Circumspection – a form of non-monotonic reasoning', *Artificial Intelligence*, vol. 13, pp. 27–39.

McCarthy, J. (1986), 'Applications of circumspection to formalizing common-sense knowledge', *Artificial Intelligence*, vol. 28, pp. 89–116.

McClelland, J.L. and Rumelhart, D.E. (1981), 'An interactive activation model of context effects in letter perception, Part 1: An account of basic findings', *Psychological Review*, vol. 88, pp. 375–407.

McClelland, J.L. and Rumelhart, D.E. (1985), 'Distributed memory and the representation of general and specific information', *Journal of Experimental Psychology: General*, vol. 114, pp. 159–88.

McClelland, J.L. and Rumelhart, D.E. (1986), *Parallel Distributed Processing: Explorations in the Microstructure of Cognition, vol. 2: Psychological and Biological Models*, Cambridge, Mass., MIT Press.

McCorduck, P. (1979), *Machines Who Think: A Personal Inquiry into the History and Prospects of Artificial Intelligence*, San Francisco, Freeman.

McCulloch, W.S. and Pitts, W.H. (1943), 'A logical calculus of ideas immanent in nervous activity', *Bulletin of Mathematical Biophysics*, vol. 5, pp. 115–33.

McDermott, D.V. and Doyle, J. (1980), 'Non-monotonic logic I', *Artificial Intelligence*, vol. 13, pp. 41–72.

McDermott, D.V. and Sussman, G.J. (1972), *The CONNIVER Reference Manual*, Massachusetts Institute of Technology, Laboratory of Artificial Intelligence, Memo no. 259.

McDermott, J. (1982), 'R1: A rule-based configurer of computer systems', *Artificial Intelligence*, vol. 19, pp. 39–88.

McKeown, K.R. (1985), 'Discourse strategies for generating natural language text', *Artificial Intelligence*, vol. 27, pp. 1–41.

Mackworth, A.K. (1973), 'Interpreting pictures of polyhedral scenes', *Artificial Intelligence*, vol. 4, pp. 121–37.

Marcus, M.P. (1980), *A Theory of Syntactic Recognition for Natural Language*, Cambridge, Mass., MIT Press.

Marcus, M.P. (1984), 'Some inadequate theories of human language processing', in T. G. Bever, J. M. Carroll and L. A. Miller (eds), *Talking Minds: The Study of Language in Cognitive Science*, Cambridge, Mass., MIT Press.

Marr, D. (1976), 'Early processing of visual information', *Philosophical Transactions of the Royal Society of London, Series B*, vol. 275, pp. 483–525.

Marr, D. (1982), *Vision: A Computational Investigation into the Human Representation and Processing of Visual Information*, San Francisco, Freeman.

Marr, D. and Hildreth, E. (1980), 'Theory of edge detection', *Proceedings of the Royal Society of London, Series B*, vol. 207, pp. 187–217.

Marr, D. and Nishihara, H.K. (1978), 'Representation and recognition of the spatial organisation of three-dimensional shapes', *Proceedings of the Royal Society of London, Series B*, vol. 200, pp. 269–94.

Marr, D. and Poggio, T. (1976), 'Cooperative computation of stereo disparity', *Science*, vol. 194, pp. 283–7.

Marr, D. and Poggio, T. (1979), 'A computational theory of human stereo vision', *Proceedings of the Royal Society of London, Series B*, vol. 204, pp. 301–28.

Marslen-Wilson, W.D. (1973), 'Linguistic structure and speech shadowing at very short latencies', *Nature*, vol. 244, pp. 522–3.

Marslen-Wilson, W.D. (1975), 'Sentence perception as an interactive parallel process', *Science*, vol. 189, pp. 226–8.

Mayhew, J.E.W. and Frisby, J.P. (1981), 'Psychophysical and computational studies towards a theory of human stereopsis', *Artificial Intelligence*, vol. 17, pp. 349–85.

Mayhew, J.E.W. and Frisby, J.P. (1984), 'Computer vision', in T. O'Shea and M. Eisenstadt (eds), *Artificial Intelligence: Tools, Techniques, and Applications*, New York: Harper & Row.

Michalski, R. (1983), 'A theory and methodology of inductive learning', in R. Michalski, J.G. Carbonell and T.M. Mitchell (eds), *Machine Learning: An Artificial Intelligence Approach*, Palo Alto, Calif., Tioga Publishing.

Michalski, R.S. and Chilausky, R.L. (1980), 'Learning by being told and learning from examples: an experimental comparison of the two methods of knowledge acquisition in the context of developing an expert system for soybean disease diagnosis', *International Journal of Policy Analysis and Information Systems*, vol. 4, pp. 125–61.

Michie, D. and Bratko, K. (1978), 'Advice table representations of chess end-game knowledge', *Proceedings of the AISB/GI Conference on Artificial Intelligence*, pp. 194–200.

Minsky, M. (ed.) (1968), *Semantic Information Processing*, Cambridge, Mass., MIT Press.

Minsky, M. (1975), 'A framework for representing knowledge', in P. H. Winston (ed.), *The Psychology of Computer Vision*, New York, McGraw-Hill.

Mitchell, T.M. (1982), 'Generalization as search', *Artificial Intelligence*, vol. 18, pp. 203–26.

Mitchell, T.M. Utgoff, P.E. and Banerji, R. (1983), 'Learning by experimentation: acquiring and refining problem-solving heuristics', in R. Michalski, J.G. Carbonell and T.M. Mitchell (eds), *Machine Learning: An Artificial Intelligence Approach*, Palo Alto, Calif., Tioga Publishing.

Moore, R.C. (1985), 'Semantical considerations on nonmontonic logic', *Artificial Intelligence*, vol. 25, pp. 75–94.

Mostow, D.J. (1983), 'Machine transformation of advice into a heuristic search procedure', in R. Michalski, J. G. Carbonell and T. M. Mitchell (eds), *Machine Learning: An Artificial Intelligence Approach*, Palo Alto, Calif., Tioga Publishing.

Newell, A. and Shaw, J.C. (1957), 'Programming the logic theory machine', *Proceedings of the Western Joint Computer Conference*, vol. 15, pp. 230–40.

Newell, A. and Simon, H.A. (1963), 'GPS, a program that simulates human thought', in E. A. Feigenbaum and J. Feldman (eds), *Computers and Thought*, New York, McGraw-Hill.

Newell, A. and Simon, H.A. (1972), *Human Problem Solving*, Englewood Cliffs, New Jersey, Prentice-Hall.

Newell, A., Shaw, J.C. and Simon, H.A. (1957), 'Empirical explorations with the logic theory machine: a case study in heuristics', *Proceedings of the*

*Western Joint Computer Conference*, vol. 15, pp. 218–30.

Nilsson, N.J. (1980), *Principles of Artificial Intelligence*, Palo Alto, Calif., Tioga Publishing.

Norman, D.A. (1980), 'Copycat science or does the mind really work by table look-up', in R. A. Cole (ed.), *Perception and Production of Fluent Speech*, Hillsdale, New Jersey, Lawrence Erlbaum Associates.

Norman, D.A., Rumelhart, D.E. and the LNR Research Group (1975), *Explorations in Cognition*, San Francisco, Freeman.

Norris, D.G. (1982), 'Autonomous processes in comprehension: a reply to Marslen-Wilson and Tyler', *Cognition*, vol. 11, pp. 97–101.

Papert, S. (1980), *Mindstorms: Children, Computers, and Powerful Ideas*, New York, Basic Books.

Perrault, C.R. and Allen, J.F. (1980), 'A plan-based analysis of indirect speech acts', *American Journal of Computational Linguistics*, vol. 6, pp. 167–82.

Peters, P.S. and Ritchie, R.W. (1973), 'On the generative power of transformational grammars', *Information Sciences*, vol. 6, pp. 49–83.

Peters, P.S. and Ritchie, R.W. (1982), *Phrase Linking Grammars*, Department of Linguistics, University of Texas at Austin, Technical Report.

Pitrat, J. (1977), 'A chess combination program which uses plans', *Artificial Intelligence*, vol. 8, pp. 275–321.

Pople, H.E. (1982), 'Heuristic methods for imposing structure on ill-structured problems: the structuring of medical diagnostics', in P. Szolovits (ed.), *Artificial Intelligence in Medicine*, Boulder, Colorado, Westview Press.

Popper, K.R. (1957), *The Logic of Scientific Discovery*, London, Macmillan.

Power, R.J. (1979), 'The organization of purposeful dialogues,' *Linguistics*, vol. 17, pp. 107–52.

Quillian, M.R. (1968), 'Semantic memory', in M. Minsky (ed.), *Semantic Information Processing*, Cambridge, Mass., MIT Press.

Quillian, M.R. (1969), 'The Teachable Language Comprehender: a simulation program and theory of language', *Communications of the Association for Computing Machinery*, vol. 12, pp. 459–76.

Ramsay, A. and Barrett, R. (1987), *AI in Practice: Examples in POP-11*, Chichester, Ellis Horwood.

Raphael, B. (1976), *The Thinking Computer: Mind Inside Matter*, San Francisco, Freeman.

Rich, C. (1984), 'The programmer's apprentice', in P. H. Winston and K. A. Prendergast (eds), *The AI Business: The Commercial Uses of Artificial Intelligence*, Cambridge, Mass., MIT Press.

Rich, E. (1983), *Artificial Intelligence*, New York, McGraw-Hill.

Rieger, C. (1979), 'Five aspects of a full-scale story comprehension model', in N. V. Findler (ed.), *Associative Networks: Representation and Use of Knowledge by Computers*, New York, Academic Press.

Ritchie, G.D. (1980), *Computational Grammar – An Artificial Intelligence Approach to Linguistic Description*, Hassocks, Sussex, Harvester Press.

Ritchie, G.D. and Hanna, F.K. (1984), 'AM: a case study in AI methodology', *Artificial Intelligence*, vol. 23, pp. 249–68.

Roberts, L.G. (1965), 'Machine perception of three-dimensional solids', in J. T. Tippett, D. A. Berkowitz, L. C. Clapp, C. J. Koester and A. Vanderburgh (eds), *Optical and Electro-Optical Information Processing*, Cambridge, Mass., MIT Press.

Roberts, R.B. and Goldstein, I.P. (1977), *The FRL Primer*, Massachusetts Institute of Technology, Laboratory of Artificial Intelligence, Report AIM-408.

Robinson, J.A. (1965), 'A machine-oriented logic based on the resolution principle', *Journal of the Association for Computing Machinery*, vol. 12, pp. 23–41.

Rumelhart, D.E. and Zipser, D. (1985), 'Feature discovery by competitive learning', *Cognitive Science*, vol 9, pp. 75–112.

Ryle, G. (1949), *The Concept of Mind*, London, Hutchinson.

Sacerdoti, E.D. (1974), 'Planning in a hierarchy of abstraction spaces', *Artificial Intelligence*, vol. 5, pp. 115–35.

Sacerdoti, E.D. (1977), *A Structure for Plans and Behavior*, New York, American Elsevier.

Sacerdoti, E.D., Fikes, R.E., Reboh, R., Sagalowicz, D., Waldinger, R.J. and Wilber, B.M. (1976), *QLISP – A Language for the Interactive Development of Complex Systems*, Artificial Intelligence Center, SRI International, Technical Note 120.

Samuel, A.L. (1963), 'Some studies in machine learning using the game of checkers', in E. A. Feigenbaum and J. Feldman (eds), *Computers and Thought*, New York, McGraw-Hill.

Samuel, A.L. (1970), 'Some studies in machine learning using the game of checkers II: recent progress', in F. J. Crosson (ed.), *Human and Artificial Intelligence*, New York, Appleton-Century-Crofts.

Schank, R.C. (1972), 'Conceptual dependency: a theory of natural language understanding', *Cognitive Psychology*, vol. 3, pp. 552–631.

Schank, R.C. (1975), *Conceptual Information Processing*, Amsterdam, North-Holland.

Schank, R.C. (1982), 'Reminding and memory organization: an introduction to MOPs', in W. G. Lehnert and M. H. Ringle (eds), *Strategies for Natural Language Processing*, Hillsdale, New Jersey, Lawrence Erlbaum Associates.

Schank, R.C. and Abelson, R.P. (1977), *Scripts, Plans, Goals and Understanding*, Hillsdale, New Jersey, Lawrence Erlbaum Associates.

Schank, R.C. and Colby, K.M. (eds) (1973), *Computer Models of Thought and Language*, San Francisco, Freeman.

Schubert, L.K., Goebel, R.G. and Cercone, N.J. (1979), 'The structure and organisation of a semantic net for comprehension and inference', in N. V.

Findler (ed.), *Associative Networks: Representation and Use of Knowledge by Computers*, New York, Academic Press.

Searle, J.R. (1969), *Speech Acts: An Essay in the Philosophy of Language*, Cambridge, Cambridge University Press.

Searle, J.R. (1980), 'Minds, brains, and programs', *Behavioral and Brain Sciences*, vol. 3, pp. 417–24.

Searle, J.R. (1984), *Minds, Brains and Science*, London, BBC.

Selfridge, M. (1986), 'A computer model of child language learning', *Artificial Intelligence*, vol. 29, pp. 171–216.

Shannon, C. (1950), 'Programming a digital computer for playing chess', *Philosophy Magazine*, vol. 41, pp. 356–75.

Shirai, Y. (1973), 'A context-sensitive line finder for recognition of polyhedra', *Artificial Intelligence*, vol. 4, pp. 95–120.

Shortliffe, E.H. (1976), *MYCIN: Computer-based Medical Consultations*, New York, American Elsevier.

Shortliffe, E.H. and Buchanan, B.G. (1979), 'A model of inexact reasoning in medicine', *Mathematical Biosciences*, vol. 23, pp. 361–79.

Sidner, C.L. (1983), 'Focusing in the comprehension of definite anaphora', in M. Brady and R. C. Berwick (eds), *Computational Models of Discourse*, Cambridge, Mass., MIT Press.

Sussman, G.J. (1975), *A Computer Model of Skill Acquisition*, New York, American Elsevier.

Sussman, G.J., Winograd, T. and Charniak, E. (1971), *Micro-Planner Reference Manual*, Massachusetts Institute of Technology, Laboratory of Artificial Intelligence, Memo no. 203a.

Thorne, J.P., Bratley, P. and Dewar, H. (1968), 'The syntactic analysis of English by machine', in D. Michie (ed.), *Machine Intelligence 3*, Edinburgh, Edinburgh University Press.

Torrance, S. (1986), 'Breaking out of the Chinese room', in M. Yazdani (ed.), *Artificial Intelligence: Principles and Applications*, London, Chapman & Hall.

Turing, A.M. (1936), 'On computable numbers, with an application to the Entscheidungsproblem', *Proceedings of the London Mathematical Society, Series 2*, vol. 42, pp. 230–65.

Turing, A.M. (1950), 'Computing machinery and intelligence', *Mind*, vol. 59, pp. 433–60.

Ullman, S. (1979), *The Interpretation of Visual Motion*, Cambridge, Mass., MIT Press.

Waltz, D. (1975), 'Understanding line drawings of scenes with shadows', in P. H. Winston (ed.), *The Psychology of Computer Vision*, New York, McGraw-Hill.

Wanner, E. (1980), 'The ATN and the sausage machine: which one is baloney?', *Cognition*, vol. 8, pp. 209–25.

Wanner, E. and Maratsos, M. (1978), 'An ATN approach to comprehension', in M. Halle, J. Bresnan and G. A. Miller (eds), *Linguistic Theory and Psychological Reality*, Cambridge, Mass., MIT Press.

Webber, B.L. (1983) 'So what can we talk about now?', in M. Brady and R. C. Berwick (eds), *Computational Models of Discourse*, Cambridge, Mass., MIT Press.

Weiss, S.M., Kulikowski, C.A., Amaral, S. and Saffir, A. (1978), 'A model-based method for computer-aided medical decision-making', *Artificial Intelligence*, vol. 11, pp. 145–72.

Weizenbaum, J. (1966), 'ELIZA – a computer program for the study of natural language communication between man and machine', *Communications of the Association for Computing Machine*, vol. 9, pp. 36–45.

Weizenbaum, J. (1976), *Computer Power and Human Reason*, San Francisco, Freeman.

Whitehead, A.N. and Russell, B. (1910), *Principia Mathematica*, vol. I, Cambridge, Cambridge University Press.

Wilensky, R. (1982), 'Points: a theory of the structure of stories in memory', in W. G. Lehnert and M. H. Ringle (eds), *Strategies for Natural Language Processing*, Hillsdale, New Jersey, Lawrence Erlbaum Associates.

Wilensky, R. (1983), *Planning and Understanding*, Reading, Mass., Addison-Wesley.

Wilkins, D.E. (1979), 'Using plans in chess', *Proceedings of the Sixth International Joint Conference on Artificial Intelligence*, pp. 960–7.

Wilkins, D.E. (1984), 'Domain-independent planning: representation and plan generation', *Artificial Intelligence*, vol. 22, pp. 269–301.

Wilks, Y. (1975), 'A preferential, pattern-seeking semantics for natural language interface', *Artificial Intelligence*, vol. 6, pp. 53–74.

Winograd, T. (1972), *Understanding Natural Language*, New York, Academic Press and Edinburgh, Edinburgh University Press (Also published in *Cognitive Psychology*, vol. 3, pp. 1–191.)

Winograd, T. (1973), 'A procedural model of language understanding', in R. C. Schank and K. M. Colby (eds), *Computer Models of Thought and Language*, San Francisco, Freeman.

Winograd, T. (1975), 'Frame representations and the declarative/procedural controversy', in D. G. Bobrow and A. M. Collins (eds), *Representation and Understanding*, New York, Academic Press.

Winograd, T. (1983), *Language as a Cognitive Process, vol. 1: Syntax*, Reading, Mass., Addison-Wesley.

Winston, P.H. (ed.) (1975a), *The Psychology of Computer Vision*, New York, McGraw-Hill.

Winston, P.H. (1975b), 'Learning structural descriptions from examples', in P. H. Winston (ed.), *The Psychology of Computer Vision*, New York, McGraw-Hill.

Winston, P.H. (1984), *Artificial Intelligence*, 2nd edn, Reading, Mass., Addison-Wesley.

Winston, P.H. and Horn, B.K.P. (1984), *LISP*, 2nd edn, Reading, Mass., Addison-Wesley.

Wolf, J. and Woods, W.A. (1980), 'The HWIM speech understanding system', in W. A. Lea (ed.), *Trends in Speech Recognition*, Englewood Cliffs, New Jersey, Prentice-Hall.

Woodham, R.J. (1981), 'Analysing images of curved surfaces', *Artificial Intelligence*, vol. 17, pp. 117–40.

Woods, W.A. (1970), 'Transition network grammars for natural language analysis', *Communications of the Association for Computing Machinery*, vol. 13, pp. 591–606.

Woods, W.A. (1975), 'What's in a link? Foundations for semantic networks', in D. G. Bobrow and A. M. Collins (eds), *Representation and Understanding*, New York, Academic Press.

Woods, W.A. (1977), 'Lunar rocks in natural English: explorations in natural language question answering', in A. Zampolli (ed.), *Linguistic Structures Processing*, Amsterdam, North-Holland.

Woods, W.A. (1981), 'Procedural semantics', in A. K. Joshi, B. L. Webber and I. A. Sag (eds), *Elements of Discourse Understanding*, Cambridge, Cambridge University Press.

Younger, D.H. (1967), 'Recognition and parsing of context-free languages in time $n^3$', *Information and Control*, vol. 10, pp. 189–208.

# Name index

# Subject index

Jeremy White
Campbell Bunk (RKP)
Brian
01-769-0582 after 9 pm